ULTIMATE
WORKSHOP
SOLUTIONS

TABLE OF CONTENTS

SECTION 1

THE SHOP

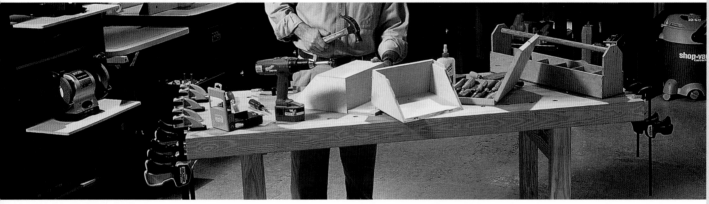
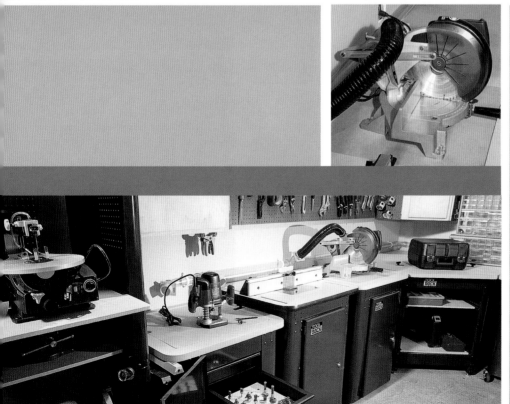

5

THE ULTIMATE
HOME WORKSHOP

Getting started in woodworking is always the hardest
part. But getting your shop set up right will make
everything that follows a little easier. This article will
show you how.

PHOTOS BY AL PARRISH

When DIY - Do It Yourself Network, asked *Popular Woodworking* to help produce its "The Ultimate Workshop" series, we sent DIY (www.diynet.com) a barrage of tips and advice the staff had accumulated over decades of professional and home-shop woodworking. We took a look at all our advice – enough to fill a book – and boiled it down into an essential guide for anyone planning their own ultimate home workshop.

But what is an ultimate home shop? It depends on you. However, whether you're going to build reproduction furniture using only hand tools, or make plywood shelves for the den, many of the ideas presented here will help you set up your ultimate home workshop the right way, the first time.

LOCATION, LOCATION, LOCATION

Most woodworkers can put their shop one of two places: the garage or (in about half the country) the basement. If you're lucky or wealthy you might have a separate outbuilding to consider.

If you're in a part of the country with basements, they can make handy shops. Basements are usually pre-wired for electrical outlets and lighting, and already have plumbing and heat. But a basement shop poses problems, too. You need to get lumber, large equipment and finished projects up and down steps. The size of your doors, the number and slope of your steps and any corners you might have to turn can make a basement shop impossible.

Another basement problem is ceiling height. Older homes may only have 6' or 7' ceilings – less than optimal when working with taller projects.

Finally, basement shops test the patience of your family with the dust and noise. Here's a tip for quieting your basement shop: If there's drywall on the ceiling, add a second layer. If the ceiling is open rafters, so much the better. Add insulation, then add a layer of drywall.

If you don't have a basement, or it's already got a pool table in it, a two-car garage makes a great workshop, offering easy access through large doors, a solid poured concrete floor and a location that's unlikely to get you in trouble when you make dust.

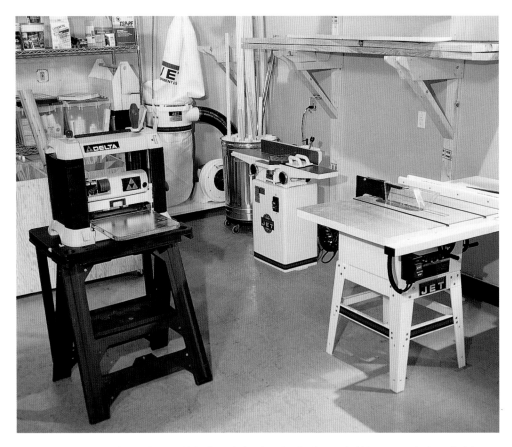

This corner essentially makes up the "machining" area in the shop. Lumber is stored within easy reach above the jointer, with the planer positioned ready to be used by simply turning around from the jointer. With the wood milled, it's a simple step to the table saw to cut the pieces to final size. The stand for the planer is designed to knock down quickly and fold flat against the wall. The planer itself stores under a cabinet, or even under the right-hand wing of the table saw. The portable dust collector is stored in the corner, but it can be attached quickly to any of the three machines in this corner for clean and safe working conditions.

With a garage shop, your first decision is whether the cars will stay out permanently or just when you're woodworking. If your workshop will include some major machinery, the cars will be experiencing some weather.

Other concerns with a garage shop include: upgrading your electrical system (more outlets and perhaps 220-volt service); plumbing and lighting the shop (and heating in colder climates).

A third option may or may not be available to you. If you have an outbuilding on your property (or the space and funds to build one) they make great shops without the noise and dust concerns. If you're building, this also allows you to get everything just the way you want it.

Once you've decided where your workshop will be, it's time to decide how it will be used.

NOT JUST FOR WOODWORKING

We all know that a lot more happens in a home workshop than just woodworking. Hundreds of home fix-up projects take place there, from painting a closet door to rewiring a lamp.

So even though you're planning on lots of woodworking, don't overlook the needs of other projects.

We know that not everyone has the same size workspace, so we thought we'd give you some templates to photocopy and cut out to plan your own shop. The grid is a 1/4" pattern in full size (one square equals 1'), which will work with most graph paper you buy in tablets at the store. (Trust me, paper tools are much lighter to move around.) Also, when organizing your tools, remember to include space for the wood on the infeed and outfeed sides.

10" Table Saw

1½ hp Shaper

16" Drum Sander

14" Band Saw

10" Miter Saw

6" Jointer

16" Scroll Saw

Router Table

16½" Floor Drill Press

10" Benchtop Drill Press

6" Belt / 12" Disc Sander

Oscillating Spindle Sander

13" Planer

1100 CFM Dust Collector

25 Gal. Vertical Air Compressor

10" Radial Arm Saw

6" Bench Grinder

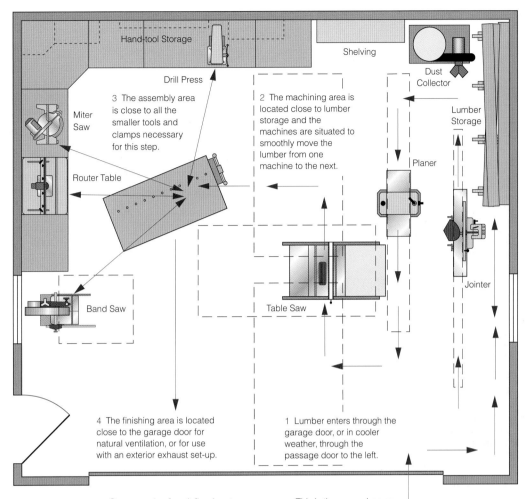

Hand-tool Storage

Shelving

Dust Collector

Lumber Storage

3 The assembly area is close to all the smaller tools and clamps necessary for this step.

2 The machining area is located close to lumber storage and the machines are situated to smoothly move the lumber from one machine to the next.

Drill Press

Miter Saw

Router Table

Planer

Band Saw

Table Saw

Jointer

4 The finishing area is located close to the garage door for natural ventilation, or for use with an exterior exhaust set-up.

1 Lumber enters through the garage door, or in cooler weather, through the passage door to the left.

Our example of work flow in a two-car garage. This is the same shop as shown in the other photos, so you know it works on more than paper. Just follow the red arrows to the easiest path for woodworking. The dotted lines show approximate infeed and outfeed room for lumber.

Plan on extra storage for paint cans, mechanic's tools and a drawer or two for electrical tools and supplies. But before we worry about storage, let's pick some tools and machines.

PICKING YOUR TOOLS

If woodworking will be an occasional activity, or space is at a high premium, consider buying benchtop machines. You can do a lot of work with a benchtop drill press, planer and band saw. While not as versatile as their floor-model big brothers, we recommend them for the small shop.

On the other hand, we don't recommend benchtop table saws for any but the tiniest of shops. While a benchtop saw might be smaller, it's also less powerful and less accurate. Find a way to squeeze a contractor saw or cabinet saw in your shop on a mobile base.

The same goes for the jointer. Like the table saw, benchtop jointers just don't satisfy the needs of most woodshops. We recommend carving out a section of floor space along the wall for a stationary 6" or 8" jointer.

With these five machines (and an assortment of portable and hand tools) you'll be ready to build cabinets and shelves. However, if turning is your passion, a lathe may be at the top of the list, and the jointer and planer may disappear altogether. It's your choice.

There are other tools that you'll want to have (or may own already), including a miter saw, scroll saw and bench grinder, but these can be added as you go along, and they don't take up much space.

PLACING YOUR MACHINES

Once you know what machines will be in your workshop, you need to determine their location. Allow for infeed and outfeed space and place them near machines they're used with most frequently.

Each machine requires space for itself and space to use the tool. With a table saw, you need to be able to maneuver a 4' x 8' sheet of plywood to the back, front and left side of the saw. This means a pretty big footprint for the machine when

The cabinets you choose for your shop can be premade kitchen cabinets, cabinets you make yourself, or cabinets designed for your woodworking needs, as shown in the photo. These cabinets offer simple drop-in platforms for a variety of benchtop tools, with slide-in/slide-out storage for easy access. Storage options include drawers and doors, depending on your needs. Each of the units is capable of easy dust collection hook-up for any benchtop tool, and one of the drop-in panels will allow the cabinet to function as a downdraft table. But don't forget the lowly pegboard for storing hand tools. It still provides the easiest, least expensive and most adjustable hanging storage around.

in use (you can overlap the "in-use" footprints of multiple machines). We've added a diagram on page 9 that shows the necessary working footprint for each major machine. We suggest you draw up your shop on graph paper, cut out the tools (at left) and start trying different arrangements to see what works.

The trick to positioning your machines in your shop is to create an orderly flow of work from raw lumber to the finished product. The work flow always starts where the wood is stored, or where it enters the workshop. Next, the lumber is prepared for use by jointing, planing and sawing to the proper dimensions. Conveniently, the machines required for these steps are also the ones that need the most power and create the most dust, allowing you to locate your power and dust collection in a "machining" area, with these machines close to one another.

From the machining phase, the next step is joinery and assembly, usually requiring hand tools, a band saw, drill press and hand-held power tools, such as a router, biscuit joiner and brad nailer. A stable workbench or assembly table are ideal for this step.

The assembly area should be located out of the way of the machining area, but not so far away that you end up carrying lots of milled lumber across the shop. Your hand and small power tools should be easily accessible (stored in handy drawers or on the wall), and quick access to clamps will make things easier as well.

Once assembly is complete, the third phase is finishing. No matter what finish you use, a clean, well-ventilated area is required.

When applying a varnish or shellac finish, the vapors

given off as the finish dries are flammable and should be kept away from any ignition points, such as water heaters or space heaters. In concentrated exposure, the vapors can also be harmful to you, so ventilation is important. Also, when storing solvent-based finishes (such as varnishes) a fire-proof storage cabinet is a must.

If you're going to use a spray-on finishing system, ventilation is even more critical to move the overspray away from your lungs.

From here, the rest of your shop will fall into place in the space left. Keep in mind that to save space, many tools can be stored under cabinets until needed.

PUTTING THINGS AWAY

While we've talked about where your lumber storage should be in the work triangle, we haven't talked about how to store it.

There are three types of wood stored in a workshop: sheet goods (such as plywood), rough or full-size lumber, and shorts and scraps. Shorts and scraps are the pieces you can't bring yourself to throw away. Not only are there usually more of these pieces, but they're harder to store than plywood or rough lumber because of their odd shapes and sizes. Let's start with the easy stuff first.

Plywood takes up the least amount of space when stored standing on edge. Most of us aren't storing more than a few sheets of plywood, so this can often be stored in a 10"- to 12"-deep rack that can slip behind other storage or machinery. This keeps it out of the way but accessible.

Rough lumber is best stored flat and well-supported to keep the wood from warping. Keeping it up off the floor also keeps it away from any water that may get into your shop.

A wall rack with a number of adjustable-height supports provides the easiest access while keeping the wood flat and dry.

Shorts are the hardest to store, but a rolling box with a number of smaller compartments holding the shorts upright allows easy access to the pieces, and it keeps them from falling against and on top of each other.

Carrying on with the storage concept, one category that deserves special attention is finishing materials. While water-borne finishes are gaining in popularity, flammable finishes in cans, bottles and jars should be stored in a fireproof storage box and kept clean and organized at all times. A tall cabinet with lots of adjustable shelf space makes room for the many sizes of finishing supplies.

Other workshop storage needs fall into the cabinet and shelving category. Just because there's a tool sitting on the floor against the wall doesn't mean you can't hang a cabinet or shelving above it. In fact, in many cases there are accessories and supplies you need near that tool that belong on a shelf right above it. And don't hesitate to go all the way to the ceiling with storage. Even though the top shelves are harder to get to, we all have things in our shops that don't get used very often.

Many of us have purchased a tool that had a base tossed in to sweeten the deal. It seems like a good idea, but if you stop and think about it, it's truly wasted space. Throw away that stamped-steel base and build a storage cabinet to go underneath the tool.

When choosing base storage cabinets, you'll have to decide whether you need drawer cabinets, door cabinets or both. If you're storing large, odd-shaped items (belt sanders, arc welders) a drawer can be a real problem. They're designed to fit only so much. A door cabinet is a better place to store bulky items.

On the other hand, if you're storing smaller items (door hinges, glue, seldom-used jigs) a door cabinet can be a great place to lose these items. Items seem to migrate to the back of the cabinet; and until you're down on your knees peering into the hole, you won't find them. While drawers can get pretty junky if you're not careful, you'll at least be able to stand up and stare down into the drawer looking for your lost metric tape measure.

Beyond doors or drawers, you have two general choices in cabinets – buy 'em or make 'em. If you make your own cabinetry, you will almost certainly get exactly what you need for the best space utilization. You'll also likely save some money, but it'll take a fair amount of time.

Buying shop-grade cabinets from a home center can work out well. There are any number of utility cabinets available in all shapes, sizes and finishes.

One other option is plastic or metal storage units, such as the Tool Dock cabinets shown below, designed specifically for a workshop. These units offer features that are set up to maximize tool use and convenience.

Beyond cabinets, open shelves are good for storage, but they're a bit of a trade-off. While you can easily see what you're looking for, so can everyone else – whether it's attractive or not.

Wire-frame shelving is not a good choice for storing small pieces. And knowing the weight limit of the shelves will keep you from picking up all of your wood screws from the shop floor when the shelf collapses. Also, while you may view deeper shelves as being capable of storing more, (which they are) recognize that smaller items on the shelf can get pushed to the back and get lost.

A good workbench is one item you should build into your plans from the start. We've put the bench in this shop so it's central to all the activity. It's just a short step away from the saw and planer, and only a few feet away from all the hand tools and other benchtop tools. And with it isolated in the center of the room, all four sides of the workbench can be used.

Here's a little closer look at the interchangeable drop-in panels and dust-collection hook-ups for the benchtop tools.

WHERE'D I PUT THAT HAMMER?

Certain hand tools (hammers screwdrivers, chisels and hand saws) are always being reached for – frequently when only one hand is free. For that reason these and other hand tools are usually stored hanging within easy reach on the wall. There are all sorts of ways to hang hand tools on a wall. Some woodworkers build special cabinets for their hand tools. The more common solution is pegboard. It's inexpensive, versatile and easy to mount. With a variety of hooks to choose from, you can make pegboard storage adapt to almost anything. And pegboard doesn't have to be dark brown. More frequently it's being offered in colored plastic, or you can simply paint your own.

But pegboard isn't the only simple option for hanging tools. You've likely seen "slat wall" in department stores holding up socks and ties. This material is essentially a 3/4" board with T-shaped grooves cut in it and a colored plastic laminate on top. It provides much of the versatility and convenience of pegboard, but looks nicer doing it. It'll cost a little more, but it's your choice.

Then there are the workshop experts who mount things right to the wall. By using drywall mollys (or covering your walls with painted particleboard) and a variety of hanging storage accessories available in any home-center store, you can make a wall of tools that will be uniquely your own. In fact, many folks add outlines of the tools on the wall (or on pegboard) so they know exactly where it belongs, and more importantly…if it's missing.

POWER, LIGHTS, VENTILATION

Now that you know where everything belongs, it's time to power it up. While it's one thing to be able to check the tool manuals for the power requirements, it's quite another thing to go about hooking up that power yourself. If you're uncertain about adding new breakers or running wiring, we recommend you get a licensed professional to help you out. But you can help them out by determining the voltage requirements for your tools, whether 110 or 220 volts, and also how many amps each tool requires.

You'll need to provide adequate amperage for each grouping of tools. A contractor's saw will usually require a 110-volt, 20-amp connection, but you can use that same circuit for your planer or jointer because these machines are seldom used simultaneously. Band saws and drill presses can also share a circuit. Another way to improve motor performance and safety is to use a heavier-gauge wire (12 gauge versus 14 gauge) for your stationary tools.

Other things to include in your power requirements are

lighting, bench outlets and any ambient air cleaners. Even if you're blessed with lots of windows in your shop, we all work on cloudy days and in the evenings. So proper lighting can be critical. Make sure you have plenty of general lighting throughout your shop, and add task lighting over dedicated work areas such as your workbench and tools that require careful attention to detail, such as the band saw or scrollsaw.

Don't skimp on power outlets. Heck, put one everywhere you can imagine plugging in a tool, radio or fan. Make sure there is a good power strip with numerous outlets mounted near your bench because cordless-tool battery chargers will use them up fast.

Wood dust is bad for the lungs. By properly using dust collection to keep the larger dust particles out of the air to start, and air cleaners to pull the smaller particles out of the air, the workshop can be a safe and lung-friendly place.

Dust collection is usually set up one of two ways – either with a central collection system using metal or plastic ductwork and a single large dust collector, or with multiple dedicated collectors (though often these can be shared by more than one machine).

A central dust-collection system is a fairly involved topic that entire books have been written about (see "Controlling Dust in the Workshop" by Rick Peters [Sterling Publications]). You need to determine the amount of air movement required to collect from the many different machines, make sure your collector is capable of that performance, and locate and use blast gates in the duct work to maximize the performance of the machine. If a central dust-collection system is your preference, you should spend some in-depth research time on the topic and maybe even consult a professional for advice.

Smaller portable dust collectors are often more affordable and can provide adequate collection for a couple of machines. By using multiple hoses and closeable gates to control which machine is being collected, one machine can do double or triple duty. Each machine is rated by the "cfm" (cubic feet per minute) of air that it is capable of handling. We've included a quick reference chart that rates each machine by the suggested cfm required to extract dust. By using the chart you can easily determine the size and number of dust collectors you need.

Ambient air cleaners pull the dust from the air that the dust collectors miss. They are designed to exchange a specific

MACHINE DUST-COLLECTION STATISTICS

Machine	Req'd CFM
12" Planer	350
13" + Planer	400
Shaper	400
Band saw	400
Radial arm saw	350
Table saw	350
Disc sander	300
Jointer	350
Drill press	300
Scroll saw	300

Static Press. Loss/ft.	
4" Duct	.055 in./ft.
5" Duct	.042 in./ft.
6" Duct	.035 in./ft.
7" Duct	.026 in./ft.
8" Duct	.022 in./ft.

amount of air determined by the size of your shop. Choose the air cleaner (or cleaners) to best serve your space, then let them go to work. Air cleaners require less attention than a dust collector, but you do need to clean or change the filters on a regular basis so they operate properly.

Another air-quality decision is finishing. Because of the volatile and harmful vapors given off by solvent-base finishing products, they will be labeled for use in a well-ventilated area. Whether that means a dedicated finishing area with appropriate air-extraction equipment, or just making sure the garage door is open and a good fan is in use, finishing should take place in an area that ensures safety from explosion, or inhalation of fumes.

SECTION 2
BENCHES

WORKBENCH

For about the cost of a quality jigsaw
you can build a bench that will retire
from woodworking long after you do.
And by the way, the price includes everything —
wood, hardware and even the vise.

By Christopher Schwarz

I've hauled my grandfather's workbench across snow-covered Appalachian mountains, down narrow stairwells and into a dirt-floored garage that should have been torn down during the Eisenhower administration. I've built a lot of good stuff on that bench, but now it's time to retire the old horse.

For starters, the bench is too low for the way I work. And the top is pockmarked with three different shapes and sizes of dog holes. And during the last few years I've become fed up with the tool tray. The only thing it seems designed to hold is enough sawdust for a family of gerbils. So I need a new bench, but there's no way I'm going to spend $1,200 to $1,400 for a high-quality bench from Hoffman & Hammer or Ulmia.

Enter Bob Key from Georgia. He and his son have been building benches using off-the-rack pine for a few years and have even built a website showing how quick and easy this is to do (visit them at www.mindspring.com/~bobkey/
beginners.htm). I was impressed with their idea. So I spent a week reading every book on benches I could find. I pored over the woodworking catalogs. And after a lot of figuring I came up with a simple plan: Build a bench for around $200.

Believe it or not, I came in less than $10 over budget and ended up with a bench that is tough, sturdy and darn versatile. I made a few compromises when choosing the hardware to keep the cost down, but I designed the bench so that it can later be upgraded with a nice tail vise. However, I made no compromises in the construction of the top or base. You can dance on this bench.

LET'S GO SHOPPING

OK friends, it's time to make your shopping list. First a word about the wood. I priced my lumber from a local Lowe's. It was tagged as Southern

8	2 x 8 x 12' Southern yellow pine boards @ $9.57 each	76.56
8	3/8" x 16 x 6" hex bolts @ 51 cents each	4.08
8	3/8" x 16 hex nuts @ 7 cents each	.56
16	5/16" washers @ 3 cents each	.48
1	Veritas Bench Dog (see Supplies for ordering information)	15.95
1	Veritas Wonder Dog (see Supplies for ordering information)	38.50
1	Veritas Front Vise (see Supplies for ordering information)	72.50
	Total Cost	$208.63

plus tax and shipping.

1 **2** **3**

PHOTO BY AL PARRISH

When you glue up your top, you want to make sure all the boards line up. Lay down your glue and then clamp up one end with the boards perfectly flush. Then get a friend to clamp a handscrew on the seam and twist until the boards are flush. Continue clamping up towards your friend, having your friend adjust the handscrews as needed after each clamp is cinched down.

yellow pine, appearance-grade. Unlike a lot of dimensional stock, this stuff is pretty dry and knot-free. Even so, take your time and pick through the store's pile of 12-foot-long 2 x 8s with care to get the best ones possible. You can hide a few tight knots in the top, but with luck you won't have to.

Here's the story on the hardware. The bolts, nuts and washers are used to connect the front rails to the two ends of the bench. Using this hardware, we'll borrow a technique used by bed makers to build a joint that is stronger than any mortise and tenon. The Bench Dog and Wonder Dog will keep you from having to buy an expensive tail vise. Using these two simple pieces of hardware, you can clamp almost anything to your bench for planing, sanding and chopping. The traditional face vise goes on the front of your bench and is useful for joinery and opening cans of peanut butter.

PREPARING YOUR LUMBER

Cut your lumber to length. You've probably noticed that your wood has rounded corners and the faces are probably less than glass-smooth. Your first task is to use your jointer and planer to remove those rounded edges and get all your lumber down to 1⅜" thick.

Once your lumber is thicknessed, start working on the top. If this is your first bench, you can make the top, then throw it up on sawhorses to build the base. The top is made from 1⅜" x 3⅜" x 70" boards turned on edge and glued face-to-face. It will take five of your 2x8s to make the top. Build the top in stages to make the task more manageable. Glue up a few boards, then run the assembly through the jointer and planer

to get them flat. Make a few more assemblies like this, then glue all the assemblies together into one big top.

When you finally glue up the whole top, you want to make sure you keep all the boards in line. This will save you hours of flattening the top later with a hand plane. See the photo above for a life-saving tip when you get to this point. After the glue is dry, square the ends of your assembled top. If you don't have a huge sliding table on your table saw, try cutting the ends square using a circular saw (the top is so thick you'll have to make a cut from both sides). Or you can use a hand saw and a piece of scrap wood clamped across the end as a guide.

BUILD THE BASE

The base is constructed using mortise-and-tenon joinery. Essentially, the base has two end assemblies that are joined by two rails. The end assemblies are built using big 1"-thick, 2"-long tenons. The front rails are attached to the ends using 1" x 1" mortise-and-tenon joints and the 6"-long bolts. Begin working on the base by cutting all your pieces to size. The 2¾"-square legs are made from two pieces of pine laminated together. Glue and clamp the legs and set them aside. Now turn your attention to cutting the tenons on the rails. It's a good idea to first make a "test" mortise in a piece of scrap so you can fit your tenons as they are made. I like to make my tenons on the table saw using a dado stack. Place your rails face down on your table saw and use a miter gauge to nibble away at the rails until the tenons are the right size. Because pine is soft, be sure to make the shoulders on

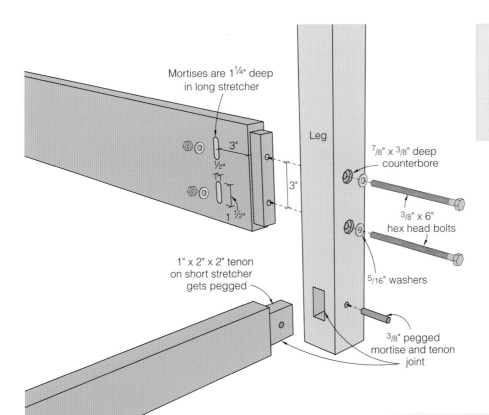

Mortises are 1¼" deep in long stretcher

3"

½"

1½"

Leg

7/8" x 3/8" deep counterbore

3"

3/8" x 6" hex head bolts

5/16" washers

1" x 2" x 2" tenon on short stretcher gets pegged

3/8" pegged mortise and tenon joint

the edges 1" wide on the upper side rails. This precaution will prevent your tenons from blowing out the top of your legs.

Now use your tenons to lay out the locations of your mortises. See the photo at right for how this works. Clamp a piece of scrap to your drill press to act as a fence and chain-drill the mortises in the legs. Make your mortises about 1/16" deeper than your tenons are long. This will give you a little space for any excess glue.

Once you've got your mortises drilled, use a mortise chisel to square the round corners. Make sure your tenons fit, then dry-fit your base. Label each joint so you can reassemble the bench later.

BED BOLTS

There's a bit of a trick to joining the front rails to the legs. Workbenches, you see, are subject to a lot of racking back and forth. A plain old mortise-and-tenon joint just won't hack it. So we bolt it. First study the diagram at left to see how these joints work. Now here's the best way to make them.

First chuck a 1" Forstner bit in your drill press to cut the countersink in the legs for the bolt head. Drill the countersinks, then chuck a 3/8"-brad-point bit in your drill press and drill in the center of the counterbore through the leg and into the mortise.

Now fit the front rails into the leg mortises. Chuck that 3/8" bit into your hand drill and drill as deeply as you can through the

Drilling the 3/8" holes for the bolts is easier if you do it in this order. First drill the holes in the legs using your drill press. Now assemble the leg and front rail. Drill into the rail using the hole in the leg as a guide (top, right). Remove the leg from the rail and continue drilling the hole in the rail. The hole you drilled before will once more act as a guide. You still need to be careful and guide your drill straight and true (right).

After you cut your tenons, lay them directly on your work and use the edges like a ruler to mark where the mortise should start and end (top, left). Use a 1" Forstner bit in your drill press to cut overlapping holes to make your mortise (left). Now square up the edges of the mortise using a mortise chisel and a small mallet (above).

leg and into the rail. The hole in the leg will guide the bit as it cuts into the rail. Then remove the leg and drill the ⅜" hole even deeper. You probably will have to use an extra-long drill bit for this.

OK, here's the critical part. Now you need to cut two small mortises on each rail. These mortises will hold a nut and a washer and must intersect the ⅜" holes you just drilled. With the leg and rail assembled, carefully figure out where the mortises need to go. Drill the mortises in the rails as shown in the photo. Now test your assembly. Thread the joint with the bolt, two washers and a nut. Use a ratchet and wrench to pull everything tight. If your bench ever wobbles in your lifetime, it's probably going to be a simple matter of tightening these bolts to fix the problem. Remember to tell this to your children.

BASE ASSEMBLY
This bench has a good-sized shelf between the front rails. Cut the ledgers and slats from your scrap. Also cut the two cleats that attach the top to the base. Now sand everything before assembly — up to 150 grit should be fine.

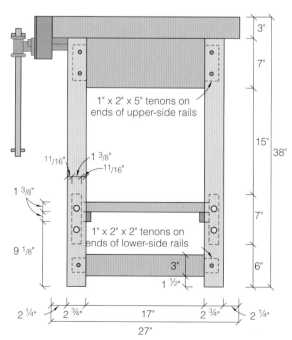

PROFILE

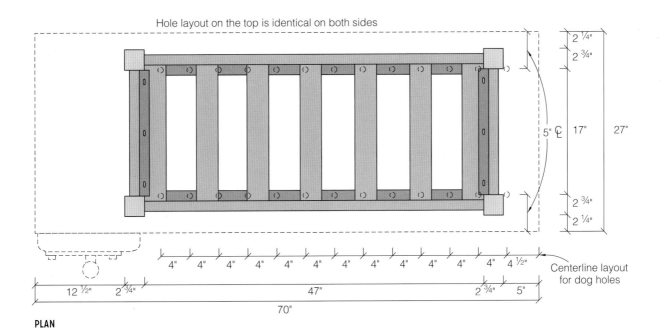

Hole layout on the top is identical on both sides

PLAN

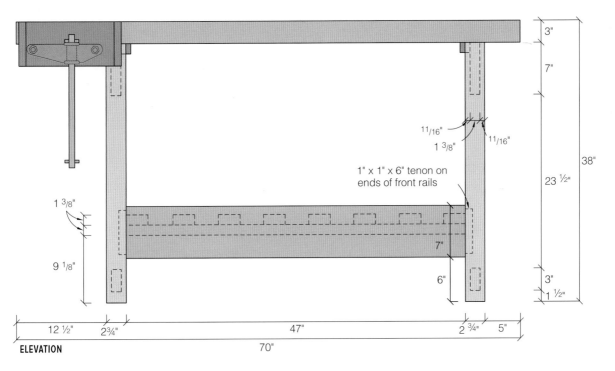

1" x 1" x 6" tenon on ends of front rails

ELEVATION

WORKBENCH			
No.	Item	Dimensions T W L	Notes
1	Top	3" x 27" x 70"	
4	Legs	2¾" x 2¾" x 35"	
2	Front rails	1⅜" x 7" x 49"	1" TBE
2	Upper side rails	1⅜" x 7" x 21"	2" TBE
2	Lower side rails	1⅜" x 3" x 21"	2" TBE
2	Ledgers	1⅜" x 1⅜" x 47"	
7	Slats	1⅜" x 3" x 18½"	
2	Cleats	1⅜" x 1⅜" x 17"	

TBE= Tenon, both ends

The mortises in the front rails are also made on the drill press. Make them 1¼" deep to make sure you can get a washer in there. If you can't, try clipping an edge off of the washer.

Begin assembly by gluing up the two end assemblies. Put glue in the mortises and clamp up the ends until dry. Then, for extra strength, peg the tenons using ⅜"-thick dowel. I had some lying around. If you don't, buy the dowel at the hardware store and add $1 to your bottom line.

Screw the ledgers to the front rails. Make sure they don't cover the mortises for the bed bolts, or you are going to be in trouble. Now bolt the front rails to the two ends (no glue necessary). Rub a little Vaseline or grease on the threads first because after your bench is together you want to seal up those mortises with hot-melt glue. The Vaseline will ensure your bolts will turn for years to come.

Screw the cleats to the top of the upper side rails. Then drill oval-shaped holes in the cleats that will allow you to screw the top to the base. Now screw the seven slats to the ledgers.

FINISHING THE TOP

Before you attach your top, it's best to drill your dog holes and attach the vise. Lay out the location of the two rows of dog holes using the diagram. I made a simple jig to guide a ¾" auger bit in a brace and bit. The jig is shown in action in the photo above.

Now position your vise on the underside of the top and

THE PLEASURE AND PAIN OF PINE

Southern yellow pine is cheap, but you probably know that it likes to twist, cup, wind and bow — everything but corkscrew. There's a way to prevent this, and it's a simple trick that will help reduce warping in all your projects.

First, after you cut your pieces to size, store them on edge with about an inch of space between them. One of the major reasons pine bows is that it's not completely dry (surprise). When you stack it flat, one side is exposed to the atmosphere and the other is not. As a result, one side dries faster than the other and the board bends. Leave a pine board alone for a night like this and the next morning you'll probably have a bowl.

Here's another tip. When you get set to assemble your top, do it all in one day. Surface all your boards and glue them up as fast as you can. If a pine board is in a lamination, it's much less likely to bow because it has other boards that may cancel out its tendency to warp.

Drilling your dog holes may seem like hard work using a brace and bit. It is. However, you get an amazing amount of torque this way — far more than you can get with a cordless drill. Sadly, I had cooked my corded drill, so this was my only option.

attach it with the bolts provided by the manufacturer. This Czech-made vise is of surprising quality, with a heavy-duty Acme-thread screw. The only downside to the vise is you are going to have to make your own wooden face. I must confess I didn't have enough wood left over from my 2 x 8s to make the face. So I made it from a small piece of scrap from another project. You'll need to drill three holes in the wooden face so it fits over the bars, but this is pretty self-evident when you pull the vise out of the box. All the European benches I've seen have a bead cut on the edges. I'm not one to argue with tradition, so I used a beading bit in a router table to cut beads on mine, too.

Make the vise's handle from a length of 1"-diameter oak dowel. My handle is 20" long, which is just the right length to miss whacking me in the head at every turn. I'm a tall guy, so you might want to make yours a bit shorter.

You are now almost done. It's necessary to flatten the top. Use "winding sticks" to determine if your top is flat.

Winding sticks are simply identical, straight lengths of hardwood. Put one on one end of the top and the other on the far end. Now crouch down so your eye is even with the sticks. If your top is flat, the sticks will line up perfectly. If not, you'll quickly see where you need work. Use a jack plane to flatten the high spots. Then sand your top and rag on a couple coats of an oil/varnish blend on the base and top.

With the bench complete, I was pleased with the price and the time it took, which was about 30 hours. However, I'm now itching to build a cabinet beneath the bench and to add a leg jack for planing the edges of long boards. Maybe I'll get to that next issue, or maybe I'll let a future granddaughter take care of those details.

STORAGE AND ASSEMBLY BENCH

When space is tight (and when isn't it?) this modular system gives you a height-adjustable assembly bench, two stands for benchtop tools and six drawers of roll-around storage. Best of all, it breaks down fast and stores in small spaces.

By David Thiel

My shop at home is a two-car garage. To make things more complicated, my wife feels pretty strongly that the two cars should be allowed to stay in the garage. What a silly idea, but it's been an interesting challenge to keep her happy and still work comfortably on my projects. At the heart of this dilemma is getting enough storage and assembly space. There's enough room in the garage to put some shallow cabinets on or against the walls, but storing my "assembly bench" (fold-up horses, planks and a partial sheet of plywood) stops me from getting to my storage. And while the fold-up horses are handy, they're not as stable as I'd prefer and I can't adjust them higher or lower. Sometimes I want to work 24" off the ground, other times 34". I decided it was time to solve my dilemma and here you see the result. When assembled, this unit offers sturdy, adjustable-height bench space with easy access to the stuff in the drawers. When not in use, the two cabinets store conveniently against the wall. You also can use them as benchtop tool stands and still have easy access to the drawers.

BUILDING BOXES

This is a basic project. The only complicated part is the height-adjustment feature of the cabinets. I haven't spent a lot of time illustrating the cabinet construction, but the illustrations and the construction description should get you there safely.

The cabinets consist of a $3/4$"-thick plywood top and bottom, rabbeted between the two $3/4$"-thick sides. The back is also $3/4$" and is rabbeted into the sides, top and bottom. Start by cutting the pieces to size, then cut $1/2$" x $3/4$" rabbets on the top, back and bottom inside edge of each side. I made the rabbets on my table saw, but you could easily use a router instead. Then cut the same rabbet on the back edge of the top and bottom pieces.

I used my 2" brad nailer to shoot the cases together, adding some glue to the joint for good measure.

STORAGE & ASSEMBLY BENCH

	No.	Item	T	W	L	Material	Notes (w/inches)
			\multicolumn{3}{Dimensions (inches)}		
Cabinets							
	4	Sides	¾	15	21¾	Birch ply	½ x ¾ rabbets, 3 sides
	4	Tops & botts	¾	15	27	Birch ply	½ x ¾ rabbet, back
	2	Backs	¾	27	21¼	Birch ply	
	2	Tops	¾	30	72	Birch ply	
	4	Support arms	¾	6	19⅝	Birch	
	2	Top plates	⅞	6	29⅛	Birch	½ x ¾ rabbets, ends
	8	Channel sides	¾	⅞	20	Birch	
	8	Channel fronts	¾	2	20	Birch	
	4	Channel botts	¾	⅞	6	Birch	
	4	Dowels	1	2½		Maple	
	4	Dowels	¾	1⅝		Maple	
Drawers							
	4	Fronts	¾	5	25⅞	Birch ply	clearance space incl.
	2	Fronts	¾	10	25⅞	Birch ply	clearance space incl.
	8	Box sides	½	4	13¼	Birch ply	¼ x ¼ groove, 3 sides
	4	Box sides	½	9	13¼	Birch ply	¼ x ¼ groove, 3 sides
	4	Box fronts	½	4	24½	Birch ply	¼ x ¼ tongue, ends
	4	Box backs	½	3½	24½	Birch ply	¼ x ¼ tongue, ends
	2	Box fronts	½	9	24½	Birch ply	¼ x ¼ tongue, ends
	2	Box backs	½	8½	24½	Birch ply	¼ x ¼ tongue, ends
	6	Bottoms	¼	13	24⁵⁄₁₆	Ply	

I used my brad nailer to tack the channel bottom in place between the two channels through the front and through the sides. Be careful about shooting too close to the end of a piece to avoid blow-outs.

After drilling the clearance holes in the cabinet sides, I used a clamp to hold the channel assembly in place while pilot drilling, then screwing the channels in place from the inside of the cabinet.

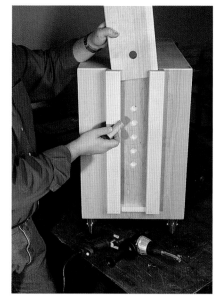

A 1" dowel is a simple and secure way to hold the support arms at the proper height. The five hole locations (and the all-the-way-down position) give you a variety of working heights.

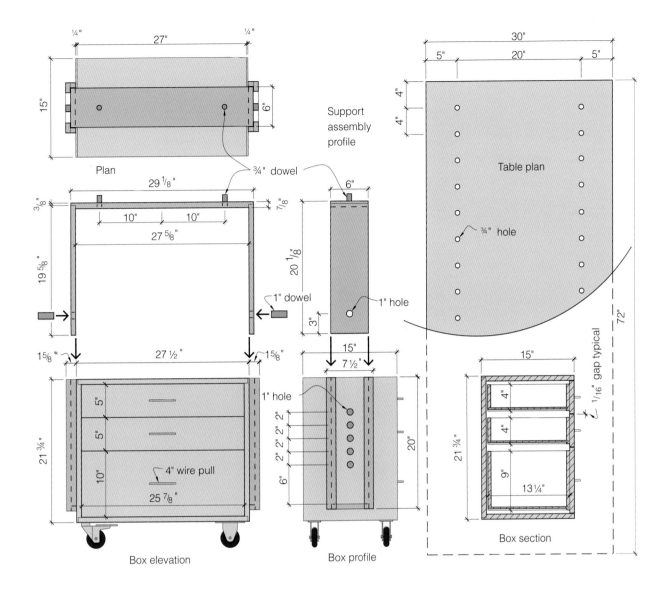

Plan

Support assembly profile

¾" dowel

Box elevation

1" dowel

4" wire pull

Box profile

1" hole

Table plan

¾" hole

Box section

Screws (#8 x 1¼") would also do the job here. Use the backs to square up the cabinets. This will be important when you install the drawers.

I was feeling pretty minimalist with this project and decided to let the utility show through by simply rounding over all the plywood edges with a ¼" roundover bit in my router. If you prefer a more finished appearance, take the extra time to apply iron-on veneer tape to the exposed plywood edges.

To make adding the height-adjustable supports easier I attached the four casters (two standard, non-swivel and two swivel locking) to the cabinets at this time.

GOING UP, GOING DOWN

I went through a lot of different ideas to make the top height-adjustable. After making it a lot more complicated than necessary, I threw away those drawings and went back to simple. The height-adjustable table supports are brought to you by the letters "U" and "L." The support arms are

U-shaped solid birch assemblies that slip into two L-shaped channels on each side of the cabinets.

Start by jointing and thicknessing all the solid birch necessary for the pieces and cut them to finished size, except for the channel pieces. Leave those pieces a little long until after they're glued up. I once again took advantage of my brad nailer to speed up the assembly process. Glue and nail the channel fronts to the channel sides, then set everything aside to let the glue cure.

While they're drying, cut the channel bottoms to length. Cut an extra one to use as a spacer while you're at it. When the channels are ready, clean up any extra glue, then get the roundover router out again. I rounded all the outside surfaces on the channels and the top lips where the support arms will enter the channels.

Glue and nail the channel assemblies together, using the extra bottom to help maintain even spacing at the top of the assembly.

To attach the channels to the cabinets, first use a

By adding smaller tops to the individual cabinets, each makes a fine tool stand with lots of storage beneath. Note the roller stand mounted on the underside of the top. Flip the top over and you've created an outfeed table for any machine.

combination square to make a line 4⅛" in from the front and back edges of each cabinet. Double-check the lines to make sure they will fall in the exact center of each of the channel sides. After checking, drill five evenly spaced ³⁄₁₆" clearance holes on each line. Countersink each hole from the inside of the cabinets, then attach the channel assemblies to the cabinets, holding the top of the channel flush to the cabinet top.

Now move to the support arms themselves. Use your drill press to make a 1"-diameter hole through each support arm, 3" up from the bottom edge and centered on the piece. On each cabinet, mark the location for five 1" holes centered on the spaces between the channels, locating the first 6" up from the inside of the channel bottom, then 2" on center from that first mark. These holes shouldn't be drilled all the way through the cabinet side, or the dowels will interfere with the drawers. Make the holes about ⅝" deep. I used a Forstner bit and used the spur tip as an indicator of depth. By drilling slowly I was able to tell when the spur poked through on the inside, and stop the hole at that depth.

Next, round over all the edges on the support arms except those on the top, then slip the arms into the channels and check the fit. If they don't move easily (though they shouldn't be too loose) adjust the fit. With the arms all the way down in the channel, take one of the top plates and lay it across the two arms. Mark the location of the arms on the top plate, allowing the arms to naturally settle in the channels. If they're pushed too tightly to the cabinet, the arms won't move easily.

Head to the table saw and cut ½"-deep rabbets on each end of the top plate using the marks for the support arms to determine the width. Then drill clearance holes, and screw the top plates to the support arms after pilot drilling the hole to avoid splitting.

You should be able to raise and lower the entire assembly with little resistance. I used simple dowels to lock the arms at whatever height I wanted. Round over the edges of the top plate, then move on to building the benchtop.

MORE THAN AN ASSEMBLY TOP

The top is made from two ¾"-thick pieces of plywood glued together. Use lots of glue spread thinly over the entire surface of one piece, then nail the corners to keep the top from slipping around while you clamp up the top "sandwich."

To give the top even more versatility, I added dog holes along the front and back edge of the top to accommodate a set of Veritas Bench Pups and Wonder Pups. These work like vises and can hold almost any workpiece. These holes also become the attachment points to hold the top in place on the cabinets.

Locate the dog holes 5" in from each edge and spaced 4" on center, starting 4" from either end. I used a ¾" auger bit to make the holes, and the photo shows a jig we've used before to make sure the holes are straight.

With the holes drilled, mark a centerline down the length of each support top plate. Then lay the benchtop on top of the cabinets and position it evenly on the top plates. Now look through a set of dog holes in the benchtop and move things around until the centerline on the plate is in the center of the holes. Use a pencil to mark the hole locations on the top plate, then remove the top.

Drill ¾"-diameter holes partway through the top plates (⅝" deep). Then drill a ³⁄₁₆" clearance hole the rest of the way through the plates, centered on the holes, countersinking the holes from the underside of the top plate. Cut four ¾"-diameter dowels to 1⅝" in length, and screw them in these holes from the underside of the top plates.

The top can now be easily located on the dowels without having to bend over. Once in place, the dowels hold the cabinets in place, and make the entire bench more sturdy. But don't forget to round everything over. Not only did I round the top's edges, but I also rounded the lips of the dog holes. This makes it easier to locate the dowels and dogs and also keeps the plywood from splintering at the sharp edges.

STURDY STORAGE DRAWERS

The drawers are the last step and are designed for basic utility. They are $\frac{1}{2}$" plywood boxes with $\frac{1}{4}$"-thick plywood bottoms and a $\frac{3}{4}$" false front. I used tongue-and-groove joinery on the drawer boxes.

Set up either a $\frac{1}{4}$" stack dado in your table saw, or a $\frac{1}{4}$" bit in your router table. Then set the fence to leave $\frac{1}{4}$" between the fence and bit or blade. Set the depth of the cut for $\frac{1}{4}$", then run the front, back and bottom inside edges of each drawer side. Also run the bottom inside edge of each drawer front.

Next adjust the fence on your saw/router table to cut the tongues on the drawer fronts and back. Check the fit, then run all the fronts and backs. The drawers are then glued and nailed together. The bottoms slip into the groove in the sides and front, and then are nailed in place to the bottom edge of the drawer back. Use the bottoms to make sure the drawers are square before nailing them in place.

The false drawer fronts are again simple and utilitarian: $\frac{3}{4}$" plywood with the edges rounded over. I held each drawer box $\frac{1}{4}$" up from the bottom edge of each front. Attach the drawer handles (simple 4" chrome pulls from almost any home center store that cost about $2 each) to the fronts, countersinking the screw heads flush to the back of the drawer fronts. The false fronts are screwed in place through the drawer box fronts. Mount the slides following the hardware instructions.

I added a couple coats of paint to the cabinets, but left the top as bare wood. I added a coat of lacquer to the top support assembly and the drawer fronts. There's only one thing left to do to make these storage cabinets all they can be. Make a couple of auxiliary tops to fit on the individual cabinets. I made mine with a piece of $\frac{3}{4}$" plywood (drilled to match the dowels). Add a roller and you have a height-adjustable outfeed table that can be used with your table saw, jointer, planer or any other machine. When not in use as a bench or outfeed table, you've now got two very handy tools stands that tuck away against the wall — right next to the cars.

The drilling jig is simply a piece of plywood with an edge stop (like a bench hook) with a guiding block screwed in position over the hole (centered 5" from the edge). You'll notice another hole drilled through the plywood in front of the block. That hole is in line with the guiding hole and lets you see your positioning line drawn on the top to know if you're in the correct location to drill.

SOURCES

Grizzly Industrial Inc.
800-523-4777, or www.grizzly.com
4 - H0689 3" fixed casters - $4.95 ea.
4 - H0693 3" swivel casters w/brake - $7.95 ea.
6 - H2902 12" full-extension slides - $9.95 pr.
Lee Valley
800-871-8158, or www.leevalley.com
2 - 05G10.02 Wonder Pups - $ 35.50 ea.
1 - 05G04.04 Bench Pups - $24.50 pr.

POWER-TOOL WORKBENCH

You can't buy a bench that does everything this one does: It's a traditional workbench, outfeed table and assembly bench. And even if you could buy one, it would be a lot more expensive than the $483 we spent on the wood, hardware and vise.

By Christopher Schwarz

In a world dominated by power tools, it's a wonder that commercial workbenches are still designed mostly for handwork. These European-style monsters are set up more for planing, mortising and dovetailing, rather than routing, biscuiting and nailing.

What's worse, most traditional benches are too big (most are 6' long) for the handwork necessary in a modern garage shop; and they are too small (usually 24" deep) to assemble sizable projects on. Plus, there's the cost. You can buy a decent workbench for $800, but nice ones will cost more than a cabinet saw.

One of our contributing editors, Glen Huey, found a solution to this problem when he set up his professional cabinet shop years ago. Glen does some handwork, but for the most part, his motto is: "If you can't do it on a table saw, it isn't worth doing."

So Glen set up his bench as part of his table saw. It attached to the outfeed side of his Unisaw and served as:
• a smaller, traditional workbench for handwork
• a spacious and solid outfeed table
• an enormous assembly bench (when you take into account the table saw and its table board)
• and a cavernous place for tool storage in the drawers and on the large shelf underneath the top.

I've watched Glen build dozens of projects with this rig – everything from corner cabinets to a drop-lid secretary – and it has never let him down.

PHOTO BY AL PARRISH

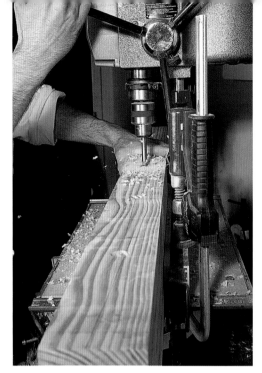

Drill the ³⁄₄"-diameter dog holes into the front edge of your bench before you put the top together. This will save you from making a jig later or having dog holes that wander if you cut them freehand.

I built the top in four-board sections and then glued those sections together. Don't skimp on the glue or clamps – the quickest way to a big old gap in your bench's top.

In a world dominated by power tools, it's a wonder that commercial workbenches are still designed mostly for handwork. These European-style monsters are set up more for planing, mortising and dovetailing, rather than routing, biscuiting and nailing.

What's worse, most traditional benches are too big (most are 6' long) for the handwork necessary in a modern garage shop; and they are too small (usually 24" deep) to assemble sizable projects on. Plus, there's the cost. You can buy a decent workbench for $800, but nice ones will cost more than a cabinet saw.

One of our contributing editors, Glen Huey, found a solution to this problem when he set up his professional cabinet shop years ago. Glen does some handwork, but for the most part, his motto is: "If you can't do it on a table saw, it isn't worth doing."

So Glen set up his bench as part of his table saw. It attached to the outfeed side of his Unisaw and served as:

• a smaller, traditional workbench for handwork

• a spacious and solid outfeed table

• an enormous assembly bench (when you take into account the table saw and its table board)

• and a cavernous place for tool storage in the drawers and on the large shelf underneath the top.

I've watched Glen build dozens of projects with this rig – everything from corner cabinets to a drop-lid secretary – and it has never let him down.

I took Glen's great idea and tuned it up a bit with an enormous tail vise, bench dogs and an extra shelf. Plus, I built this bench using Southern yellow pine for the top, legs and stretchers, and I used birch plywood for the tool box. (If you live in the West, you'll have to substitute fir for pine for this project.) The total cost of the wood, hardware and vise was $483 and change – less than half the price of an entry-level commercial workbench. If that's still too rich, you can

POWER-TOOL WORKBENCH						
No.	Item	Dimensions T W L			Materials	Notes
1	Top*	3	26	52	SYP	
4	Legs	2½	2½	31	SYP	
4	End rails	1⅜	3	22	SYP	1¼" TBE
2	Frt/bk rails	1⅜	7	40	SYP	¾" TBE
2	Vise jaws	1¾	7⅛	26	Maple	
2	Toolbox sides	¾	23⅝	16	Ply	¾" x ½" rabbet for back
2	Toolbox top/bott	¾	23⅝	37	Ply	¾" x ½" rabbet for back
1	Toolbox divider	¾	14½	22⅞	Ply	
1	Toolbox back	¾	15½	38	Ply	
2	Top drw false frts	¾	6½	18⅛	Ply	
4	Top drw sides	½	5½	21½	Ply	½" x ¼" rabbet on ends
2	Top drw front	½	5½	16⅝	Ply	
2	Top drw back	½	4¾	16⅝	Ply	
2	Top drw bott	½	16⅝	21¼	Ply	in ½" x ¼" groove
2	Low drw false frts	¾	8	18⅛	Ply	
4	Low drw sides	½	7	21½	Ply	½" x ¼" rabbet on ends
2	Low drw front	½	7	16⅝	Ply	
2	Low drw back	½	6¼	16⅝	Ply	
2	Low drw bott	½	16⅝	21¼	Ply	in ½" x ¼" groove

* The top is made from 20 individual boards. With most of the 2x material I managed to get 1⅜" of usable thickness, however other boards were a bit corkscrewed and ended up thinner. You should be able to get a 26"-wide top with the material list for this project. TBE=Tenon, both ends. SYP=Southern yellow pine.

PLAN

¾"-diameter bench-dog holes

3"

10"

52"

PLAN, TOP REMOVED

Drawer fronts set back ¼" from face of case

DELUXE BENCH
- Six 2 x 8 x 12' Southern yellow pine (or fir) boards @ $10.58 each: $63.48
- One sheet of ¾" birch plywood: $42
- One sheet of ½" birch plywood: $35
- One Veritas Twin-screw vise: $229
- One set of Veritas Special Bench Bolts: $29.50
- Four Veritas Bench Pups: $24.50
- Four pairs of 20"-long full-extension drawer slides: $60

TOTAL PRICE: $483.48

MORE BASIC BENCHES

If that's still too rich for you, it's easy to make this bench for less.

- Less-Expensive Vise: Make the deluxe bench with a simpler vise (see Supplies box) and make your own bench dogs.

- Nice Vise But No Tool Box: Make the deluxe bench without the tool box and make your own bench dogs.

- Total-Economy Model: Make the bench with the less-expensive vise, no toolbox and use hex bolts (see Supplies box) instead of the Veritas bench bolts.

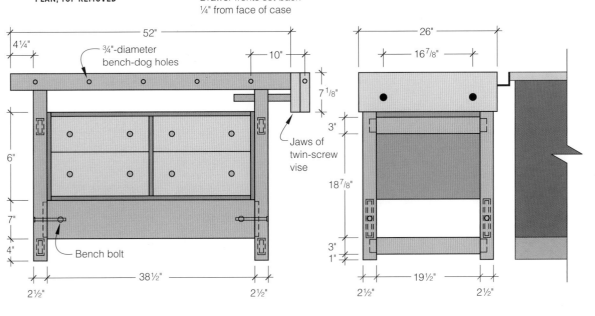

ELEVATION

52"

4¼"

¾"-diameter bench-dog holes

10"

7⅛"

Jaws of twin-screw vise

6"

7"

4"

Bench bolt

38½"

2½"   2½"

PROFILE

26"

16⅞"

3"

18⅞"

3"

1"

19½"

2½"   2½"

The easiest way to make clean mortises using your drill press is to first drill a series of overlapping holes (right). Then go back and clean up the waste between these holes several times until the bit can slide left to right in the mortise without stopping (far right). Then you only have to square up the ends with a chisel.

make this bench for less. See the supplies box at the top, right of page 33 for more details.

As shown, this bench is designed for a Delta Unisaw equipped with the short 30" fence rails. By lengthening the bench's legs up to 3", you can accommodate any table saw on the market today with the same shopping list and basic bench design.

When completed and attached to your saw, this bench will give you a huge area for project assembly – more than 19 square feet. I call it the "assembly acre."

If you have a contractor-style saw, this bench can be adapted easily to accommodate the motor hanging out the back. If you build the bench without the toolbox, the legs will clear the motor with no changes to the design for most contractor-style saws. I checked half a dozen right-tilt contractor saws to make sure this is true. If your saw is the exception, all you have to do is shift the top left before attaching it to the base. If you want some storage beneath, I suggest making one bank of drawers for the left side only and leave the right side open for the motor.

No matter which bench you build, it will change the way you work. You can assemble large cabinets on the saw and bench instead of on the floor or driveway. You will have a dedicated outfeed table for your saw instead of a tipsy roller stand. And you will have a bench for handwork that has all the bells and whistles. With a set of bench dogs, the excellent Veritas tail vise will handle every common clamping and holding chore. So let's get started.

START AT THE TOP

If you don't have a workbench, build the top first, throw that on sawhorses and construct the rest of the bench there. The first task at hand is to cut down your six 12'-long 2 x 8s into manageable lengths. Here's how I did it.

With five of the 2 x 8s, crosscut them at 54" and 108". Then rip all the pieces down the middle. This will give you the 20 boards you need to make the top. You then can glue up eight of the shorter fall-off pieces face-to-face to make the bench's four legs, and use the remaining two fall-off pieces for the end rails. With the sixth 2 x 8, you can get the front and back rails, a couple more end rails and have some scrap left over for cutting test joints.

If you have a planer and jointer, dress all the wood so it's true and then cut it to final size on your table saw. If you don't have these machines, use your saw to rip off the

I cut my tenons using a dado stack as shown. I like this method because it requires only one saw setup to make all the cuts on a tenon. First define the tenon's face cheeks and shoulders (right). Then define the edge cheeks and shoulders (below left). Finally, check your work using the test mortise you cut earlier (below right).

Drawboring is an easy way to make a heavy-duty joint. Begin by drilling a 3⁄8"-diameter hole through the mortise as shown above. Now clamp the tenon into the mortise and mark the center point of the hole using a drill bit and a mallet (right). Now drill a hole in the tenon that's 1⁄32" in toward the shoulder from the mark you just made.

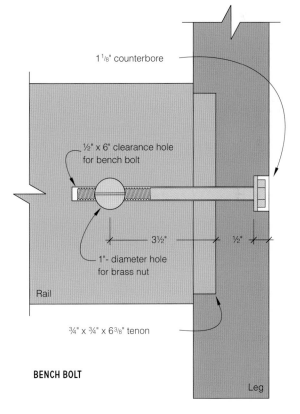

Drill hole through leg at a point ½" from the shoulder

Drill hole through tenon at a point $^1/_{32}$" in toward the shoulder

Rail

½"

$^{15}/_{32}$"

Tenon shoulder

Leg

DRAWBORING THE TENONS ON THE END RAILS

rounded edges. Now borrow some extra clamps from your neighbor and make sure you have a lot of glue on hand. It's time to assemble the top.

Here's some hard-won advice for you on these tops: Assemble the top a few boards at a time. Yes, it takes longer, but the result will be a top that has no gaps between the boards and is more likely to be flat in the end. Assemble your top using four boards at a time, using plenty of glue and clamps (I needed almost three 8-ounce bottles for the job). Here's one more important tip: If you are going to flatten the top using a hand plane (as opposed to a belt sander), arrange all the boards for the top with the grain running in the same direction. This will reduce any tearout when planing.

After the glue has dried on each section, it's a good idea to dress each assembled section of your top with your jointer and planer. This will make assembling the top easier and the end result a lot flatter. If you don't have these

1 ⅛" counterbore

½" x 6" clearance hole for bench bolt

3½"

½"

1"- diameter hole for brass nut

Rail

¾" x ¾" x 6³⁄8" tenon

BENCH BOLT

Leg

Once you've drilled the counterbore and the through-hole for the bench bolt, mark its location on the end of the tenon using a brad-point bit.

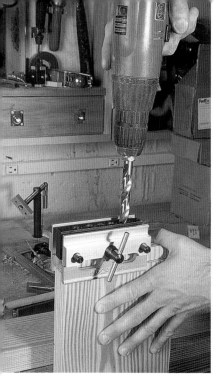

Drill a hole for the bench bolt using a doweling jig and a $\frac{1}{2}$"-diameter drill bit. It's a deep hole, so you might need an extra-long bit to do the job.

machines, be careful during your glue-ups and flatten the entire top at the end. Before you glue all the sections together, pick out the section that will be the front and drill the $\frac{3}{4}$"-diameter dog holes now for the front edge. It's much easier now than when the top is assembled.

After drilling those dog holes, glue the five sections together, clamp and wait for things to dry.

A MORTISE-AND-TENON BASE

The base of this bench is built entirely using mortise-and-tenon joints. The two ends are glued and assembled using an old-school process called "drawboring," which I'll show you how to do. The ends are attached to the front and back rails using an unglued mortise-and-tenon joint and bench bolts, which essentially are heavy-duty knockdown hardware that is similar to bed bolts. These bolts are better than any glued joint and can be tightened throughout the life span of the bench.

The first step is to make a practice mortise in a piece of scrap that you can use to size all your tenons. I made my mortises on a drill press using a $\frac{3}{4}$"-diameter Forstner bit and a fence. You can make amazingly clean mortises this way. See the photos above for details. After you've made your test mortise, head to the table saw to make the tenons.

I make my tenons using a dado stack in my table saw. The fence determines the length of the tenon; the height of the dado blades determines the measurement of the tenons' shoulders. Set the height of the dado stack to $\frac{5}{16}$", cut a tenon on some scrap as shown in the photos at left and see if it fits your test mortise. If the fit is firm and smooth, cut all the tenons on the front, back and end rails.

Now use your tenons to lay out the locations of your mortises on your legs. Use the diagrams as a guide. Cut your mortises using your drill press. Now get ready to assemble the ends.

To accurately position the hole for the brass nut shown in the photo, build a simple jig like the one shown here using $\frac{1}{2}$" dowel, a scrap of wood and a nail. The nail is located where you want the center of the brass nut to go (top). Insert the dowel into the hole in the rail and tap the nail (bottom). Now drill a 1"-diameter hole there and your joint will go together with ease.

DRAWBORING EXPLAINED

Before glues were as reliable as they are today, 18th-century craftsmen would "drawbore" a mortise-and-tenon joint to get a more mechanical fit. It's not at all difficult to do and reduces the chance of having a gap in your joint, too.

The key to a drawbored joint is a wooden peg or dowel that pulls the tenon into the mortise. Begin by drilling a $\frac{3}{8}$"-diameter hole for the peg through the mortise only, as shown in the photo above. The hole should be located $\frac{1}{2}$" from the edge of the leg and go just a little deeper than the wall of the mortise.

Now assemble the joint without glue and clamp it up. Take a $\frac{3}{8}$"-diameter brad-point bit and place it in the hole you just drilled. Use a mallet to lightly strike the bit to mark the center of the hole on the tenon's cheek. Remove the tenon and make a mark for a hole through the tenon that's in the same location as the mark you just made but $\frac{1}{32}$" closer to the tenon's shoulder as shown in the illustration at right.

Drill a $\frac{3}{8}$"-diameter hole through the tenon at that second mark. When you are ready to assemble the ends you will glue and clamp up the end rails between the legs, put some glue in the holes and then pound in some $\frac{3}{8}$"-diameter dowels. The offset holes will pull the joint together instantly. Hold off on this final assembly step until after the bench bolts are installed.

BENCH BOLTS ARE FOREVER

The set of bench bolts for this project cost $20, but they are worth it. They are easier to install than traditional bed bolts. And they are much easier to install than using off-the-rack hex bolts, nuts and washers.

Begin installing the bench bolts by drilling a $1\frac{1}{8}$"-diameter counterbore in the legs that's $\frac{1}{2}$" deep. Then drill a $\frac{1}{2}$"-diameter hole in the center of that counterbore that goes all the way through the leg and into the mortise. Now dry-assemble the ends and the front and back rails and clamp everything together. Use a $\frac{1}{2}$" brad-point drill bit to mark the center of your hole on the end of each tenon.

Disassemble the bench and clamp the front rail to your top or in a vise. Use a doweling jig and a $\frac{1}{2}$" drill bit to continue cutting the hole for the bench bolt. You'll need to drill about $3\frac{1}{2}$" into the rail. Repeat this process on the other tenons.

Now you need to drill a 1"-diameter hole that intersects the $\frac{1}{2}$" hole you just drilled in the rail. This 1"-diameter hole holds a special round nut that pulls everything together. To accurately locate where this 1" hole should be, I made a simple jig shown in the photos at left that I picked up from the instruction book for the vise. It works like a charm. Sometimes drill bits can wander – even when guided by a doweling jig – and this jig ensures your success.

Plane or sand all your legs and rails and assemble the bench's base. Attach the top to the base. You can glue dowels in the top of the legs and drill holes in the underside of the top, or you can use metal desktop fasteners with $2\frac{1}{2}$"-long screws. Either way, be sure to leave some way for the top to expand and contract.

I nailed the divider in place in the toolbox so I could check and double-check its position before fixing it in place.

THE MODERN TOOLBOX

After all that traditional joinery, I was ready to fire up the biscuit joiner. You can build this toolbox using one sheet of ¾" plywood and one sheet of ½" plywood.

Cut your parts to size and start construction by cutting a ¾" x ½" rabbet on the back edge of the sides, top and bottom to hold the back. The best way to do this is on your table saw. Cut biscuit slots to join these four parts, then glue and clamp up the case. Once the glue is dry, cut the case divider to its finished size, position it inside the case and nail it in place. Screw the back into its rabbet and iron on birch edge tape to cover the plywood edges. Screw the toolbox to the front rail and legs of the bench's base.

Build the drawers using ½"-thick plywood. Most drawers have ¼"-thick bottom panels, but because these drawers have to stand up to extra abuse, I chose to use ½" plywood instead.

With the drawer boxes built, it's time to hang them in the case. Installing drawer slides is easy if you know a couple tricks. Most professionals simply will scribe a line on the inside of the case and screw the slide there. You'd do it this way too if you installed slides every day. For the rest of us,

it's easier to make spacers using scrap plywood that hold the slide in position as you screw it to the case. Install the slides for the top drawer first. Put your spacer in place and put the slide on top. Screw it in place using the holes that allow you to adjust the slide forward andback.

Now install the slides on the drawer sides using the holes that allow you to adjust the slide up and down. Put the drawer in the case and check your work. Adjust the slides and, when satisfied, add a few more screws to lock that position in place. Hang the remainder of the drawers.

FALSE DRAWER FRONTS

Installing false fronts also can be tricky with inset drawers such as these. The best two tools for the job are some shims that you can buy at any home center and the drawer-front adjusters that install on the back side of the false fronts.

Begin by ironing on edge tape to the plywood edges (if desired) and installing the screws for your drawers' knobs. Now get set to install the false fronts on the lower drawers. Remove the drawer boxes from the top of the case and clamp the false fronts to the lower drawer boxes. Using

Use spacers to position your drawer slides for installation. They take an extra few minutes to make, but they act like a third hand when securing the slides to the case.

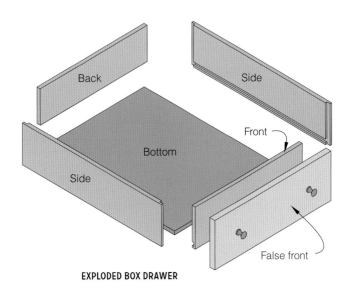

EXPLODED BOX DRAWER

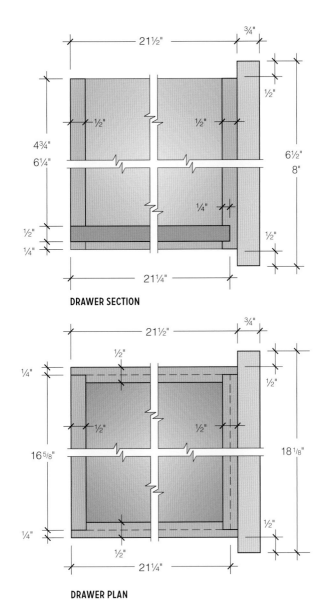

DRAWER SECTION

DRAWER PLAN

Here you can see a drawer-front adjuster installed in the backside of a false front. The machine screw can wiggle a bit in the plastic housing, which allows you to move the drawer front slightly for a perfect fit. Here's a tip: You can plane the white plastic easily if the adjuster isn't flush with the false front.

Drill two pilot holes in the drawer boxes and install screws in them so the points stick out about $\frac{1}{16}$". Now position your drawer front where you want it using shims.

Once your drawer front is in position, press it against the screw tips. This will mark the wood for the location of your drawer-front adjusters.

the shims, adjust the false fronts until you have a $^{1}/16$" gap on the sides and bottom. You might have to trim the false fronts a bit using a plane or sandpaper for a good fit. Once satisfied, nail the false fronts in place, then secure them with a few screws.

Now put the top drawer boxes back into the case. Drill a couple pilot holes into the front of the drawer box and put screws into the holes so the points poke out about $^{1}/16$". Take a top drawer false front and carefully put it into position and add shims to get it close. Press the false front against the drawer box until the screw points bite into your false front. Remove the false fronts.

Drill 25mm holes in the back of the false front for the drawer-front adjusters and pound them in place as shown in the photo on the next page. Now replace the screws in your drawer box with the screws for the drawer-front adjusters and attach the false front. You'll be able to shift the false fronts around a bit until you get a consistent gap all around. When you're happy, add a couple more screws to lock the false front in position.

DETAILS: DOGS AND THE VISE

The spacing of the $^{3}/4$"-diameter dog holes on the top of the bench are determined by the type of vise you purchase. If you are using the Veritas Twin-screw vise, drill your dog holes every 10" as shown in the diagrams and chamfer the openings of the holes. I purchased four Veritas Wonder Pups to use as dogs in this bench. You also could make your own dogs by gluing a $^{3}/4$" dowel into a small block of $^{3}/4$"-thick wood.

Installing the tail vise is a project unto itself and requires a long afternoon and some precision drilling. The instructions supplied with the vise are first-rate – as is the vise itself – so there's no need to go into detail here. If you mount this vise as shown, it's remarkably versatile. It excels at clamping boards so you can work on their ends, such as when dovetailing. With the dogs, you can clamp large panels to your bench for sanding. And with the dog holes drilled on the front edge of the bench and vise as shown, you can secure long boards (up to 61" long) to work on their edges.

If your work is both long and wide (for instance, a large cabinet door) you can pull out one of the drawers in the toolbox below for additional support while you work on its edge. The drawer slides are rated to hold up to 100 pounds, so you should be able to tackle all but the heaviest panels.

One of your last acts on this bench is to flatten the top. I removed the high spots with a No. 7 jointer plane, cutting diagonally across the top in both directions. Then I cleaned up my work with a random-orbit sander. Check your progress occasionally using a straightedge or winding sticks. A belt sander will take the place of a jointer plane if you prefer.

Once you load up the toolbox with tools, it's not going anywhere, so there's little need to attach it to the back of your saw. If you do find yourself pushing the bench around, you could add a shelf between the front and back rails of the bench base (below the toolbox) and load that up with more tools or sand bags. Or you can cobble up a way to attach the bench to your saw's table board and sheet-metal frame.

Once you get your bench where you like it, you'll want to rout out a couple channels in the bench's top to accommodate your miter gauge's bar. For my saw, these slots measured $^{3}/8$" deep, $1^{1}/8$" wide and 10" long. Measure the bar of your miter gauge with the longest bar and add a little extra for good measure.

For me, the only real problem with this new workbench is that it begs the question: What do I do with my old bench? Natural selection just weeded it out.

24-HOUR WORKBENCH

Most woodworkers need a workbench that is sturdy, inexpensive and doesn't take a month of Sundays to build. This is that bench.

By Christopher Schwarz

Whenever we leave beginning woodworkers to work alone in the shop, it's a fair bet that when we return to check on them, they're working on the shop's floor.

We have at least five workbenches in our shop – not counting the assembly tables – but the new people always seem to prefer the wide expanse of the concrete floor more than the benches. Of course, I shouldn't talk. When I started woodworking I had my grandfather's fully outfitted bench. But my first few projects were built on the floor of our back porch, my assemblies propped up on a couple of 4x4s. I can't for the life of me remember why I chose the floor instead of the bench.

Since those early years, I've built a few workbenches. And I've been striving to make each one more versatile, solid, inexpensive and quick to build than the last. I think I've finally got it. To test my theory, Associate Editor Kara Gebhart and I built this bench with a budget of under $200 and just 24 hours of working time in the shop.

That $200 includes the wood, the vise and the hardware. And that 24 hours includes everything, too, even the two hours we spent picking out the wood and sawing it to rough length on a dolly in the parking lot of The Home Depot. (But once again, I was working on the ground. Oh, drat.)

The real beauty of this bench (besides getting you off the floor) is that it can be completed using tools you likely already have in your shop.

For this project, your must-have tools are a table saw, a drill press, a corded drill and some basic hand tools. If you have a jointer and planer, the project will go faster because you can easily dress your lumber to size and eliminate any bowing or warping. But don't be afraid to work with the lumber as it comes from the lumberyard. Just make sure you buy the straightest pieces you can.

START WITH THE ROUGH STUFF
TIME: 0:00 TO 5:06

In a nutshell, here's how the bench goes together: The top is made of four pieces of Baltic birch plywood that are laminated together with a pine "skirt" glued around the edge. On the bench's pine base, the end rails are joined to the legs using pegged mortise-and-tenon joints. The end assemblies attach to the front and back rails using an unglued mortise-and-tenon joint with big bench bolts – it's quite similar to a bed in construction.

When we first went to the lumberyard, it seemed like a good idea to buy 4x4 posts for the legs. But when we got there (and later called around to other nearby lumberyards) we discovered that the only 4x4s available in

CAULS

Use whatever clamps are on hand to glue the top together. If you're low on clamps, you can use 5-gallon buckets of water (they are quite heavy) in the middle, the four cauls discussed in the article and C-clamps along the edges.

yellow pine were #2 common, which has more knots than the #1 pine (also sold as "prime" or "top choice" in some yards). If you can't get yellow pine where you live, you can just look for fir. (To find yellow pine in your area, visit southernpine.com.)

After picking through the mound of knotty 4x4s, we decided to instead make the legs by ripping a 2x8 and gluing up the legs to the thickness that we needed. It took longer to make the legs this way, but now they have almost no knots.

Crosscut and rip the parts you need for the base of the bench and the skirt that goes around the top. If you have a planer and jointer, dress your lumber. Now glue up and clamp the parts for the legs and get out your clamp collection and some buckets (yes, buckets) to glue up the top.

TOP-DOWN CONSTRUCTION TIME: 5:06 TO 6:29

I've built a few of these benches and have come up with a pretty easy way to make the top: Just sandwich all the plywood into a nearly 3"-thick slab. We glued it up one layer at a time to keep things under control and to ensure we could eliminate all the gaps on the edges.

You're probably going to need at least four 8-ounce bottles of yellow glue for this part of the project, plus a scrap of plywood ($\frac{1}{4}$" x 4" x 7" worked for us) to spread the glue evenly. Squirt a sizable amount onto one piece of plywood and spread the adhesive until you've got a thin and even film. Place the plywood's mating piece on top and line up the edges. Now drive about a dozen #8 x 1$\frac{1}{4}$" screws into the

two pieces. Space the screws evenly across the face of the board, but you don't need to get scientific about it. The object is to pull the two pieces together without gaps. After 30 minutes of drying time, remove the screws and add another layer of glue, plywood and some more screws.

Because you don't want a bunch of screw holes staring at you every time you use the bench, you'll likely want to attach the final layer with clamps, clamping cauls and anything else heavy you have in your shop.

We used four cauls (a clamping aid) across the width of the top to put even more pressure in the middle. The cauls should be about 2" x 2" x 32". Plane or sand a $\frac{1}{16}$" taper toward each end to give each caul a slight bow. When you clamp the bow against the top, this will

24-HOUR WORKBENCH						
NO.	ITEM	DIMENSIONS (INCHES)			MATERIAL	NOTES
		T	W	L		
1	Top*	3	24$\frac{1}{4}$	58$\frac{1}{4}$	Baltic birch plywood	
2	Top skirt, ends	1$\frac{3}{8}$	3	27	Southern yellow pine	
2	Top skirt, front & back	1$\frac{3}{8}$	3	61	Southern yellow pine	
4	Legs	3	3	31	Southern yellow pine	
4	End rails	1$\frac{3}{8}$	3	23$\frac{1}{2}$	Southern yellow pine	2" TBE
2	Front & back rails	1$\frac{3}{8}$	7	40	Southern yellow pine	$\frac{3}{4}$" TBE
1	Vise jaw	2$\frac{3}{4}$	6	15	Southern yellow pine	

* The top is laminated using four layers of $\frac{3}{4}$"-thick Baltic birch plywood.
TBE=Tenon, both ends.

put pressure in the middle of your slab.

Finally, use whatever other clamps you have to clamp the edges (C-clamps work well).

When all four layers are glued together, cut your top to its finished size using a circular saw and a straight scrap of wood to guide it. Because the top is so thick, you'll have to cut from both faces, so lay out cutting lines with care.

SKIRT WILL TEST YOUR SKILLS
TIME: 6:29 TO 11:49

Now gather the skirt pieces and begin laying out the finger joints for the corners. These joints are mostly decorative. Butt joints or miters will do just as well (and save you some time). And if you want to make this

process even easier, use $\frac{1}{2}$"-thick material for the skirt, which is a whole lot easier to clamp in place because it is more flexible than some of the thicker material.

Here's how we suggest you cut the finger joints: First lay out the joints on the end pieces with just one tongue or finger sticking out. Each finger is 1$\frac{3}{8}$" long and 1" wide. Cut the waste away using a hand saw or band saw and check the fit against your top. When it fits perfectly, use these joints to lay out the mating joints on the long skirt pieces. Cut the notches on the long skirt pieces and check the fit of your joints. Tune them up using a chisel, a rabbet plane or a shoulder plane.

Now glue the skirt pieces to the top. Because each "ply" in plywood runs the opposite direction of the ply above it, there's actually a fair amount of long

The skirt pieces can be joined using finger joints, a miter or just wood screws. If you choose finger joints, your best bet is to lay out and cut the joint on one member and then use that joint to lay out your cut lines on its mate.

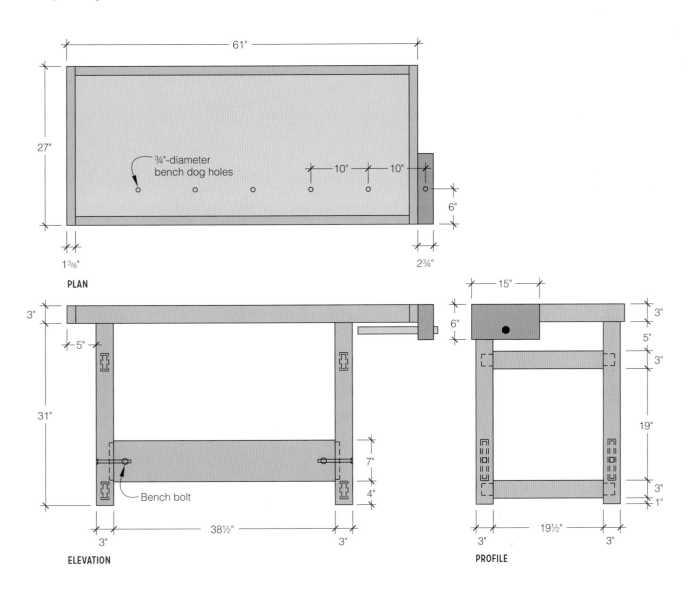

PLAN

ELEVATION

PROFILE

grain on the edges of your top. This means the skirt will stay stuck just fine using only glue. Add as many clamps as you can. While that glue dries, start reading the directions for installing the vise, because that's the next step.

The instructions that come with the Veritas vise are complete and easy to follow; it just takes some time to get everything moving smoothly. Before you begin, be sure your drill press's table is square to the chuck – this will save you lots of frustration. Once you get your vise installed, place the top on a couple of sawhorses (you'll need a friend's help) and get ready to build the base.

A STOUT BASE
TIME: 11:49 TO 14:54

The base of this bench is built with mortise-and-tenon joints. The two assembled ends are glued together and then pegged using dowels. The ends are attached to the front and back rails using an unglued mortise-and-tenon joint plus bench bolts.

The first step is to make a practice mortise in a piece of scrap that you can use to size all your tenons. We made our mortises on a drill press using a $^{3}/_{4}$"-diameter Forstner bit and a fence. You can make really clean mortises this way. After you've made your test mortise, head to the table saw to make all of your tenons.

I make my tenons using a dado stack in my table saw. The fence determines the length of the tenon; the height of the dado blades determines the measurement of the tenons' shoulders. Set the height of the dado stack to $^{5}/_{16}$", cut a tenon on some scrap as shown in the photos and see if it fits your test mortise. If the fit is firm and smooth, cut all the tenons on the front, back and end rails.

Now use your tenons to lay out the locations of your mortises on the legs. Use the diagrams as a guide. Cut mortises using your drill press and get ready to install the bench bolts.

BIG BAD BENCH BOLTS
TIME: 14:54 TO 18:59

The set of bench bolts for this project set us back $30, but they are worth it.

We cut our tenons using a dado stack. We like this method because it requires only one saw setup to make all the cuts on a tenon. First define the tenon's face cheeks and shoulders (above). Then you can define the edge cheeks and shoulders. Finally, check your work using the test mortise you cut earlier (right).

The easiest way to make clean mortises using your drill press is to first drill a series of overlapping holes. Then go back and clean up the waste between these holes several times until the bit can slide left to right in the mortise without stopping. Then you only have to square up the ends with a chisel.

Once you've drilled the counterbore and the through-hole for the bench bolt, mark its location on the end of the tenon using a brad-point bit.

SUPPLIES

LUMBER:
- 3 • 2 x 8 x 12' boards, preferably Southern yellow pine (if available in your area) or vertical-grade fir. We paid $8.58 for each board ($25.74 total).
- 2 • sheets of ¾" Baltic birch, Finnish birch or Appleply. This material comes in 60" x 60" sheets. Have the lumberyard rip them down the middle so you end up with four sheets of ¾" x 30" x 60". We paid $27.93 per sheet – what a bargain ($55.86 total).

HARDWARE:
- 4 • 5" corner braces. We paid $1.87 each ($7.48 total).

LEE VALLEY TOOLS
800-871-8158 or leevalley.com
Prices do not include any sales tax or shipping.
- 1 • set of four Veritas special bench bolts #05G07.02, $29.50
- 1 • large front vise #70G08.02, $72.50
- 1 • vise handle #05G12.03, $6.50

TOTAL PRICE: $197.58
Prices as of publication deadline.

There are less expensive alternatives to this specialty hardware, but none are as easy to put together.

You can begin installing the bench bolts by drilling a 1⅛"-diameter x ½"-deep counterbore in the legs that's centered on the location of the rail. Then drill a ⅝"-diameter hole in the center of that counterbore that goes all the way through the leg into the mortise you cut earlier.

Now dry-assemble the ends plus the front and back rails and clamp everything together. Use a ⅝" brad-point drill bit to mark the center of your hole on the end of each tenon.

Disassemble the bench and clamp the front rail to your top or in a vise. Use a doweling jig and a ⅝" drill bit (as seen in the photo below) to continue boring the hole for the bench bolt. You'll need to drill about 3¾" into the rail. Then repeat this process on the other tenons.

Now you need to drill a 1¼"-diameter hole that intersects the ⅝" hole you just drilled in the rail. This 1¼"-diameter hole holds a special round nut that pulls everything together. To accurately locate where this 1¼" hole should be, I made a simple jig (shown in the photos) I picked up from another project. This works like a charm and I recommend you use one. Sometimes drill bits can wander – even when guided by a doweling jig – and this simple jig ensures success.

Plane or sand all your legs and rails, then assemble the bench's base. First glue the end rails between the legs. Glue and clamp that assembly.

When it's dry, drill a ⅜"-diameter hole through each joint that's about 2" deep. Then glue and hammer a peg through the tenons using 2⅛"-long sections of ⅜"-diameter dowel stock into each hole. Then install the bench bolts and use a ratchet and socket to snug your bolts and bring everything together.

Now screw the 5" braces to the legs using the photo at right as a guide. Turn the top upside down on the sawhorses and place the assembled base in position. Screw it down.

DOG HOLES AND DETAILS
TIME: 18:59 TO 23:02

Dog holes on a bench are essential for clamping large panels, holding table legs and even clamping difficult-to-clamp assemblies. Most round dog holes are ¾" in diameter so they accept

To accurately position the hole for the brass nut shown in the photo, build a simple jig like the one shown here using ⅝" dowel, a scrap of wood and a nail. The nail is located where you want the center of the brass nut to go. Insert the dowel into the hole in the rail and tap the nail. Then just drill a 1¼"-diameter hole there and your joint will go together with ease.

a wide range of commercial dogs.

We made our own dogs for this bench to keep us from blowing our $180 budget. (If your budget isn't as strict, we recommend the Veritas brass Bench Pups. They cost $14.95 for a pair. Ask for item # 05G04.04. Contact Lee Valley at 800-871-8158 or leevalley.com.)

Our homemade dogs are made using 3"-long sections of ¾" dowel screwed to ⅝" x 1½" x 1½" pieces of scrap hardwood.

First drill the dog hole in your tail vise's jaw using your drill press. While you have the vise jaw off the bench, go ahead and add the edge detail of your choice to the ends. We chose a traditional large bead. A chamfer would be quicker if you're pressed for time.

Now put the vise's jaw back on and lay out the locations of your dog holes in the top. They can be anywhere from 8" to 11" apart. You'll have to build a simple jig to cut the holes. It's made from three pieces of scrap and is shown in action in the photo at the far right.

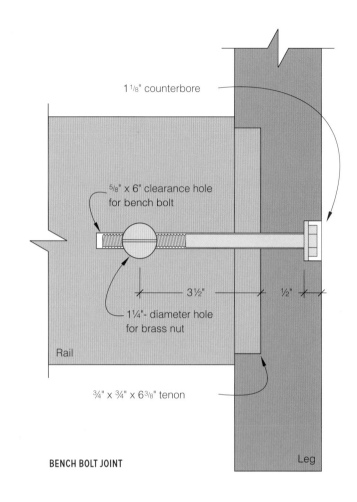

1 ⅛" counterbore

⅝" x 6" clearance hole for bench bolt

3½"

½"

1¼"- diameter hole for brass nut

Rail

¾" x ¾" x 6⅜" tenon

Leg

BENCH BOLT JOINT

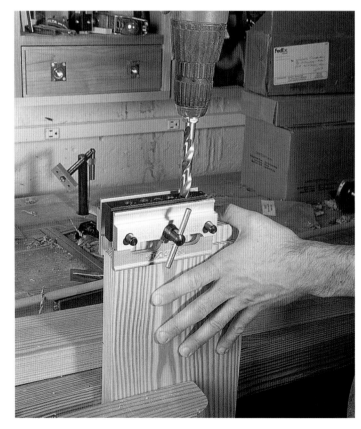

Drill a hole for the bench bolt using a doweling jig and a ⅝"-diameter drill bit. It's a deep hole, so you might need an extra-long bit to do the job.

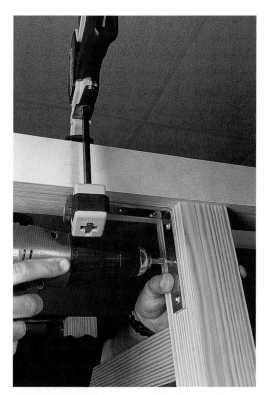

Installing the brackets that secure the top to the base is simple with this trick. Lay a scrap board across the legs and clamp the bracket to it. Now screw the bracket to the leg.

Here you can see our dog-hole drilling jig in action. There are two $\frac{3}{4}$" holes in the plywood base: one for the bit and the other to allow us to see the layout marks on the benchtop.

We bored the dog holes using a $\frac{3}{4}$" auger bit in a corded drill. Use a low speed on your drill for this operation because you need buckets of torque.

Now chamfer the rim of each dog hole; this prevents the grain from ripping up when you pull the occasionally stubborn dog from its hole (bad dog!). You can just use a chamfer bit in your plunge router to make this cut. Or you can simply ease the rims using some coarse sandpaper.

We sanded the top by using #120-grit sandpaper in a random-orbit sander and called it a day. Break all the sharp edges using #120-grit sandpaper. You don't need a fancy finish on this bench – just something to protect it from spills and scrapes. We took some off-the-shelf satin polyurethane, thinned it down to three parts poly and one part mineral spirits and ragged on two coats. Allow the finish to dry at least four hours between coats. (No, the four hours of drying time isn't included in our total time.)

Then we turned the stopwatch off and checked our time: 23 hours and 2 minutes. We had just enough time left to sweep the floor in case someone else needed to work down there.

FLATTEN A WORKBENCH'S TOP

Is it necessary? And if so, what are the best techniques?

By Christopher Schwarz

Like any tool or machine, a workbench requires accessories (jigs, fixtures, appliances) and occasional maintenance to actually do anything of great value. A bench without a bench hook is a dining table. A bench with a cupped work surface is an exercise in bewilderment and wasted effort.

There are a variety of ways to go about flattening a workbench top, including some that are patently nuts. But before I march down that list of your options, I ask: Does the top need to be flat?

Whenever I'm in an old barn, workshop or even an antique mall, I can't resist poking around the guts of any old workbenches I find. When my wife and I take the kids on a hayride, I end up in the chicken house checking out the 18th-century wooden screws on a face vise. When we visit living history museums, the kids are chasing the animals, and I'm asking the guy dressed as a cooper if I can poke around the undercarriage of his bench.

I've found little evidence that these benches were flattened regularly. Many of them bear toolmarks that are deep and of varying ages. I've seen benches that are so worn from use that the edges look as round as a pillow. One bench I saw in Columbus, Ohio, was so worn away in one spot that its 3"-thick top was less than an inch thick.

And when I check the 19th- and early 20th-century books, there's very little attention given to the workbench top. While there is detailed instruction on sharpening, tool maintenance and the act of building a bench, flattening its top isn't often listed as routine shop maintenance. At most, they'll note that the top should be flat.

Like an oil change. Flattening my benchtop is routine maintenance. How do I know when it's time? My handplanes stop giving me predictable and flat results. That usually tells me it's time to true the top.

1 In the right light. Move your bench so that one end points to a window. This makes it easier to read your winding sticks as you look for gaps underneath them and for alignment across their lengths.

2 Look for warp. My winding sticks here are 36"-long aluminum angle. Place one winding stick at the far end of your bench and the other one about 24" away. Sight across them both, looking for high and low spots. Move the far winding stick to the other end of the benchtop and repeat.

There are several explanations for this:

1. Workbench flatness is overrated and a product of our modern obsession with granite surface plates and dial calipers.

2. Early woodworkers would use "planing trays" – a disposable workshop appliance that attached to the bench and allowed woodworkers to plane cabinet-scale parts at a variety of angles.

3. Or a flat workbench was so important to those who handplaned panels and furniture components that its flatness was a given.

I don't have the answer, but I suspect that all three are true to some degree. If you've ever done any handwork on a bench that was cupped, bowed or twisted, then you know that it's not a good way to work. The downward pressure from a handplane (particularly wooden-bodied planes) can bend your

work into a low spot in the bench. When using long planes in particular, a low spot will prevent you from ever planing the board flat.

You can use small wooden wedges under your stock to support it and prevent it from bending into a low spot on your bench, but the problem is that you will have difficulty knowing when your board is flat. A workbench top that is fairly flat is also a fair way to gauge of the flatness of other boards.

TWO SOLUTIONS FOR TOPS

So my recommendation is that if you can wield a handplane (even just enough to be trouble), then you should either use a planing tray or strive to keep your top fairly flat. You can overdo this. It's not necessary to flatten the top using methods that involve a machinist's straightedge and feeler gauges. And I would ward you away from methods that use a router that runs on a carriage

suspended over your bench. I've watched people do this, and it is a lot of trouble to build these devices.

I think there are two smart paths: Learn to use a jointer plane (flattening a workbench top is the best practice for this) or remove your benchtop and take it to a cabinetshop that has a wide-belt sander.

(Side note: Some workbench designs can be flattened using home woodworking machines. One such design has a benchtop that is made of two thick 10"-wide slabs with a 4"-wide tool tray screwed between them. Simply remove the screws and run each 10"-wide slab through your portable planer. Reassemble! Side, side note: I dislike tool trays, a.k.a. hamster beds.)

I can hear the workbench purists squirming from where I perch. Won't sending a workbench top through a wide-belt sander embed it with grit that will mar the workpieces of future

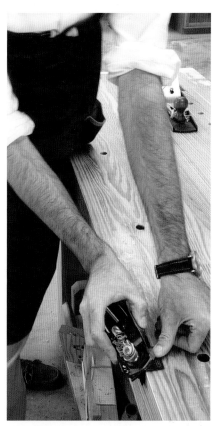

3 Cup or bow? Now that I know the geography of the top, I'll drag one stick all along the top and watch the gap under the winding stick. This quick check confirms my suspicions about where the high spots are (and they are usually along the long edges of the top).

4 Stop spelching. Before I get down to business, I'll cut a small chamfer ($1/16$" to $1/8$") on the long edges of the top. This will prevent the grain from blowing out (the British call this spelching) when I plane cross-grain.

5 In my cups. In general, my tops become cupped in use. So I remove the two high hills by working directly across the grain. In this instance the cup is slight, so I started with a jointer plane. If the cup is severe, start with a jack plane so you can take a thicker shaving.

6 Across and down. Every stroke across the top should overlap the stroke before. The shavings will give up easily (though I am told that the iron will dull more quickly). Work from one end of the top to the other. Then back down. Repeat until the plane's cutter can touch the hollow in the middle.

7 Diagonal makes a difference. Work across the top diagonally now, overlapping your strokes as before. Take care at the starting corner and stopping corner – your plane's sole won't have much support. You can proceed with speed during the middle strokes.

8 And the other way. Switch directions and work diagonally the other way across the top. Repeat these two types of passes until you can make shavings at every point in a pass.

9 Finish planing. Now reduce your depth of cut and use your jointer plane along the grain of the top. Overlap your stokes and repeat your passes until you are getting full-length shavings.

10 For the obsessed. You don't have to smooth-plane your benchtop, but it's good practice with a large laminated surface. You can begin smooth-planing with the grain; there is no need for cross-grain or diagonal strokes.

projects? Not in my experience. Once you dust off the top and put a finish on it, such as an oil/varnish blend, the grit becomes part of the finish.

Plus, even if there is a little #220-grit in my benchtop, that fine grit is a lot kinder to my workpieces than what else gets embedded in my bench during my normal work: bits of dried glue, dyes, pigments and occasional stray metal filings.

FLATTEN IT WITH A HANDPLANE

Because I don't have a wide-belt sander, I prefer to use a handplane to do the job. Once you do this a couple times, you'll find that it's a 30-minute job – and a lot less lifting than carting a top across town. The first time I ever tried to flatten a benchtop with a handplane (years ago) I was 100 percent successful, and I just barely knew what I was doing.

Flattening a benchtop is like flattening a board on one face. First you remove the high spots. These high spots could be at the corners or there could be a hump all along the middle (though I have never had one of these in my benchtop). Find the high spots using two winding sticks – parallel lengths of hardwood or aluminum angle that are longer than your bench is wide.

Mark any high spots in chalk or pencil and work them down with a bit of spirited planing using a jack, fore or jointer plane set to take an aggressive cut and equipped with a cambered iron. Get things close. Check your results with your winding sticks.

Fetch your jointer plane and work the entire top using diagonal strokes that overlap. Repeat that process by going diagonally back the other way across the top. After each pass, your shavings will become more and more regular. When your shavings are full length, your top is flat (enough). Now plane the entire top with the grain and use slightly overlapping strokes. It should take two or three passes to produce regular full-length shavings. You are finished. So finish it with some oil/varnish blend and

get back to work.

Need details? Visuals? I've prepared a pictorial essay of the process that should help you get started. My digital camera codes each photo with the time it was taken. The first photo was snapped at 10:46 a.m. By 11:44 a.m. I was done. And remember: I'd stopped to take photos about the process, and each photo had to be illuminated with our photographic lights. I think the photography took longer than the actual work.

11 Cross-grain shavings. When working across the grain, this is what your shavings should look like. Take the heaviest cut you can manage and keep your handplane under control.

12 Diagonal shavings. Full-length shavings taken at 45° will look like thick ribbon. Shoot for a thickness of .005", or perhaps a bit more.

13 For the obsessed II. If you smooth-plane your benchtop, set your tool to take a shaving that is .002" or less. You can take even more if your top is behaving and it is a mild wood.

14 Wipe on, wipe off. Rag on two coats of an oil/varnish blend. When everything is dry, a coat of wax will help your top resist glue, but it will make it slippery (a bad thing – handtool users don't want their stock sliding everywhere).

SECTION 3
ROUTERS

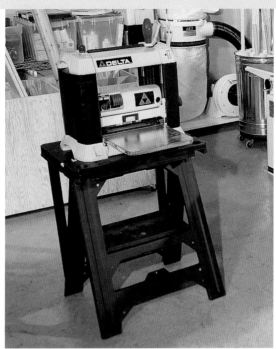

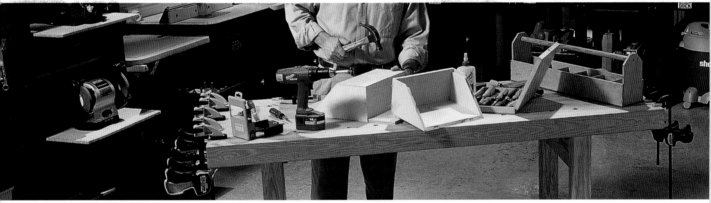

ONE-WEEKEND ROUTER TABLE

By David Thiel

I think it might have been seeing a $1,000 router table setup at a recent woodworking show (it's very cool, but $1,000?). Or maybe it was realizing that our shop's router table's cabinet mostly takes up space and fills with dust. Either of these observations was enough to get us rethinking our router table needs.

Essentially you need a stable, flat working surface that can support most work. You need a fence that guides, supports and moves easily for adjustments (both the fence location on the table and the faces themselves toward the bit). You also need easy access to the router for bit changing and height adjustment. Other than that, it just needs to be up off the floor, hence the cabinet.

So we decided that a lightweight, easily stored router tabletop that would still offer all these benefits would be preferable. Oh, and we wanted to be able to make it in a weekend for a reasonable price. How about $200? No problem!

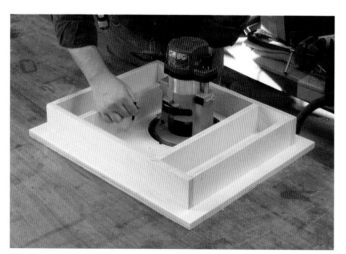

Allowing the proper clearance for your router is critical. You can see that I've removed the handles from the tool to allow as much space as possible. Mark out the space and then assemble the frame to fit.

AN INGENIOUS DESIGN

For a stable, lightweight top the solution that made sense was a torsion box made of high-density plywood. The size that seemed most functional was a 20"-deep x 24"-wide platform that only needed to be about 4" tall. The box itself has an open center section on the bottom to accommodate the router body. There are two lengths of T-track installed front to back on the tabletop to easily reposition the fence.

The fence itself is a variation of one we've built half-a-dozen times. The fence base is almost a torsion box – more of a torsion corner – that provides stable support for the laterally adjustable fence faces and allows for dust hook-up.

For the router itself, we went shopping. After looking at a number of router lifts and router table plates we chose the Milwaukee 5625-29, a $3\frac{1}{2}$ horsepower router that offers through-the-base height adjustment. And, no, the price of the router is not included in the $120 figure. You don't have to use this router, but in our opinion it has the horsepower you want to swing large panel-raising bits on your router table, and the through-the-base adjustment means you don't need to buy a router lift. The variable speed is also a big plus.

We chose a circular router plate from Veritas because it replaces the sole plate on your router and allows you to still use the router freehand or in the table without changing the base. The base also fits into the table without the use of any tools, and slips in and out from above in seconds.

Now the fun part: To bring the router table up to height, but still make it compact, we designed a brace that is mounted to the table and then the entire thing is simply clamped in your bench vise. Instant router table!

TORSION TOP CONSTRUCTION

The top itself is very simple to make. A frame made of $\frac{3}{4}$" x 3" plywood pieces is sandwiched between two pieces of $\frac{3}{4}$" plywood. The bottom piece is notched to accommodate

Router table cabinets can be a waste of space. This compact, vise-mounted unit stores easily and is just the right size.

your router (you'll need to test fit your router to locate the center frame pieces and the notch). The top piece extends 1½" beyond the frame on all sides to allow for clamping featherboards or other guides to the top surface.

Start by cutting out the top, bottom and seven frame pieces. If you opt to use the Veritas plate, the instructions are very clear on how to cut the hole in the tabletop to fit the plate. Otherwise, follow the instructions for your individual router plate.

We chose to locate the router plate closer to the front of the table rather than in the center of the table. Most router table work happens within 6" of the fence and this location keeps you from having to lean across the table for operations. If you have a larger piece to run, the fence can be reversed on the table to give you a larger support surface.

With the router plate located in the top, suspend the router from the top and locate the two center frame members the necessary distance to clear the router. Make a note of that dimension, then lay out your frame accordingly.

I used glue and an 18-gauge brad nailer to assemble all the pieces for this project. While perhaps not the height of joinery, it's fast and reliable.

With the frame assembled, place the frame on the bottom, and mark and notch the center section to allow clearance space for the router body. You could leave the center section open, but the extra strength along the back of the tabletop is worth the effort.

Attach the bottom the same way you assembled the frame.

Before fastening the top to the table, you need to install the aluminum T-track inserts for fence adjustment. I used a dado set on my table saw to run the grooves before attaching the top.

Next, attach the top, centering it on the frame assembly. Pay extra attention when attaching the top to keep the fasteners below the surface of the tabletop. This will keep you from scratching your work, or worse, allowing your wood to hang up on a brad head during an operation.

DOWN AND DIRTY FENCE

The fence is also absurdly simple to make. Accuracy is important to make sure it sits square to the tabletop, but other than that, it's brads and glue.

Start construction on the fence by cutting out the base, sub-face, faces and braces. All but the braces are very straightforward. The braces are actually triangles. The best method is to rip a piece of plywood to 3" wide, then head to the miter saw. First miter both ends of the strip at a 45° angle, then reset the miter saw for a 90° cut and cut the 3" triangles from the strip. Repeat this process and you've got four braces.

The sub-face and base need to have a 3"-wide half-circle cut at the center of each piece along one edge as shown on page 74. This space will be the opening for the router bits.

The sub-face is then glued and nailed to the base. Then glue the braces into the corner formed by the sub-face and base. Make sure to locate the braces as shown to avoid interference with any of the fence handles. I again used brad nails to hold the braces in place.

For the router table to be as useful as possible it needs dust collection. This is achieved by building a simple hood to surround the bit opening in the fence. Drill a hole in the hood back piece. Adjust the hole size to fit your dust collection hose,

More marking: With the frame assembled and resting on the bottom piece, mark out the notch that will allow the router to extend through the top.

With the bottom notched, simply glue and nail it in place on the frame.

After cutting the grooves for the T-track, tap it in place using a backing block. If you have to tap too hard with the hammer, your groove is too small. Attach the track with ½" x #4 flathead screws. Pre-drill and countersink each hole.

usually 1¼" in diameter.

Then attach the hood sides to the hood back, holding the sides flush to the top edge of the back. Then add the top to the box.

The next step is to locate and drill the holes for the cam clamps that hold the fence to the table and for the knobs that hold the faces. Place the fence assembly over the table and orient the cam clamp holes so they fall in the center of the T-tracks in the top. There can be a little bit of play, but not too much.

Secure the fence to the table with the cam clamps so it seats tightly. Use an engineer's square to check the fence against the top. If it's not square you need to adjust the base slightly, either by shimming or removing material from the underside of the fence base to make it square.

Next, drill the holes for the fence knobs, again avoiding the braces so the knobs can be easily turned. The holes should be 2" up from the tabletop.

The fence faces are next. To allow the best fence clearance near the bit, I beveled the inside lip of each of the faces at 45°. Next you need to rout two, 2½"-wide stepped slots in the front of each fence face. These will allow the faces

to be moved left-to-right to accommodate different bit sizes.

The easiest way to do this is on a router table, but if you're building your first, you can use a drill press with two different bits. Use a ½"-diameter Forstner bit to first cut a ¼"-deep slot. Then change to a 5/16"-diameter bit to drill through to the back of the fence face. This will create a slot that will let a ½"-hex-head bolt drop into the slot, recessing the head, but capturing the sides of the bolt head to keep it from spinning.

I also added a T-slot fixture to the front of each face. This allows you to attach featherboards, a guard to protect your fingers and other guides. Again, you can use a router or your dado set in the table saw to make the slot (about 1" down from the top of the fence).

Attach the fence faces using the bolts, washers and knobs.

THE MOUNTING SUPPORT

To make the whole thing work, you need to be able to secure the table in your bench vise, but still have access to the router motor. We used a U-shaped support screwed to the sides of the table. The actual size of the support will depend on your

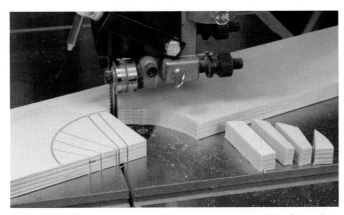

Cutting out the bit clearance hole on the band saw is made simple by first cutting "spokes" toward your line. These relief cuts allow the pieces to fall out in small chunks, rather than fighting with one bigger piece.

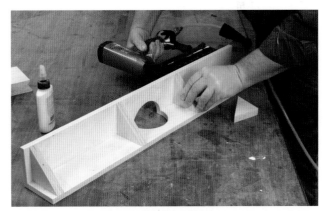

With the sub-face and base assembled, add the four triangular braces with glue and brads. Space them adequately to support the fence, but make sure you leave room for the knobs.

The dust collection hood completes the router table fence. It should seal tightly around the fence to provide the best dust collection, so don't skimp on the glue here.

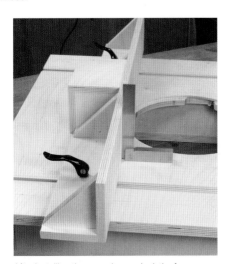

After installing the cam clamps, lock the fence in place on the top and check for square. If adjustment is necessary, you can do it by sanding the base or adding thin shims. You don't want to add shims behind the fence faces because they're moving parts. Adjust the base.

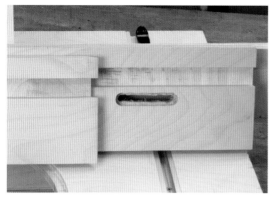

Seen from the front, the fence faces have been grooved for the T-tracks, and the clearance holes to attach and adjust the faces are drilled. Note that the face slot shows the rough edges from the overlapping holes made on the drill press. A few minutes with a file and some sandpaper will clean up the slots so the bolt will move smoothly.

After drilling clearance holes, you can locate the holes in the fence faces and add the knobs.

ONE-WEEKEND ROUTER TABLE

NO.	LET.	ITEM	DIMENSIONS (INCHES)			MATERIAL
			T	W	L	
1	T1	Top	¾	20	24	Plywood
1	B1	Bottom	¾	17	21	Plywood
2	B2	Frame F&B	¾	3	21	Plywood
4	B3	Frame dividers	¾	3	15½	Plywood
1	B4	Frame divider	¾	3	10½	Plywood
2	B5	Support stems	¾	3	7	Plywood
2	B6	Support braces	¾	3	21	Plywood
2	F1	Fence faces	¾	4	14	Plywood
1	F2	Fence sub-face	½	3½	28	Plywood
1	F3	Fence base	½	3	28	Plywood
4	F4	Fence braces	¾	3	3	Plywood
1	F5	Hood top	½	5	3½	Plywood
2	F6	Hood sides	½	2½	3	Plywood
1	F7	Hood back	½	5	3	Plywood
2	H1	Fence T-tracks	⅜	¾	14	Aluminum
4	H2	Hex-head bolts	¼"-20	1½"		
4	H3	Star knobs				
2	H4	Cam clamps				
2	H5	Table T-tracks	⅜	¾	20	Aluminum

Here you can see the fences in place and the fence attached and ready to run. The T-tracks in the fence faces can be used for featherboards and you can use them to attach a simple guard to keep your hands a safe distance from the bit.

The support brace (customized for my bench vise) holds the router top firmly in place with plenty of clearance (and no wasted space).

bench vise, but you want the tabletop to rest on the vise as much as possible. In fact, if you can also get the top to rest on the vise at the rear of the table, that's even better support. Our larger router forced us to move the support all the way to the rear of the table. This is something else that can be individualized on your table.

You'll see in the photo that we used two support braces to catch the vise at both the top and bottom of the jaws for more support. Your vise may require a different arrangement, so give it a test run to make sure it's held tight.

FINISHING TOUCHES

With the support mounted you can put your table to work. But you may want to add a step – finishing. While a bare plywood surface will perform reasonably well, a slicker surface will make things move easier. You can add a topcoat of spray-on lacquer (as we did), or simply add a coat of oil or shellac.

Some other simple additions for your table can include some shop-made featherboards (that will fit nicely in the T-tracks on the fence face) and if you're really industrious, you could actually add a couple of storage drawers to either side of the opening in the top. Customize the project to meet your needs.

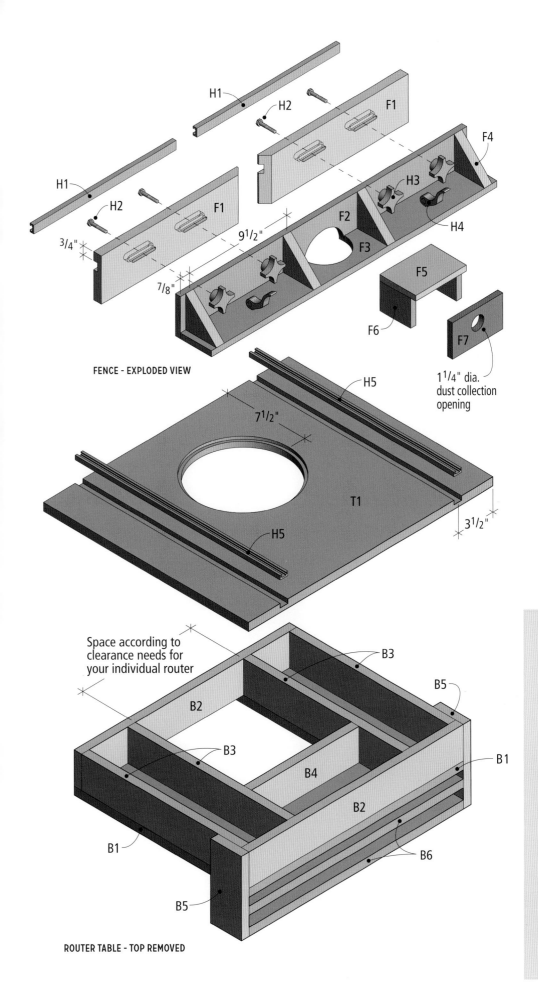

H1

H2

F1

H1

H2

F1

3/4"

7/8"

9 1/2"

F2

F3

F4

H3

H4

F5

F6

F7

1 1/4" dia.
dust collection
opening

FENCE - EXPLODED VIEW

H5

7 1/2"

T1

H5

3 1/2"

Space according to
clearance needs for
your individual router

B2

B3

B3

B4

B3

B5

B1

B2

B1

B2

B6

B5

ROUTER TABLE - TOP REMOVED

DIRT-SIMPLE ROUTER JIGS

Improve your router techniques with simple, shop-made jigs that are easy to use and just as simple to build.

By Glen Huey

I'm a power-tool woodworker. Sure I use hand tools for some parts of furniture building, specifically when cutting dovetails. But I doubt you'll ever catch me with a Bridge City Tool Works VP-60, Veritas router plane or a Lie-Nielsen shoulder plane if I'm trying to complete a project quickly. It's just not my thing. The jobs completed with those tools, I accomplish with my router and a router jig.

The next time you venture into your shop to work on a project, take a survey of what's stacked around your shop. I'll bet you have the material to create a boatload of simple, useful jigs that, when combined with your router, will increase your woodworking abilities. The routing techniques shown in this article are a combination of the correct router bits along with dirt-simple jigs made from leftover pieces from other projects, such as scraps and plywood.

A SQUARE-PLATFORM JIG

We all know you can guide your router by placing the router's base against an edge to make a straight cut, but who wants to calculate the offset of the base each time you go to use it or struggle with clamping requirements? If you use my favorite router jig along with a pattern bit, you have a setup that is a multi-tasker and is as easy as can be to position for accuracy.

That jig I call a square-platform jig. To make the jig, start with two pieces of plywood cut to the same size. Attach the two with glue and a few brads (keep the brads away from the edges), then add a third piece to the front edge to act as a lip – similar to a bench hook – and the jig is ready for work. The key is to keep the edges of the jig straight and square with that third piece, which I call a catch rail.

This jig is best when used for cutting dados for shelves or for creating a dovetailed socket for drawer dividers. Due to its usefulness, I have more than a few of these jigs in my shop made in different sizes and thicknesses for different techniques and for use with different router bits, but my favorite setup is a 1"-thick jig (two pieces of $\frac{1}{2}$" plywood). This thickness is perfect for working with a $\frac{3}{4}$"-diameter, top-mount bearing router bit with a 1" cutting length.

The greatest thing about this jig is the ease of clamping. No longer is it necessary to use more than a single clamp. One clamp holds the jig to the workpiece and does not allow any movement of the jig. When a clamp is positioned at the lower left-hand corner of the jig as shown in the photo below, the jig cannot move away from the workpiece due to the clamp. And the jig cannot slip to the left because the front piece acts as a catch. As long as the clamp is secure, no amount of force will allow a shift in the jig. This makes it easy to clamp and quick to adjust from one work area to the next.

To use this jig, do any layout work, then slide the jig into position, always aligning the jig to the left of the work area because the normal operation of a router pushes the tool to the left (if the jig were set to the right of the work area, it would be a struggle to hold the router firmly against the jig in use). Next, add a clamp keeping a clear path for your router base and allow the pattern-bit bearing to ride along the edge of the jig. With this setup, wherever the jig is, the router bit follows.

Keep it square. The key to this jig is to keep the edges perfectly square with the catch rail that is attached to the bottom face of the jig. Glue and brads are the joining force.

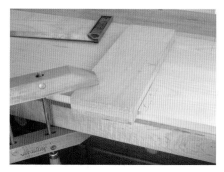

Quick and secure. The design of the platform jig allows a single clamp to hold the jig in place. This allows the jig to move to the next layout line quickly. Once the clamp is tight, it's all but impossible to slide the jig in either direction.

Tricky joint; simple jig. Three pieces of plywood are all you need to cut a housed sliding dovetail socket.

USE THE SAME JIG FOR DADOS

I began using this jig due to the ghastly dado bottoms produced by my older dado stack. My stack had exterior blades that were slightly higher than the chippers and this caused an unwelcome profile at the bottom of the dado. When bookcase shelves were routed through, that shape showed – and it wasn't pretty.

Because most bookcase units I built were 12" or less in depth, I made my first platform jig 16" long. At that length, the jig stretched across the entire width of the sides and created a dado in a single pass.

To make the cut, allow the router base to sit on top of the jig while the bearing rolls against the jig's edge. Use a pattern-routing bit that is ¾" in diameter and the resulting cut is exactly ¾" wide with a bottom that's flat. There is no ghastly profile to try and hide. Cut one dado or 100 dados and the results are the same – predictable and accurate.

PERFECT SLIDING DOVETAILS

Having so much success creating dados with this jig, I wondered what other operations I could make easier by using this setup. One area that came to mind was drawer dividers. Most chests I build use sliding dovetails for joining dividers to the case sides. How could I adapt this jig?

What I discovered was that I had to change the router setup, not the jig.

One-pass dado. The correct router bit along with this jig provides a simple and quick method for cutting dados that are through, or simply stop before reaching the end of the workpiece to create a stopped dado.

I typically use a ¾" dovetail bit when cutting the socket for my dividers, but I didn't have a bearing to ride against the jig. I had tried bearings on dovetail bits, but I wasn't satisfied with the results. So I turned to a ¾" outside-diameter bushing. You might think it's impossible to use a ¾"-diameter dovetail router bit with a ¾" outside-diameter bushing, but if the bit extends below the bushing (aim for at least a ½"-deep socket into the case sides), everything works perfectly.

Again, simply align the jig with your layout marks, add a clamp, then cut the dovetail socket into your workpiece. Cut into the case side to the width of your divider and you're golden. This creates a perfect sliding-dovetail socket, and

it's a simple move from a completed socket to the next socket area. Additionally, remember to use the same router bit to create the male part of the joint. The second half of this operation is completed at a router table.

If you're wondering about hogging out the waste with a straight bit prior to cutting with a dovetail bit, I seldom, if ever, take the time to work this way. My router bits are sharp and able to make this cut without difficulty. If this extra step is important to you, I would mount a ¾" bearing on a ½" straight bit so I was always registering off the jig.

How about housed dovetail sockets? The beauty of this jig is that you simply make a first pass with the ¾" pattern bit to make the shallow dado. Then follow up with the dovetail bit in a second router, as shown in the opening photo of this article. The entire operation is completed with one clamping setup.

Also, here's a tip: Create the dovetail slots while your case sides are wider than the final dimension by ⅛". Once the joinery is complete, trim the extra material from the edges to leave a clean front edge.

Are you wondering why I suggested you keep the brads located away from the edges of the jig? When you nick the jig's edge – and you will ding it with your router bit spinning – you can simply take a pass at the jointer to straighten the jig's edge.

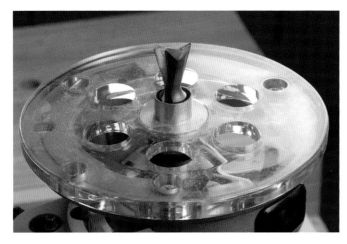

Designed to fit. The equal width of the bushing and the widest portion of the dovetail bit is what makes this setup work. The dovetail bit cuts exactly to the outside edge of the bushing. As the bushing travels the edge of the jig, the dovetail slot is perfectly aligned.

A SIMPLE JIG FOR SMALLER ROUTER BITS

Another jig I use, which is not far from the design of the platform jig, is based off of a circular saw guide's jig. When using those saw guides, the base of the saw rides on top of the guide while the blade cuts at the edge. This setup is great for aligning the guide to the cut line. I adapted this idea to use with my small router bits in lieu of guide bushings or bearings. It works great for plowing small grooves or dados such as when routing out cubbyhole dividers in desk interiors.

Constructing jigs such as these is simple. Here, too, I have a few scattered about the shop that work with specific router bits. I even take the time to label each jig so I know with which bits it works. Begin with a piece of 1/8" tempered hardboard or 1/4" plywood that's about 5" wide and 10" or so long. Next, add a piece of 3/4" material along one edge of the plywood to act as a fence. Add a front piece to this setup just as in the platform jigs – it's important to keep the relationship of the front piece at an accurate 90° to the fence piece.

To complete the building of the jig, install a router bit into the router, set the depth of cut to a bit stronger than the hardboard or plywood, then with the router base running against the fence, make a cut. The newly created edge is the exact cutline of the router bit and aligning this jig is as easy as clamping to your layout lines.

A SIMPLE STRAIGHTEDGE JIG

Not all the best shop-made jigs are pieces of plywood arranged in some design. One of the most useful jigs is simply a straight piece of stock or two pieces stacked together, what I call a straightedge jig. There are a couple operations where these shine. One use is for simple straight cuts on pieces too large or too awkward to hoist onto the table saw. A second use is to create a tenon for installing breadboard ends on a tabletop. Or, you can use this to create everyday, run-of-the-mill tenons.

Each of these operations works with a pattern bit; the depth of cut determines the layers of plywood needed for the jig. If I plan to create

No bearing is no problem. Design this simple jig to have the base plate rub the fence as the cut is made. Make one for each router bit.

No guesswork needed. Once built, the jig is a snap to align with layout lines; hit the mark every time.

Ideal edge treatment. A pattern bit matched with a single layer of plywood is a perfect way to trim ends of wide panels or large tops. With the bearing running along the guide, a clean, straight cut is achieved.

a smooth cut across an edge, a single thickness of plywood is best. This style of jig allows the standard pattern bit with a 1" cutting length to extend completely through a ¾"-thick workpiece while the bearing rubs the jig.

For example, if I were trying to cut the angled slope on a case side of a slant-lid desk, it would be nearly impossible to hoist the panels up to a band saw, or to control a panel at a table saw. But trim close to the line with a jigsaw, clamp a plywood straightedge at the layout line, then make a pass using your router while the pattern bit rides smoothly along the guide. The completed cut is square and needs little sanding or smoothing before finish – it's that smooth.

The same operation is perfect for squaring large panels, too. You know how hard it can be to trim a large top with a panel-cutting sled. Once you achieve parallel sides at a table saw, use a square to lay out one end cut, position a plywood straightedge at the layout line, clamp the jig in place and trim the end square. Repeat the same steps at the opposite end of the top.

I don't like to perform this operation with a circular saw – as you may have seen done a number of times – due to the sometimes-wonky finish of the cut. It's easier to sand a routed cut than that of a circular saw – but I will trim the end close with a jigsaw prior to routing.

Two layers for tenons. A second layer of plywood builds the jig to make it possible to rabbet the end. This is a great setup for the first step for breadboard ends.

CHANGE THE THICKNESS, CHANGE THE CUT

If you require a cut that's not a through cut such as making a tenon, you will need to stick two pieces of plywood together because of the cutting length of the router bit. A single thickness of plywood is sometimes not thick enough to allow the bearing to ride against the guide without cutting into the workpiece too deeply. A second thickness of plywood remedies that problem. Now it's possible for the bearing to ride the jig and set the depth of cut where needed.

I use this two-piece setup to create tenons on large panels or tabletops. I cut a 1¼"-long tenon to create a

pattern for bracket-style feet and cut the design using my router. It's more efficient to create the feet other ways, but this works if needed. Furthermore, I use this technique for high chest aprons and sculpted drawer dividers such as those on block-front or serpentine chests.

MORE WORK FOR A PATTERN BIT

As you can tell, I use a pattern bit with plywood jigs for many operations. And bit diameter is not important. I use a ¾"-diameter bit as well as a ½"-diameter router bit. Additionally, I use bits with either a top- or bottom-mount bearing.

Until now we've primarily discussed work accomplished with straight jigs. However, plywood is also where I turn for intricate work with patterns. I've built quite a few tea tables over the years and the most fancy was a Massachusetts design with extremely scalloped aprons at both ends and sides.

Instead of transferring the design onto each apron separately, I drew the design one time onto plywood – use a piece that's ½" thick at minimum – and used that to repeat the layout on each piece. But the plywood pattern did double duty. Not only could I use the piece to trace the pattern onto the aprons, I used the plywood and a pattern bit to cut the intricate design at a router table.

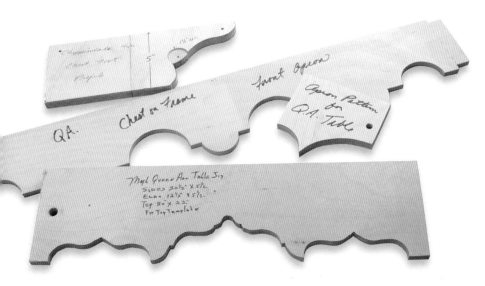

Possibilities abound. Teaming plywood patterns with a pattern-routing bit opens the door to design and detail – and it makes repeatability achievable.

If you attach the plywood pattern on top of the workpiece, you'll need a bottom-mount bearing, but a top-mount bearing is used if the pattern is positioned below the workpiece. As you make the jigs for this type of work, make sure to extend the ends of the pattern an extra inch or more to allow contact between the bit and pattern prior to cutting the work.

There are a number of techniques where this setup works great other than table aprons. Before I added a spindle sander to my shop, I would create a pattern for bracket-style feet and cut the design using my router. It's more efficient to create the feet other ways, but this works if needed. Furthermore, I use this technique for high chest aprons and sculpted drawer dividers such as those on block-front or serpentine chests.

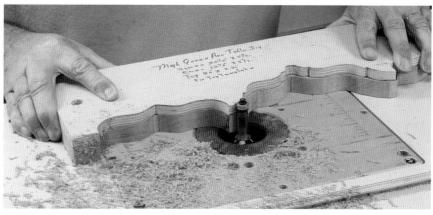

Fundamental pattern routing. A bottom-mount bearing follows the pattern as a smooth and accurate cut is made on the workpiece below.

RUNNING IN CIRCLES

Step into most woodworking stores and you'll find many commercially made jigs for cutting circles of all sizes. In fact, these jigs are so involved that you have to read the instructions before beginning work (something we all hate to do). For the most part we use a few sizes of circles specific to our work. We don't need all those settings. I looked for something different.

My first circle-cutting jig was an elongated base added to my plunge router. I used the existing bolts to affix the base to the router, then cut a circle. Seemed easy enough. But I ran into an issue. With the router bolted to the jig, there's a point as you rotate and make a cut that you have to let go of the handles in order to complete the circle because the router doesn't turn as you spin the jig. Your hands should always be in control as you use a router.

To eliminate the handle problem, I turned to a guide bushing. Again using plywood, I fashioned a jig for circle cutting. This time, instead of affixing the jig to the router base, I positioned a ¾"-diameter hole where the router bit would be located. The hole, which could be sized to match any size guide bushing, allows the bushing that's installed in the router to spin freely as a circle is cut. The ability to spin during use means my hands stay in contact

with the router throughout the cut.

Using the jig is a walk in the park. Select a guide bushing that matches the hole in the jig, then install the desired router bit and the bushing to the tool. Measure accurately for your needed diameter and pin the jig to the workpiece with a dowel. All that's left is to cut a circle. Use a plunge router for this technique and step through the cutting process; don't try to complete the cut in a single pass.

You don't need scads of money. You don't need complicated commercial jigs. You don't even need to keep the jig once it serves its purpose. All you need is a few pieces of plywood used in conjunction with certain router bits and you can increase productivity in your shop. It's as simple as plugging in a router.

Safe and secure. The guide bushing turns in the hole as the circle is cut. At no time is it necessary to remove your hands from the router. Elevate the workpiece or the bench is will also get a groove.

Another simple setup. One hole in the middle of the circle-cutting jig, plus a guide bushing, equals a great method for creating circles.

NO-NONSENSE ROUTER TABLE

A great router table for little cost and just a few hours to build.

By Robert W. Lang

The original version of this router table was born out of necessity. I needed a router table at a job site, and I didn't have the space or the desire to carry my large one. I cobbled it together quickly, screwed the router's baseplate to the bottom of the tabletop, and made a simple fence. A dozen years later, it still serves me well.

It's easy to get carried away when making a router table, building something the size of a 5-horsepower shaper, full of drawers for storing every router bit in the catalog and accessories for every imaginable circumstance. If you'd rather keep things simple, or need a second table in your shop, this will do everything you need without taking much time or space. And if you want to jazz it up, this is a good starting point.

The top measures 16" x 24" – large enough to handle all but extremely large panels and small enough to store below a bench or on a shelf. The small size also helps to keep the top from sagging,

a common issue with super-sized router tables.

The height of the table will be a compromise between a comfortable working height, and ease of getting the router in and out to change bits. I chose a router that clamps in a fixed base and can be quickly removed for changing bits. I left plenty of room for this operation, which leaves the top a bit high when placed on my workbench, but just right when set on sawhorses.

Begin construction by cutting the top, sides and back from $\frac{3}{4}$"-thick plywood, particleboard or MDF. The two rails across the front are $\frac{3}{4}$" x $2\frac{1}{2}$" hardwood.

On each of the two side pieces, mark a line $2\frac{1}{2}$" in from each edge. Use a compass to draw a $2\frac{1}{2}$" radius in each corner, and cut inside the lines with a jigsaw. The curves in the corners add strength, and these cutouts in the sides make the structure lighter. More important, they provide room for F-style clamps. Clamps are used at the top to

hold the fence, and they can also be used at the bottom to secure the table to a bench or sawhorses.

The back goes in between the sides, secured with glue and #8 x $1\frac{3}{4}$" screws. To keep everything lined up, assemble the parts on the flattest surface available. The top of the table saw is a good choice for this. After the first three parts are assembled, cut the rails to length, and glue and screw them between the sides. The edge of the top rail is flush with the top of the sides.

I placed the lower rail so $\frac{3}{4}$" is below the bottom edge of the sides. This allows me to clamp it in my bench vise, quickly securing the router table. If you don't plan on using the router table in conjunction with a vise, place the bottom edge of the lower rail even with the bottom of the sides. Always secure the router table before using it; you don't want it sliding around in the middle of a cut.

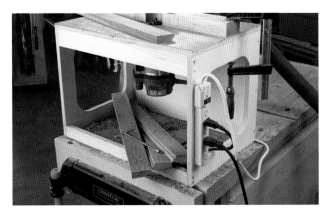

Not fancy, but functional. A good router table features a flat, solid top and a straight fence. With those in place, there isn't a need for much more.

Start flat to end flat. Assembling the frame on a flat surface makes it easier to align parts, and ensures a flat surface for mounting the top.

FRONT AND CENTER

Before attaching the top to the frame, decide where and how to attach the router base to the table. If you have a drill press, it will be easier to align the mounting and center holes, but these can be carefully positioned using a handheld drill. I centered the router front to back and side to side. This provides adequate area in front of the bit, and makes access to the router easier. Moving the router back a few inches will provide more table area in front of the bit, but be sure there will be room inside for the router.

Draw a center mark on the tabletop, and position the baseplate of the router over it. Mark the locations for the mounting screws and with a Forstner bit, make a counterbore deep enough for the screw heads at each screw location. Different routers will use different size screws, and you'll likely need to make a trip to the hardware store to get some screws ¾" longer than the stock mounting screws. Drill the holes with a bit that is larger in diameter than the screws. The oversized holes and counterbores will allow you to move the router base around to help line up the holes.

The center hole should be about ¼" larger in diameter than your largest bit. Make the hole with a Forstner bit at the drill press, or with a hole saw and a handheld drill. If you need to enlarge the hole at a later time, cut around the perimeter with a rabbeting bit, then switch to a straight bit with a bearing mounted above the cutter. This will preserve the round shape of the hole, and if you want to use smaller inserts, they can be placed in a rabbet.

Mounting the router directly to the top involves a trade-off. It is quick and easy compared to making a large cutout for an insert plate, and keeping the top at full thickness means a stronger top that is less likely to sag over time. The disadvantage is that you lose some depth of cut.

How much depends on your particular router, the bit you use and the cut you want to make. For most cuts this won't be an issue, but if it becomes one, you can always add an insert plate later.

When the holes have been placed, go ahead and attach the baseplate to the bottom side of the top. The top can be held to the frame with screws from above, but a stronger and neater attachment will be to place ¾" cleats on the top inside edges of the frame, and attach the top from below with #8 x 1¼" screws.

Again, working on a flat surface is a must, so put the top face down on your table saw, then run a bead of yellow glue around the perimeter. Put the assembled frame on the top, screw the cleats down and leave it alone while the glue dries.

The fence is also simple, a 1¾"-thick x 3"-wide piece of hardwood, carefully jointed with flat faces and straight edges. One end is held to the table with a ⁵⁄₁₆"–18 machine screw and nut. The fence swings on this screw to adjust the distance between the fence and the bit, and the opposite end of the fence is held down with a clamp.

I made the cutout in the fence by cutting a 2½"-diameter semi-circle at the band saw, smoothing the recess with a spindle sander. If I want a continuous fence, I can flip this over, or if I want to close down the opening, I can screw a couple pieces of scrap on each side of the opening.

There isn't any need for the fence to be parallel to the edge of the table, nor is there a need for a miter slot. Operations that move the wood on end across the bit may be performed by using a block of scrap wood held against the fence as a guide.

Other than knocking off the sharp edges, the only sanding I did was to go over the top with #150-grit paper in a random-orbit sander. I ragged on a couple coats of shellac, and when that was dry I scuffed the top with a nylon abrasive pad and applied a coat of paste wax to reduce friction.

I added a fitting to the top of the fence for dust collection, and a power strip to turn on the router and the shop vacuum simultaneously. It isn't fancy, but it functions well, and it didn't take a lot of time or money to build.

Insert? Don't need it. Foregoing a thin insert for mounting the router will yield a stronger top and save construction time.

Nice and flat. The weight of the router helps during final assembly, it keeps the top flat as the cleats are screwed in.

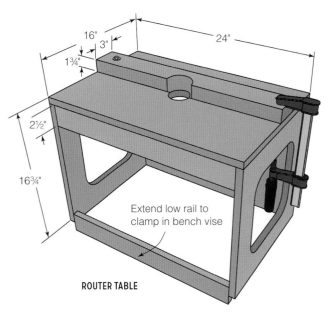

16"
3"
1¾"
24"
2½"
16¾"

Extend low rail to clamp in bench vise

ROUTER TABLE

ROUTER FENCE FOR A TABLE SAW

If you've got a table saw, you've got the beginnings of a versatile router table system and edge jointer.

By Jim Stuard

Your table saw is a router table and jointer just waiting to happen. Replace one of the saw's wings (or adapt your existing table board) to hold a router table insert, and you're in business. Add this router fence to your table saw's fence and you get a router fence with the capacity to handle boards few commercial router tables could even touch. Make a couple quick adjustments to the fence and you can edge-joint boards for gluing up panels — no jointer necessary.

This fence was designed for the Little Shop Mark II, a rolling workshop that was featured in the September 1999 issue of **Popular Woodworking** (#110). However, this fence will work with just about any contractor- or cabinet-style table saw.

IT'S IN THE HOLE

This fence is essentially two long plywood boxes with hardwood face fronts on them. The space between the boxes is where the router bit spins. One of the boxes stores router bits, the other acts as a dust collection chute. Though construction isn't complex, study the diagrams carefully before you begin.

First cut the hole for the insert in the top of your saw's table. If you've built the Little Shop Mark II, use the end of the long top for your table. For contractor's saws, you can use the table board on the right side of the saw. Or you can replace one of your saw's wings with a piece of laminate-covered plywood. Lay out the spot for the router table insert. I put the

insert in the middle of the width of the table and between the back and front rail from the end. Cut the opening for the insert as shown in the photos. Mount the insert to the router. Drop it in the opening and adjust it so it's flush with the table.

MAKING THE FENCE

First you build the body of the fence, and then you attach the fence faces afterward. Begin by cutting the opening for the bit on the front piece. Use a rasp to round over the inside right edge of the opening to help deflect chips into the box that will later be connected to a shop vacuum. Next cut the bottom piece for the right box and cut a 45-degree chamfer on the end next to the opening for the bit, again to deflect chips.

Assemble the boxes like this: First attach the two end pieces of the left box to the left bottom piece. Then attach the larger end piece for the right-side box (with the dust collection hole) to the bottom piece for the right box. Now nail the front and back pieces to the left and right assemblies. Be sure to hold the bottom edges flush. For the top part of the fence, keep in mind there are three fixed pieces — one on each end and one in the middle. And there are two removable pieces that give you access to the bit storage, the dust collection tube and the wing nuts that will hold the fence faces in place. Attach the three fixed top pieces and the support.

Now drill the holes in the back piece to accept the $1/4$" x 20 t-nuts that attach the router fence to the saw fence.

MAKE IT ADJUSTABLE

Now it's time to cut slots in the front piece that will be used for attaching the fence faces to your box and allow the fence faces to be adjustable. Rout the $1/4$" x 2" slots for adjusting the fence faces according to the diagram. Drop-cut plunge routing is something I'll only do with larger assemblies such as this. Smaller pieces don't have enough mass to absorb a kickback. If you're unsure about this process, then use a less accurate, but safer, method of drilling two $1/4$" holes and connecting them with a jigsaw. The object is to get a $1/4$"-20 bolt to slide smoothly throughout the length of the 2" slot. Now cut a 45-degree angle on the ends of the fence faces, leaving a $1/8$" flat end on the miter for durability. Lay out and drill the relief holes for the $1/4$" x 20 bolt heads then follow these holes with $1/4$" holes for the bolt shanks.

TINY BUT TOUGH FINGERS

The last step is to make finger boards. The method I use is to rip a piece of $3/4$" wood to $3\,1/8$" and about 8" long. When doing this, it's actually safer to have the blade height up a little higher than usual to prevent kickback. A good rule is to move your fence $1/4$" after each cut until you've completed the finger board. The fingers on this board are thick enough to take a beating, but thin enough to flex with some strength. Make three finger boards. One for both sides of the fence and one for the router table insert, with its center right at the insert opening.

ROUTING THE PLATE OPENING

A good way to get a parallel and square opening is to use the saw fence as a guide for two of the cuts. Measure the offset from the edge of the router base to the side of the spiral bit and use this in setting the fence for each cut, parallel to the fence. Clamp a square piece of wood in place as a guide for the sides of the opening, perpendicular to the saw fence.

Next form the rabbet that holds the insert in place by using the same procedure and bit you used to cut the opening (right).

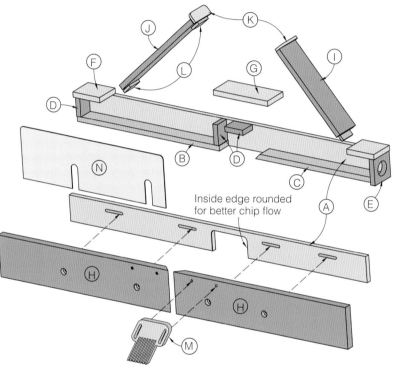

Inside edge rounded for better chip flow

ROUTING SLOTS IN THE FENCE

Clamp a stop to the saw fence to stop the assembly at the end of its cut. Drill a 1/4" hole at the beginning of the cut and with the router running, lean the fence assembly against the stop, touching the table and lever it down over the hole that you just drilled. Gently push the assembly to the end of its cut and lever-lift the assembly off the table.

JOINTER INSERT

For edge jointing, cut a piece of laminate to the size of one fence face. Make it a little tall so you can pull it out from between the fence face and the fence. Cut two slots to clear the bolts on the fence. Chuck a straight bit in the router and set it flush with the offset fence face and you've made an edge jointer. Pull the spacer out to resume normal operation.

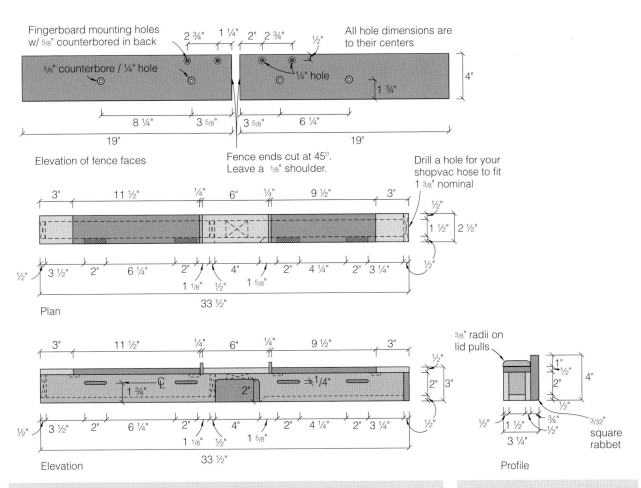

Fingerboard mounting holes
w/ 5/8" counterbored in back

2 3/4"   1 1/4"   2"   2 3/4"   1/2"

All hole dimensions are to their centers

5/8" counterbore / 1/4" hole   1/4" hole

4"

1 3/4"

8 1/4"   3 5/8"   3 5/8"   6 1/4"

19"   19"

Elevation of fence faces

Fence ends cut at 45°.
Leave a 1/8" shoulder.

Drill a hole for your shopvac hose to fit
1 3/8" nominal

3"   11 1/2"   1/4"   6"   1/4"   9 1/2"   3"

1/2"   1 1/2"   2 1/2"

1/2"   3 1/2"   2"   6 1/4"   2"   4"   2"   4 1/4"   2"   3 1/4"   1/2"

1 1/8"   1/2"   1 5/8"

33 1/2"

Plan

3"   11 1/2"   1/4"   6"   1/4"   9 1/2"   3"

3/8" radii on lid pulls

1 3/4"   2"   1/4"

1/2"   2"   3"

1"   1/2"   2"   4"   1/2"

1/2"   3 1/2"   2"   6 1/4"   2"   4"   2"   4 1/4"   2"   3 1/4"   1/2"

1 1/8"   1/2"   1 5/8"

33 1/2"

Elevation

1/2"   1 1/2"   3/4"   3/32"   1/2"   square rabbet

3 1/4"

Profile

SCHEDULE OF MATERIALS: LITTLE SHOP ROUTER FENCE				
NO.	LTR.	ITEM	DIMENSIONS T W L	MATERIAL
2	A	Front & back	1/2" x 2 1/2" x 33"	Plywood
1	B	Bottom	1/2" x 1 1/2" x 15 3/4"	Plywood
1	C	Bottom	1/2" x 1 1/2" x 13 1/8"	Plywood
3	D	Ends & support	1/2" x 1 1/2" x 2"	Plywood
1	E	End	1/2" x 2 1/2" x 2 1/2"	Plywood
2	F	Tops	1/2" x 2 1/2" x 3"	Plywood
1	G	Top	1/2" x 2 1/2" x 6"	Plywood
2	H	Fence faces	3/4" x 4" x 19"	Maple
1	I	Lid	1/2" x 2 1/2" x 9 1/2"	Plywood.
1	J	Lid	1/2" x 2 1/2" x 11 1/2"	Plywood
2	K	Pull	1/4" x 1" x 2 1/2"	Plywood
4	L	Index blocks	1/4" x 1" x 1 1/2"	Plywood
2	M	Finger boards	3/4" x 3 1/8" x 8"	Maple
2	N	Jointer spacers	5" x 16"	Plas. Lam.

SUPPLIES

ROCKLER WOODWORKING

800-279-4441

WWW.ROCKLER.COM

T - Knob, 71506, $1.99/each.
Insert a 2" x 1/4"-20 hex bolt into this knob to create knobs for attaching the router fence to the saw fence.

Router table insert, 25843/$64.99.

OTHER HARDWARE:

10- 1 1/2" x 1/4"-20 hex bolts
10- Lock washers for 1/4" bolts
10- Flat washers for 1/4" bolts
10- 1/4"-20 wing nuts
2- 1/4"-20 t-nuts

5/8

1/8 SLOTS

FINGER BOARDS

Cut a 30-degree angle on the end of the board. Cut two parallel, 1/4" slots in the board as shown in the photo. Mark a line 2 1/2" from the end of the miter cut. Cut out the 5/8" notches in the sides and then cut out 1/8" fingers with a 1/8" spacing, ripping to the 2 1/2" pencil mark. Stop and back the board out of the cut.

JIG FOR ROUTING ELLIPSES

Using this jig is so much fun it's almost a crime.

By Jim Stack

An ellipse is an angled cross section of a cone and has constantly changing radii. This jig will enable you to cut patterns, grooves and templates. A perfect ellipse will be the result every time.

This jig can easily be sized larger. Determine how large your ellipse will be and cut the base plate to size. The grooves for the guide blocks will be the same size regardless of the base plate dimensions.

To begin, cut the base plate to size. Then set up a dado cutter in your table saw and cut the grooves for the guide blocks. Center the grooves on the base plate.

Cut out the pivot arm. Use a router mounted under a router table to cut the $\frac{1}{4}$" slot in the pivot arm. Next, cut out the guide blocks and drill them to accept the machine screws. (See the illustration for details.)

The mounting plate for the router that attaches to the pivot arm will vary in size and shape according to the size of your router.

Waxing the guide blocks and the guide block grooves will allow this jig to operate smoothly.

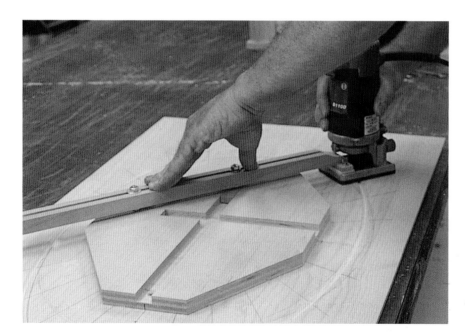

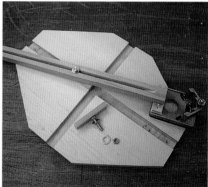

1 This photo shows the router base mounted to the pivot arm and one of the guide blocks, with all its parts. The mounting plate for the router will vary from router to router. The router base shown here is for a trim router.

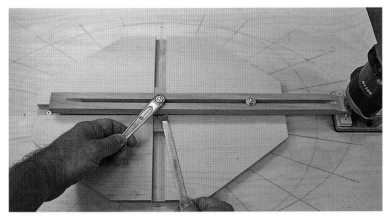

2 When setting up the jig, adjust the guide blocks to the length and width of the ellipse. Tighten the nuts so the blocks are locked in place on the pivot arm. Remember that the guide blocks need to be able to turn freely.

HARDWARE

2	2" × ¼"–20 (51mm × 6mm–20) oval head bolts
4	¼"–20 (6mm–20) hex nuts
6	¼" (6mm) flat washers

INCHES (MILLIMETERS)

REFERNCE	QUANTITY	PART	STOCK	THICKNESS (MM)	WIDTH (MM)	LENGTH (MM)
A	1	base plate	plywood	³/₄ (19)	11 (279)	16 (406)
B	1	pivot arm	hardwood	³/₄ (19)	1¼ (32)	20 (508)
C	2	guide blocks	hardwood	½ (13)	³/₄ (19)	3 (76)
D	1	mounting plate	hardwood	½ (13)	³/₄ (19)	3 (76)

Dimensions of base plate can be adjusted to fit your particular needs.

16"

¾"

Front View

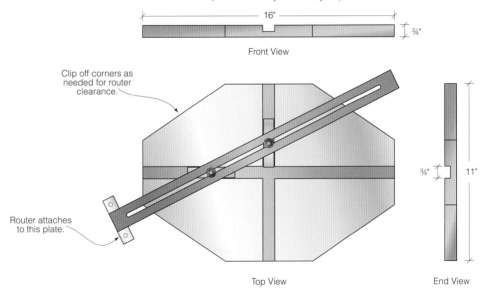

Clip off corners as needed for router clearance.

Router attaches to this plate.

Top View

¾"

11"

End View

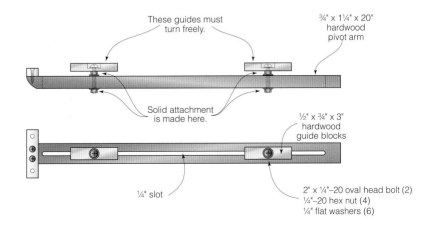

These guides must turn freely.

¾" × 1¼" × 20" hardwood pivot arm

Solid attachment is made here.

½" × ¾" × 3" hardwood guide blocks

¼" slot

2" × ¼"–20 oval head bolt (2)
¼"–20 hex nut (4)
¼" flat washers (6)

TABLE SAWS

TABLE SAW TENON JIG

By Glen Huey

Several years ago my brother-in-law was thinking about buying a commercial tenoning jig because he was having trouble keeping his work flat against his table saw's small fence while cutting tenon cheeks.

"Don't do that," I told him. "I'll show you how to build a jig from a few pieces of scrap that will do the job just fine." So I built the jig in the photo above and have used it just about every day in my shop to cut tenons on my table saw and sliding dovetails on my router table. The high side and back keep my tenons in position as I cut the cheeks. It's difficult to mess up a tenon with this jig.

When I decided to retire the old jig and build a new one, I thought about adding some fancy features. Then I realized that simple is best, and I stuck with my original design. This jig is built to be used with a commercial Biesemeyer fence. If you don't have a Biesemeyer, you'll have to change the dimensions of the top and side runners, but that's simple to do.

SIMPLICITY ITSELF

Basically, this jig is two pieces of plywood in an "L" shape that have a couple pieces of wood screwed to them to allow them to ride the table saw's fence. After settling on the dimensions that are right for your fence, cut all your pieces to size. First clamp the side piece and top runner in position on your fence. Mark where the two pieces intersect and screw and glue the two pieces together. Be sure to countersink the screw heads in the side piece. Position the side runner in place under the top runner. You want it to be tight against the fence — but not too tight. Screw it into place.

Now glue and screw the large back piece to the side piece. You want the angle to be 90 degrees between the two pieces, so check your work. Later you'll add a corner brace that will keep this angle fixed at 90 degrees. Attach the two triangular braces to the side and runners. Attach the braces with nails and glue.

Now miter the corner brace to fit. Put an engineer's square between the back and side and adjust the brace until it holds these pieces at exactly 90 degrees. Now nail the brace in place.

SET UP AND USE

Before you go cutting tenons, wax the areas of the runners that come in contact with your fence. If your jig won't slide, unscrew the side runner and take a light jointer pass on it. When the jig slides smoothly, add some glue to the joint between the side and top runner to make it permanent.

Cutting tenons is now simple. First use your miter gauge and fence to define your shoulders. Then put your jig up on the saw and make your cheek cuts.

The first tenoning jig I built years ago. It's seen a lot of use on my table saw and my router. When I went to build a new jig, I realized that this one served me so well that I didn't need to add any more features to make it more useful.

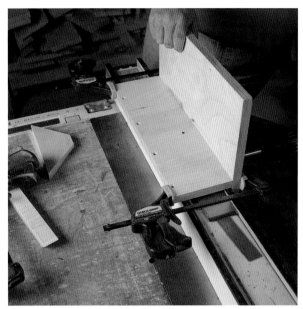

Here's the side piece held in place against the top runner. You want the top runner to be snug against the top of your fence (above). The triangular braces (right) keep the side and top runner square and sturdy for years to come.

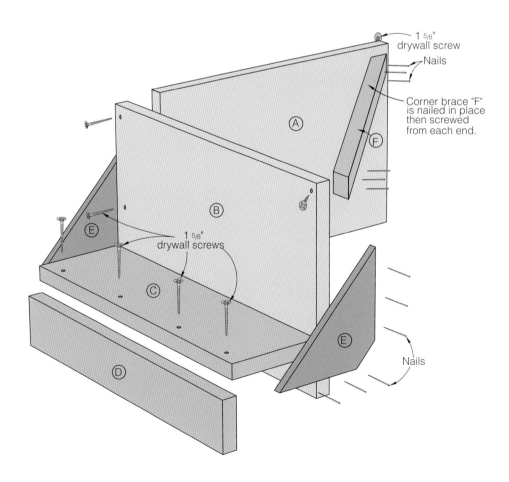

1 5/8"
drywall screw

Nails

Corner brace "F"
is nailed in place
then screwed
from each end.

A

F

B

E

1 5/8"
drywall screws

C

D

E

Nails

Take your time fitting the corner brace between the side and back pieces. You want it to hold these pieces at exactly 90 degrees.

Furniture wax works great to keep the runners moving smoothly over your fence. Be sure to reapply wax when the jig starts to get a little stiff after use (below).

The curly maple board attached to my miter gauge minimizes tearout when I make the shoulder cuts for my tenons.

After making my cheek cuts (which is shown in the opening photo of the article), reset the saw to define the tenon's edge cheeks (above).

Mortise-and-tenon joints are the staple of my custom woodworking business. I use this jig on every piece of furniture I build. The jig's simplicity and sturdiness have made it one of the workhorses in my shop (right).

SCHEDULE OF MATERIALS: TENON JIG

NO.	LTR.	ITEM	DIMENSIONS T W L	MATERIAL
1	A	Back	¾" x 10" x 15¼"	Plywood
1	B	Side	¾" x 10" x 16"	Plywood
1	C	Top runner	¾" x 4¾" x 16"	Plywood
1	D	Side runner	¾" x 2½" x 16"	Plywood
2	E	Triangular braces	⅜" x 3" x 7½"	Plywood
1	F	Corner brace	⅞" x 1" x 21"	Hardwood*

* Piece is long; cut to fit.

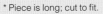

TABLE SAW OUTFEED TABLES

Don't let the simplicity of these tables fool you. When used together they make many operations easier and serve many other tasks that aren't immediately obvious.

By Steve Shanesy

You can find all sorts of devices for sale to support your stock as you feed it over your table saw. Some sport rolling pin-style rollers, some have a series of roller balls. Some attach directly to your saw, others offer micro-adjustment to level it to the precise plane of your saw table.

My humble outfeed table offering has no such features. In fact, they are about as "plain Jane" as you can get. Remove them from the shop and no one would take them for anything other than what they are — a pair of trestle tables.

So what's the big deal? Well, if you operate in a small shop space, say a garage or basement, these tables will serve so many useful purposes you'll wonder how you ever did without them.

I've been using a pair of tables just like these in my basement shop for the past five years. They surround my table saw and can be easily repositioned for ripping long stock, crosscutting a full sheet of plywood and supporting long crosscuts using my table saw's sled (and they give me a place to hang the sled when it's not in use). But wait, there's more.

These tables also serve as stock support for both sides of my compound miter saw. I use them as smaller assembly tables, for stacking stock while I'm planing or jointing it. Sometimes I finish projects on them. And because they are also the same height as my regular assembly table, I can put larger objects on both.

I arrived at the trestle-style design because it's not only stout and material-efficient, but it keeps the base enough "inboard" so that you're not bumping table legs with your feet. It also keeps the weight down and makes them easy to slide on your shop floor.

GETTING SET FOR BUILDING

Before you start construction, measure the distance from the floor to the top of your table saw. There can be as much as an inch or two variance in heights. The plans given here are for a saw that is just over 34" high. You should make your tables' height $\frac{1}{8}$" less than your saw's height and reduce the height by as much as another $\frac{1}{8}$" if your shop floor isn't very level around the saw. What can make these tables useless is if they are even a bit higher than the saw table. In my book, being slightly under doesn't matter.

And if you wonder why I didn't use levelers, I'll tell you. It's just not worth the hassle of adjusting them every time you move a table, let alone two of them. And you'd have to do this every time, owing to variations in the floor or the fact that most screw-adjustable levelers will wind or unwind just by dragging the table across a floor. When maintaining a plane in critical work, perhaps with a miter saw, shims or wedges are quick and easy.

CONSTRUCTION DETAILS

I built these tables using both mortise-and-tenon joints and dowel joints. You could use only dowels if your shop isn't set up with mortising equipment. And in fact, my original tables were constructed entirely using biscuit joints and screws and are no worse for the heavy service they have seen. If you don't use mortises, remember to deduct the length of the tenons from the parts list.

I used stout white oak for the bases because I had some 8/4 stock on hand. But since I finished it out to $1\frac{1}{2}$" thickness, you might want to consider using ordinary 2 x 4s. Just don't use twisted ones.

Follow the diagrams and cutting list to prepare your stock in the correct sizes, making any allowance for a difference in table saw height in the leg parts.

Next take the feet, top rails and legs for Table 1 and lay out the mortise locations as shown in the diagram. All tenons are $\frac{1}{2}$" thick by $1\frac{1}{4}$" wide by $1\frac{1}{4}$" long. Make the mortises the same dimensions except in depth. Make them $\frac{1}{16}$" deeper so the tenons don't bottom out before they seat home.

LAYOUT TRICK: WORK FROM THE CENTER OUT

When I do layout work I often find it handy to use a couple tricks. Take the top rails and feet of Table 2, for

example. It's really important that the mortises and dowel joints line up perfectly for the legs. To pull this off, I group all the parts together so their ends align perfectly. You can even throw a square on the group to make sure they aren't creeping out of alignment. Clamp them so they can't move.

Next, locate and mark from each end the center of the leg locations (7$\frac{1}{8}$") on one of the parts. Since the feet get mortises that are 1$\frac{1}{4}$" wide, measure out $\frac{5}{8}$" from each side of the center lines. Now take a square you know to be true and transfer these lines to the other parts. For the top rail, use the same lines to align your doweling jig. Later, you can transfer these lines onto the leg parts for identical jig alignment. Grouping parts

and measuring from the center out cuts down on simple errors of missed or inconsistent measuring on common parts. The beauty of this method is that even if you are off slightly, everything remains off consistently. After laying out the mortises, cut them all.

CUT THE TENONS

Next cut the tenons, fitting them to the mortises. I use the table saw for this job, setting up the saw using scraps of fall-off from the actual parts so their dimensions are consistent with the materials I'm working with.

I cut the cheeks using the table saw's fence, standing the parts on end to run them over the blade. Use a back-up block to support the tall stock when making these cuts. To finish the tenons I band saw off most of the

waste from the cheek cut. I then set the table saw fence to establish the final length of the tenon. With the stock on its side and guided by a slot miter gauge, trim the remainder of the cheek waste. Then turn the part to the other side and make the shoulder cut.

In this project, since there weren't a lot of tenons, I just made a series of passes over the rest of the shoulder to cut away the waste. Otherwise, I would have set up a dado stack to do the work more quickly.

Before you make the final shapes on the top rails and feet, lay out and drill for the pair of dowels at the top of the leg-to-rail joint on Table 1. Position them so they straddle the mortise in the rail as shown in the diagram.

Next make the angle cuts on the rails and feet, and the cutout on the

Joining the top stretcher to the top rail and the leg to the top rail on Table 1 requires the dowel placement to straddle the mortise.

OUTFEED TABLES						
NO.	ITEM	DIMENSIONS (INCHES)			MATERIAL	
		T	W	L		
TABLE 1						
1	Top (A)*	$\frac{3}{4}$	15	47	birch plywood	
2	Top rails (B)	$1\frac{1}{2}$	$2\frac{1}{4}$	14	white oak	
2	Top-Bot stret (C)	$1\frac{1}{2}$	$2\frac{1}{4}$	$39\frac{1}{2}$	white oak	
2	Legs (D)	$1\frac{1}{2}$	$2\frac{1}{4}$	$29\frac{1}{4}$	white oak	
2	Feet (E)	$1\frac{1}{2}$	3	14	white oak	
2	Solid edging	$\frac{3}{4}$	$\frac{1}{2}$	48	any hardwood	
2	Solid edging	$\frac{3}{4}$	$\frac{1}{2}$	15	any hardwood	
TABLE 2						
1	Top (F)*	$\frac{3}{4}$	25	47	birch plywood	
2	Top rails (G)	$1\frac{1}{2}$	$2\frac{1}{4}$	20	white oak	
1	Top stret (H)	$1\frac{1}{2}$	$2\frac{1}{4}$	$39\frac{1}{2}$	white oak	
4	Legs (J)	$1\frac{1}{2}$	2	$29\frac{1}{4}$	white oak	
1	Shelf (K)*	$\frac{3}{4}$	$15\frac{1}{2}$	36	birch plywood	
2	Solid edging top	$\frac{3}{4}$	$\frac{1}{2}$	48	any hardwood	
2	Solid edging top	$\frac{3}{4}$	$\frac{1}{2}$	25	any hardwood	
2	Solid edging shelf	$\frac{3}{4}$	$\frac{1}{2}$	37	any hardwood	
2	Solid edging shelf	$\frac{3}{4}$	$\frac{1}{2}$	$15\frac{1}{2}$	any hardwood	

*Dimension given does not include $\frac{1}{2}$"-thick solid edging to be added.

bottom of the feet. Follow the layout in the diagram, then band saw out the waste. Smooth the rough band-sawn edges.

Before gluing up, make a dry-run assembly to make sure everything is right before you get to that panic glue-up stage. After making any adjustments, start gluing up, but don't try to do everything at once. First glue up and clamp the leg/rail end sections. Once those are dry, glue the stretchers to the ends. Although this takes a bit longer, it allows you to make sure your glue ups are square and flat. A twist in a table base is a real pain.

Once the base is completely assembled, you can call it done or rout a $\frac{3}{8}$" radius profile on all the edges except where the feet meet the floor and the top rail and stretcher attaches to the top. I did this on my tables and think it makes them appear more "finished."

The tops and shelf are straightforward. Cut plywood to the sizes given, then glue and tack on $\frac{3}{4}$"- x $\frac{1}{2}$"-wide solid edging. Tack below the center point so you can rout a $\frac{1}{4}$" radius profile on the top edges. This detail isn't optional; the rounded edge helps prevent stock from catching on

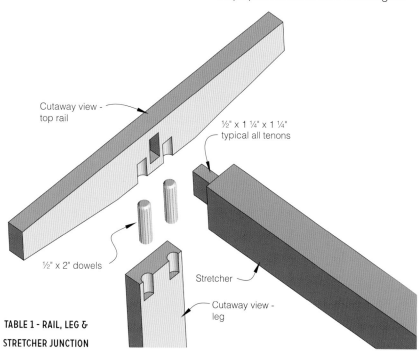

Cutaway view - top rail

$\frac{1}{2}$" x 1 $\frac{1}{4}$" x 1 $\frac{1}{4}$" typical all tenons

$\frac{1}{2}$" x 2" dowels

Stretcher

Cutaway view - leg

TABLE 1 - RAIL, LEG & STRETCHER JUNCTION

The top rails are joined to the legs using two $\frac{1}{2}$" dowels for each leg while the bottom uses a mortise and tenon. Other joinery options include dowels only, mortises only or biscuits.

the edge when the tables are in use.

Before attaching the shelf on the larger table, sand the base and tops to your satisfaction. I didn't bother with a finish on my tables. These are for the shop, after all.

To attach the shelf, use corner braces at each of the four legs. If you change the height of the shelf for any reason, just make sure it won't interfere with your table saw's motor hanging out the back of your contractor saw.

And by the way, if you are already set up and happy with an outfeed system for your shop, remember that you can always change the height of these tables and use the design and joinery for any number of other trestle-style tables.

It may take a little "persuading" to seat the tenons in their mortises, but if properly fit should only require tapping in place.

When gluing up, assemble the ends first and let them dry before completing the table base assembly by gluing the stretchers to the ends.

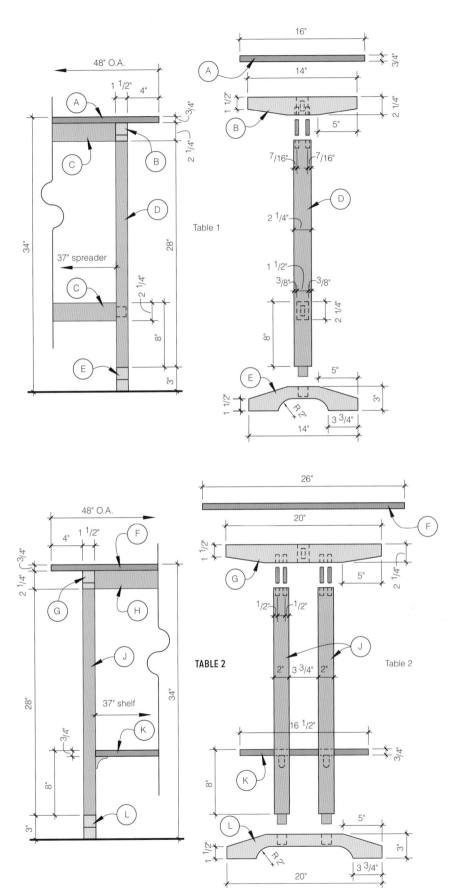

UNDER-THE-SAW CABINET

By Steve Shanesy

The space below your table saw is a prime storage area that's likely been doing little more than gathering scraps.

In my eternal quest to find more shop space, I discovered a respectable piece of real estate right under my nose, err, well my table saw anyway. Yes, right below the table board was a beat-up box of odd cut-offs that were about as valuable as ice cubes are to Eskimos.

After noodling around with design ideas I settled on the rig you see here. Not only does it provide a lot of useful storage, but it has really helped me organize my blades and accessories that weren't always at my fingertips. There's even extra storage on the "outfeed" side of the cabinet.

The Shaker-style flat-panel doors gave me a chance to try out some new router bits. We've included a special pull-out poster that provides all the details for making these doors, or other doors, that will make a handy reference when hung in your shop.

BUILD THE CASE

Cut out the plywood for the sides, top, bottom, the common back, partition, front rail and full bottom that goes below the router-bit storage tray.

On the two sides, cut a rabbet on the top edge that's $\frac{1}{2}$" deep by $\frac{3}{4}$" wide that will hold the top. For the bottom, make a dado $\frac{1}{2}$" deep by $\frac{3}{4}$" wide that starts 3" up from the bottom edge.

Next will be several $\frac{1}{4}$" by $\frac{1}{4}$" dados and grooves. These joints join the common back to the sides, the partition on the "infeed" side of the cabinet where it joins the common back, and where the rail and full bottom form the drawer openings. Refer to the drawings for the

placement of each of these dados. Remember to stop the dado on the cabinet side for the router bit section bottom so it doesn't pass beyond the common back.

For the corresponding parts, cut $\frac{1}{4}$" tongues on the edges. On the back, these are on the two sides; for the partition, they're on the back edge. The 4" rail has tongues on both ends, and the full bottom on both long edges.

Now, before you begin assembly, notch the bottom corners of the sides to create the setback for the toe kick. The height of the kick is the same as the lower edge of the dado you cut for the cabinet's bottom.

DRY FIT, THEN ASSEMBLE

Dry-assemble the case to check the fit of the joints. Make sure that during the real assembly you have all the parts oriented in the right direction so you don't turn a part with a $\frac{1}{4}$" tongue around and create a cabinet that won't go together.

When you are ready for final assembly, have a friend around or assemble the parts in stages.

Before nailing the top in place, screw two cleats into the sides of the router bit opening that are $\frac{1}{2}$" up from the bottom. Make sure a $\frac{1}{2}$" piece of plywood will slide smoothly in the space because this will be the simple slide method for the router bit pull-out tray. When done, install the top. Next, turn the cabinet upside down and nail or screw through the bottom into the bottom edges of the common back and partition.

While the case is in this position, nail on the kick pieces after edging the ends with hot-melt glue-backed veneer tape. While the iron is hot, veneer the other edges of the cabinet and shelves to conceal the plywood core.

MAKE, INSTALL THE DRAWERS

The project requires one regular drawer and two pull-out trays. All three are made the same except the trays have a cut-out front. The router bit storage be hind the other drawer front isn't really a drawer at all, but another kind of tray. Here's how to make the regular drawer and trays.

Cut out the parts according to the cutting list. On the drawer fronts and backs, cut rabbets that are $\frac{5}{16}$" deep by $\frac{1}{2}$" wide. These accept the sides. The back is $\frac{1}{2}$" narrower in width than the sides and front. This allows the bottom to slip in $\frac{1}{4}$" x $\frac{1}{4}$" grooves cut in the sides and front, $\frac{1}{4}$" up from the bottom edge. Before assembling the trays, make the cutout on the front. Make the cut $2\frac{1}{2}$" in from the side and the top edge. To assemble, use glue and nails. After the glue has dried, slip the bottoms in place, then check for square before nailing the bottom in place.

Install the drawers following the instructions for the type of drawer slides you use. The drawers are sized to use common $\frac{1}{2}$"-thick drawer slides.

The tray for the router bits is just a $\frac{1}{2}$" piece of plywood glued into a $\frac{3}{8}$" x $\frac{3}{8}$" groove in the drawer front that starts $\frac{5}{16}$" up from the bottom edge.

Position the plywood to allow for the drawer front gap on the right side of the front. Later, add another layer of plywood with holes cut to stand your bits in place, then screw this second layer to the tray bottom.

Now turn to the vertical pull-out panel. It is simply ½" plywood that runs in grooves on top and bottom to guide it. A hole near the front edge gives you a place to grasp and pull. Cut two pieces of stock 1¼" x 2⅞" x 21¾", then cut a groove ¾" deep by ½" wide that's 1¾" from the edge. Screw these to the cabinet in the upper and lower corners.

MAKE AND INSTALL THE DOORS

Turn to the center spread of this issue for a special pull-out poster containing complete details for building the doors.

Mortise the butt hinges on the stiles to the thickness of one hinge leaf. I used a router with a ¼"-diameter bit. Use a chisel to square up the mortise corners. To swage the hinges, see the photo at right.

Screw the hinges on the doors after drilling pilot holes. Use paraffin on the screw threads and a screwdriver if you're using brass screws, which are quite soft.

Position the doors in the opening and use shims to set the door up from the bottom. Carefully pencil the hinge locations, then mark and drill the pilot holes for the hinges and install.

To complete the project, drill holes for the adjustable shelves. I spaced mine 1½" in from the front and back, then from the bottom, up 8½", 10", 11½", 17", 18½" and 20". Before finishing, install door catches, and the door and drawer pulls.

For finish, your cabinet deserves a little protection so give it a clear coat of your favorite finish material.

Before assembly, handsaw 3"x 3¾" notches in the sides at the bottom corners to make the toe kick space.

UNDER-THE-SAW CABINET

NO.	ITEM	DIMENSIONS (INCHES) T	W	L	MATERIAL	COMMENTS
2	Sides	¾	31	30¾	birch ply	rabbet top edge
1	Common back	¾	25	26¼	birch ply	rabbet both sides
1	Partition	¾	20¹⁵/₁₆	26¼	birch ply	rabbet back edge
2	Top/bottom	¾	25½	31	birch ply	
1	Rail	¾	4	16¼	birch ply	
1	Full bottom, router area	¾	8½	20¾	birch ply	rabbet 2 long edges
2	Toe kicks	¾	3	26	birch ply	
2	Shelves	¾	7⁵/₈	24⁵/₁₆	birch Ply	
1	Pull out panel	½	20¾	19½	birch ply	
2	Panel guides	1¼	2⁷/₈	19½	solid hardwood	
1	Drw front	¾	5³/₈	8³/₈	solid birch	
1	Drw front	¾	5³/₈	16¹/₈	solid birch	
1	Router bit tray bottom	½	7¹⁵/₁₆	21	birch ply	tongue, 1 short end
1	Drw sub front	½	4¼	14³/₄	birch ply	rabbet 2 short ends
1	Drw back	½	3¾	14³/₄	birch ply	rabbet 2 short ends
2	Drw sides	½	4¼	19⁵/₈	birch ply	
1	Drw bottom	¼	14¼	19³/₄	birch ply	
4	Sides, pull out trays	½	4½	20	birch ply	
2	Fronts, pull out trays	½	4½	13⁹/₁₆	birch ply	rabbet 2 short edges
2	Backs, pull out trays	½	4	13⁹/₁₆	birch Ply	rabbet 2 short edges
2	Bottoms, pull out trays	¼	13¹/₁₆	19³/₁₆	birch ply	
4	Door stiles	¾	1½	20⁷/₈	solid birch	
2	Door rails	¾	1½	6¼	solid birch	tongue 2 short ends
1	Door panel	½	6³/₁₆	18¹¹/₁₆	solid birch	
2	Door rails	¾	1½	14	solid birch	tongue, 2 short end
1	Door panel	½	13¹⁵/₁₆	18¹¹/₁₆	birch ply	
4	Door stiles	¾	1½	26¼	solid birch	
4	Door rails	¾	1½	10¹/₈	solid birch	tongue, 2 short end
2	Door panels	½	10¹/₁₆	24¹/₁₆	birch ply	

Apply a hot iron to hot-melt-glue backed edge veneer, then file off any veneer overhang using the teeth on your file's edge. It works just like a saw.

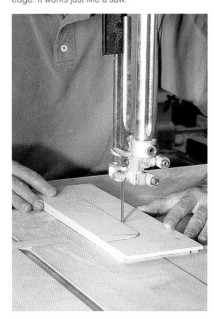

Mark the cutout on the fronts of the pull-out trays and then band saw to the line and sand. Then go ahead and assemble the trays.

Both the pull-out panel and the pull-out tray are guided by simply creating grooves for them to slide in and out.

Use your router and an edge guide to mortise the hinges on the door stiles. I set my hinges 3" from the stile ends.

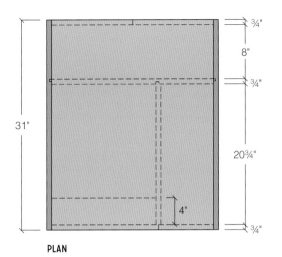

PLAN

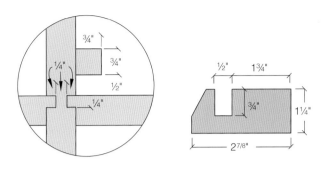

VERTICAL-PANEL GUIDE PROFILE

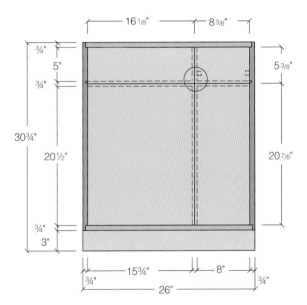

PARTITION DETAIL

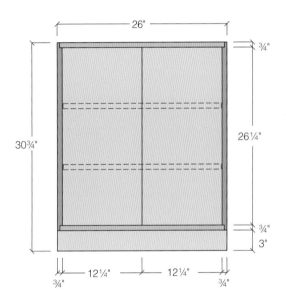

SEE DETAIL ABOVE RIGHT

Swaging hinges will allow a better door fit. Place the hinge on a solid surface, cover the leaves with a piece of steel up to the hinge barrel, then give it a good whack with a hammer.

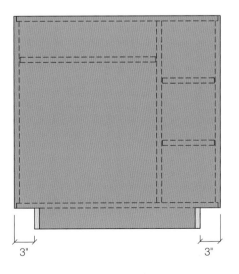

PROFILE

MULTIPURPOSE SAW SLED

It takes just nine pieces of wood to turn your table saw into a precision crosscutting and tenoning machine.

By Nick Engler

For many years I had the pleasure of working with Jim McCann, a craftsman I admired as much for his ingenuity as his considerable skill. Jim and I designed projects of all sorts, but we had a special fondness for jigs. It was a challenge for us to create a shop-made tool as simple and as functional as possible. This sliding table or saw sled was one of our best efforts. There are really four jigs here — the sliding table itself, a micro-adjustable fence stop for duplication and accuracy, an auxiliary table to prevent binding and kickbacks, and a tenoning jig to hold stock vertically — just nine wooden parts to do dozens of sawing chores.

SLIDING TABLE

The table is a large base with a long fence that slides across the saw table, past the saw blade. A miter bar attached to the underside of the base guides the jig. This is the one special piece of hardware you need to make this jig — a miter bar to fit the slot in your particular table saw. (Most are ⅜" deep and ¾" wide.) Attach the bar to the base with machine screws, countersinking the heads so they're slightly below the surface of the base. Position the bar so that when you saw with the jig for the first time, the blade shaves about ¹⁄₁₆" from the edge of the sled's base.

Make the fence from a single piece of straight-grained hardwood. Tip: To make a long, slender part such as the

fence as stable as possible, rip it in half parallel to the annual rings. Rotate one part 180° and glue the parts back together so the annual rings cup in the opposite directions. This will help the fence stay straight and true.

Rip the board for your fence down the middle, joint both halves straight, and cut two grooves in each half — a ¾"-wide, ⅜"-deep groove followed by a ¼"-wide groove all the way through the stock, as shown in the Elevation

Section A drawing and the shaded area of the Fence Detail drawing on a following page. The grooves in the front half should run almost the complete length of the fence, while the grooves in the back half need to be only a few inches long. When you glue the fence halves back together, the grooves will form T-slots. Use the long T-slot on the front of the fence to mount the fence stop and the tenoning jig. The shorter slot on the back stores the stop and keeps it handy.

Mount the fence to the base with ³⁄₈" hex bolts. Drill counterbores for the heads of the bolts so they don't protrude from the underside of the base. The bolt nearest the saw blade serves as a pivot, should you need to angle the fence to cut miters. The other bolt secures the fence and provides a small amount of angle adjustment. The shank hole for this bolt is ⁷⁄₁₆" in diameter. That extra clearance lets you move the fence back and forth a few degrees to adjust it square to the blade. Once the fence is adjusted, draw a pencil line to mark the position of the fence on the base. If you ever need to change the angle of the fence, the pencil line will make it easy to square it up again.

Since 95 percent of your saw cuts are made at 90°, and another 4½ percent are made at 45°, I suggest you drill holes and counterbores so you can secure the fence at 90° and 45°, and leave it at that. For those odd angles, you can either drill holes as you need them or resort to your miter gauge.

To help measure as I cut, I added a scale to the front of the fence, inset in a ¹⁄₃₂"-deep rabbet. Note that the scale is upside down. It's easier to read when I lean over the fence.

AUXILIARY TABLE

One of the few drawbacks to a sliding table is that the base raises the work off the saw table, leaving it unsupported on the far side of the saw blade. Because of this, the wood will drop down as you finish the cut, binding the blade. This in turn may

In addition to everything else it does, the sliding table also makes an excellent base for other sawing jigs that you might need. Here I've attached a special fence and clamp-downs to make scarf joint in the spars for a reproduction of a Wright Brothers' flyer.

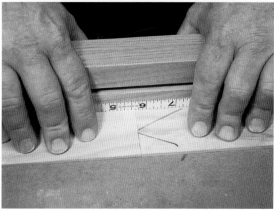

Tip: To adjust the fence so it holds the wood precisely square to the saw blade, take a scrap piece and rip it so the edges are parallel. Mark one face, saw through the mark (top), and flip one part over. Bring the cut ends together, holding the edges against the fence (right). If the seam between the parts gaps at the top or bottom, the fence is not square to the blade.

cause the cut-off part to kick back.

The auxiliary table (shown in the opening photo on page 92) prevents this. It's a second base the same size as the first, but without a fence or a miter bar. Instead, there is a cleat at the front edge that hooks over your saw table and prevents the auxiliary table from sliding forward as you work. Depending on the design of your saw, cut the cleat so that you can secure it with a clamp either to the fence rail or the front of the saw.

FENCE STOP

The stop is a block of wood you can mount anywhere along the length of the fence and can make duplicate cuts without having to measure for each cut. A ¼" carriage bolt secures the stop in the T-slot, and a ¼"-diameter dowel prevents it from pivoting. To get the stop to slide smoothly you'll need to do a little file work. The head of a carriage bolt is stamped so there is a curved transition or fillet between the head and the square section at the beginning of the shaft. This fillet

wedges itself in the slot and makes it difficult to move the stop. To fix this, file the carriage bolt to remove the fillet, creating a square shoulder between the head and the shank of the carriage bolt.

I also added a micro-adjustment to my stop. Drill a 5/32"-diameter hole through the stop that's parallel to the bottom edge and thread this hole with a 10-32 tap. (A dense hardwood such as hard maple will take these small threads no problem.) Countersink the end of the hole nearest the blade (when the stop is mounted to the fence). Turn a 10-32 flathead machine screw into the threaded hole and tighten a jamb nut and a knurled nut on the other end so you can turn the screw easily. One turn of the screw will advance the head precisely 1/32", allowing you to make extremely accurate adjustments.

TENONING JIG

The tenoning jig is two pieces of wood joined at 90°. This makes a cradle to hold boards vertically to the saw blade — just place the board in the corner

formed by the two parts and secure it with a clamp. Don't waste good wood on this jig; make it from scraps. The tenoning jig is a "disposable" fixture — it eventually gets eaten up by the saw blade, and you'll have to make a new one. Mount the jig to the fence with two ¼" carriage bolts, much the same way you mounted the fence stop.

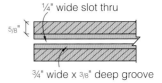

¼" wide slot thru

5/8"

¾" wide x 3/8" deep groove

Elevation Section A

3/8"

¼"

7/8"

¾"

2"

5/8"

¾"

1½"

End view

Fence Detail

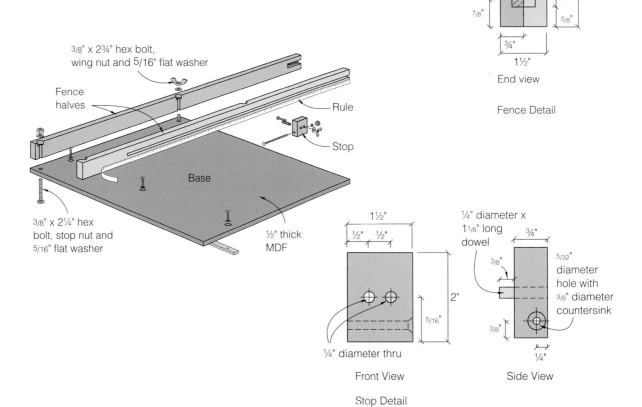

3/8" x 2¾" hex bolt, wing nut and 5/16" flat washer

Fence halves

Rule

Stop

Base

3/8" x 2¼" hex bolt, stop nut and 5/16" flat washer

½" thick MDF

1½"

½"   ½"

2"

5/16"

¼" diameter thru

Front View

Stop Detail

¼" diameter x 1 1/8" long dowel

¾"

3/8"

5/32" diameter hole with 3/8" diameter countersink

3/8"

¼"

Side View

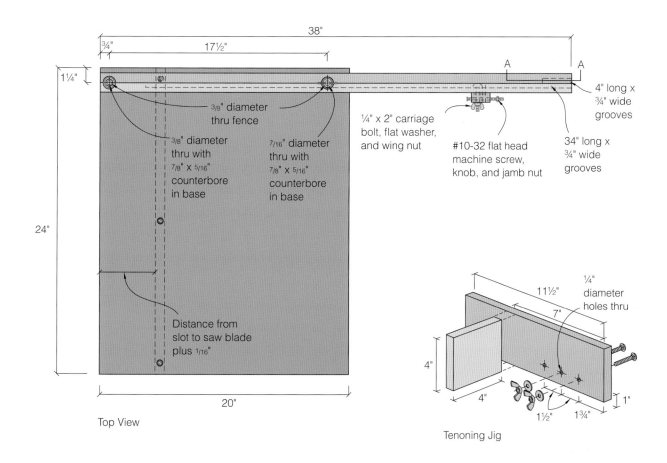

38"

¾"

17½"

1¼"

24"

20"

A   A

3/8" diameter
thru fence

3/8" diameter
thru with
7/8" X 5/16"
counterbore
in base

7/16" diameter
thru with
7/8" X 5/16"
counterbore
in base

¼" x 2" carriage
bolt, flat washer,
and wing nut

#10-32 flat head
machine screw,
knob, and jamb nut

4" long x
¾" wide
grooves

34" long x
¾" wide
grooves

Distance from
slot to saw blade
plus 1/16"

Top View

11½"

7"

¼"
diameter
holes thru

4"

4"

1½"   1¾"

1"

Tenoning Jig

Use the tenoning jig and the fence stop in
combination. Slide the tenoning jig into the T-slot,
then slide the fence stop right behind it. Turn the
micro-adjustment screw until it's snug against
the end of the jig. Clamp a piece of wood in the
cradle, make a test cut, and check the results. If
you need to adjust the position of the jig, loosen
the carriage bolts and rotate the adjustment
screw. In this manner you can make very fine
adjustments, getting the cut just right.

JIM TOLPIN'S UNIVERSAL RIP FENCE

A simple fixture lets your table saw cut curves, patterns and tenons in one pass.

By Jim Tolpin

My universal fence fixture – the heart of my table saw system to which an entire galaxy of accessories can be attached – greatly expands the utility and ease of use of the table saw. With this system you can easily create a wide variety of joints with speed and precision: from tenons to tongue-in-groove and spline joints, to raised panels and rabbets.

It revolves around a single auxiliary fence that quickly bolts to my table saw's existing Biesemeyer-style rip fence. Used by itself, this fixture (which is generally left in place as it does not interfere with most table saw operations), guides wide stock on edge through the blade. This fixture also incorporates a T-slotted aluminum extrusion that accepts the $\frac{1}{4}$" x 20 attachment bolts of two or more shop-made hold-downs to keep stock flat to the table.

BUILDING THE FIXTURE

I recommend building the fixture from a high-quality grade of hardwood plywood that's free of voids and warp. Generally speaking, the more laminations the better.

Take your time to get the cuts straight and square, and securely glue and screw the fixture together. I use biscuits to strengthen the butt joints – full-length shop-made splines would give even more strength if you want to take the extra effort to make them. Careful construction of this fixture will ensure that the accessories that depend on it will run smoothly and accurately.

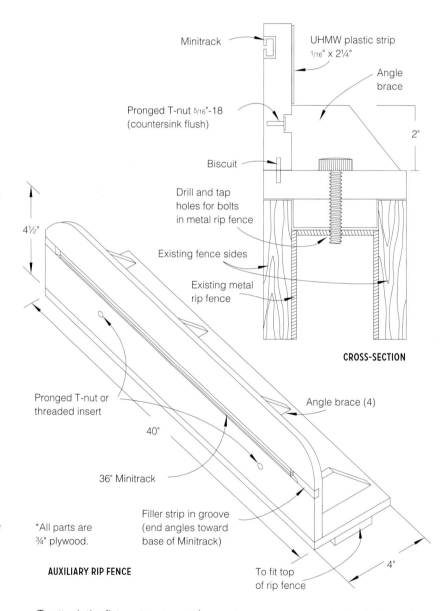

CROSS-SECTION

Labels: Minitrack · UHMW plastic strip $\frac{1}{16}$" x $2\frac{1}{4}$" · Angle brace · Pronged T-nut $\frac{5}{16}$"-18 (countersink flush) · 2" · Biscuit · Drill and tap holes for bolts in metal rip fence · Existing fence sides · Existing metal rip fence

AUXILIARY RIP FENCE

Labels: $4\frac{1}{2}$" · Pronged T-nut or threaded insert · 40" · 36" Minitrack · *All parts are $\frac{3}{4}$" plywood. · Filler strip in groove (end angles toward base of Minitrack) · Angle brace (4) · To fit top of rip fence · 4"

To attach the fixture to your saw's rip fence, you may need only to drill and tap a hole in its metal top surface to accept the hold-down bolts as I did with the Biesemeyer fence at left. If, however, your particular rip fence is not a square steel box, you may have to get a little creative and extend the vertical face of the fence to run down past the face of your rip fence all the

way to the saw table. You can then run bolts horizontally through the wood fence (with the bolt heads buried into a countersink) and through your table saw's rip fence.

To reduce friction (on this and all other fixtures), note that I use $1/16$"-thick strips of ultra high molecular weight (UHMW) plastic on the bearing surfaces of the fixtures where they run against each other or on the table surface. These strips and the aluminum extrusions (which I set into grooves to accept attachment bolts for accessory fixtures) are available from suppliers listed on page 88.

In this article I will introduce you to three of my favorite accessories that I regularly use with my universal rip fence fixture system: the rip fence sled, the pattern fence and the rabbet fence.

THE RIP FENCE SLED
The most versatile of the fixtures is the rip fence sled, which nests and slides on top of the basic fixture. It offers a

multitude of uses depending on how it is set up. It can act as a short rip fence; a tenon jig with integral clamps and replaceable backing strips; an end-bevel cutting and shaping jig; and a feather spline miter-joint carriage (for frames).

An adjustable guide system allows you to tweak the amount of sliding friction. The use of this sled brings precision, efficiency and control to these processes.

Here I will explain just a couple of its applications: cutting tenons on the end of a board and creating a feather spline joint in the corner of a mitered frame.

CUTTING TENONS WITH THE RIP FENCE SLED
I often use the rip fence sled to cut tenons vertically. It's a fast and accurate process.

To cut both cheeks of the tenon at once, I install two identical blades. The one caveat is that your saw must have sufficient power (2 horsepower

minimum is recommended) to run two blades simultaneously through the type of material you are cutting. I also recommend using a 24-tooth, thin-kerf rip blade – here you'll need two, of course – to ensure best results. If you do not have these blades, you could use the two outer blades from a standard stack dado set. Be aware, however, that they won't cut as efficiently as the thin-kerf rip blades and will require more step cuts.

Setting up the double blades requires a plywood washer (don't use solid wood, as its thickness can change with the humidity) augmented by paper or plastic dado-blade washers for fine-tuning the width. Note that the washer width must be greater than the tenon width to account for the fact that the blades' carbide tips are wider than the saw-blade plate. I install a fresh throat plate and set the fence to a story stick. (A story stick simply is a scrap piece of wood with a project's dimensions transferred to it.)

Begin by test-cutting a scrap of

stock. When satisfied, clamp the stock in place and begin making the cuts in steps, never more than 1" in height at a pass – less if dense hardwood. On the last cut, in which the blades reach the shoulder cuts, push the sled all the way past the blade and turn off the saw. After you cut these cheeks, then finish the tenons by cutting the shoulders.

CUTTING FEATHER SPLINE JOINTS WITH THE RIP FENCE SLED

I often use "feather spline" joints on the corners of a frame to add decoration and strength to an existing miter joint. I often make the feathers out of a contrasting hardwood (with the grain running perpendicular to the miter line for strength).

To simplify things, I make the spline the same thickness as the kerf of one of my saw blades. Of course, if you want a thicker feather, you can use a dado blade. Just be sure the slot isn't too tight or there won't be any room for glue when it's time for assembly – you want a slip fit, not a pounding fit.

To set up to cut these feather joints on the rip fence sled, I install a pair of stock supports (with attachment bolts that fit into the sled's integral T-slot shown above). These will carry the frame at an exact 45° angle to the table surface. In this way, the slot made by the blade will cut an even distance along each side.

Set the first support up with a drafting triangle as shown in the photo above left. The second support is then set up square to the first using a carpenter's framing square. Then lock the supports tightly against the sled. Tape a piece of thin hardwood to the face of the rear support to serve as a replaceable backing board for the exiting blade. This helps prevent tear-out.

Set the distance between the sled and the blade by measuring to a story stick and then lock down the rip fence. Make test cuts in scrap to ensure accuracy. At this point it's

simply a matter of setting the frame (which I previously glued together – it's fragile but strong enough for this operation) in the crotch of the two supports, clamping it down and pushing the sled along the universal fixture. Use a series of cuts if the slot is going to be more than ¾" or so deep.

THE PATTERN FENCE

Pattern-sawing on the table saw offers a quick and accurate way to create duplicates.

The pattern fence (below and illustrated on the next page) acts as an index for a template so that the blade makes its cut in the stock precisely along the perimeter of the template. Slotted holes in the fixture allow it to be adjusted to the blade at any height. The pattern fence also can make long straight cuts and gentle

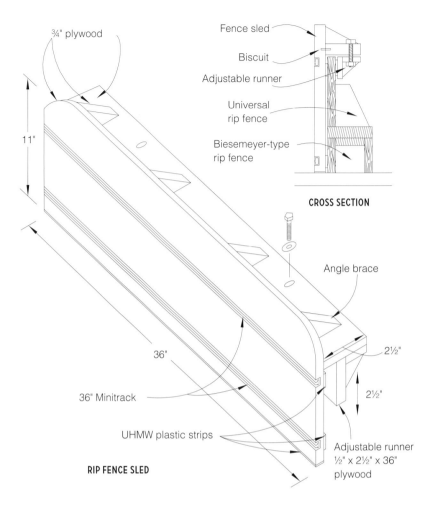

¾" plywood

11"

36"

36" Minitrack

UHMW plastic strips

2½"

2½"

Adjustable runner ½" x 2½" x 36" plywood

RIP FENCE SLED

Fence sled
Biscuit
Adjustable runner
Universal rip fence
Biesemeyer-type rip fence

CROSS SECTION

Angle brace

The rip fence sled, set up with a vertical back stop and clamp, carries a board on end through a set of double blades to create a tenon.

Set up the fixture to cut the feather splines. A drafting triangle set between the underside of the stock support (attached to the sliding rip fence fixture) and the saw table makes quick work of securing the first support at a precise 45° angle.

Use a 24" framing square, such as the one shown above, to set the second support square to the first.

curves.

I start by making an exact template of the shape I want to reproduce. Be careful to get it right because all the other pieces will be its clones. I usually add a handle to the template to provide a more secure grasp.

The next step is to rough-size the workpiece within 1" of its finished shape. Try to avoid a larger waste margin as the offcuts might get trapped between the blade and the fence.

Next, attach the template to the workpiece with protruding pins (brads) or screws if their hole marks are not going to show on the finished workpiece. If both sides must be clean, I use a vacuum clamp system or go the easy route with double-stick carpet tape. The tape will last for five or six cuts before it needs replacing. To help the tape stick better, I sand the bottom of the template and brush or spray on several coats of shellac or other sealer. To ensure a good grab to the carpet tape, I tap the template onto the workpiece with a rubber-faced mallet.

To set up for the cut, raise the height of the low fence fixture equal to the thickness of the workpiece, plus another ¼" (use a piece of ¼" plywood as a spacer). Next, move the fence system over until the outside reference edge of the low fence comes flush to the outside of the

blade, then set the height of the blade to just a fraction below the fence base; it should almost touch. Make a note of the cursor reading on the rip fence for future reference.

The magic is now ready to begin. Index one facet of the template against the fence ahead of the blade and, with a steady motion, move the template (with the rough-cut workpiece below) forward through the blade. Work carefully to keep the edge of the template tight to the fence. Then rotate the workpiece counterclockwise to the next facet and cut again. Repeat this process until you have cut all around the template. In just moments, you have created a perfect replica of the template – it's that simple. If you've used carpet tape, remove the

template by lightly tapping the side with a hammer.

STRAIGHT-EDGE RIPPING WITH THE PATTERN FENCE

The pattern fence system is also an excellent way to gain a straight edge on a board of any length, without using a jointer. Just attach a known straightedge to the board precisely along the cut line.

On any work more than 1' long I recommend screwing (rather than carpet-taping) the guide in place. Screws are more secure. If the guide board is wide enough (the longer the board, the wider it needs to be, about 1" per 2½' of length), you need to screw the guide board only at the ends. If your guide board is

In combination with the pattern fence, a template attached to your workpiece quickly and accurately clones the shape.

perfectly straight (be sure to check its bearing surface against a known straightedge) and you are careful to keep the guide against the pattern fence, you will come up with an edge as true as one you would gain from a jointer.

CURVED CUTS WITH THE PATTERN FENCE

I was happy to discover that it's possible to cut a curve on the table saw – up to ¾" per foot arc in ¾"-thick stock. (I do not recommend cutting curves in stock thicker than ¾", as the forces involved become huge.)

I discovered the use of the table saw for curve-cutting when I set out to cut planks for a small boat from 4' x 10' sheets of plywood. I found that I could cut these planks nearly four times faster on the table saw than with a jigsaw or circular saw. I also discovered that the table saw produced such an accurate cut that no trimming (other than a bit of hand planing) was necessary to make the planks fit precisely.

The trick to making curved cuts is to use a curved-edge template, or batten, fixed to the stock, in conjunction with the pattern fence and a 40-tooth combination blade (don't use a thin-kerf blade). If you keep the curves shallow, the kerf cannot bind on the blade because the offset of the carbide tips keeps the concave side of the kerf away from the blade plate. The saw blade doesn't care that the cut line runs along a curve as long as you carefully control the stock so it can't back into the blade. This is where the pattern fence comes into play.

The first step to making a curved cut is to lay out the curve. At this point you have two procedural options: You can fix a batten in place to points directly on the workpiece (which leaves little nail holes to fill but is remarkably fast), or you can lay out and then cut a curved template in a piece of sheet stock. You can attach this with screws or carpet tape. Screws do leave small holes but in the long run, they're more secure. The

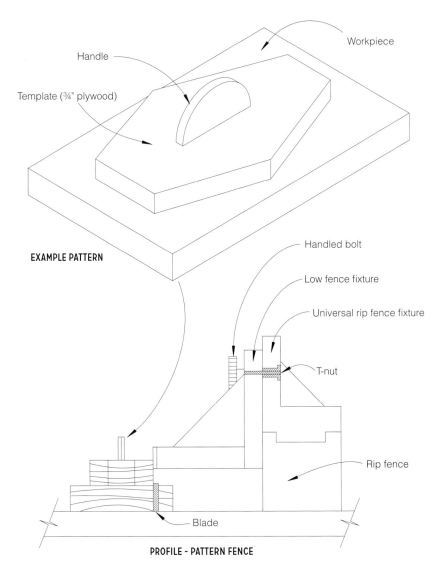

EXAMPLE PATTERN

Handle

Template (¾" plywood)

Workpiece

Handled bolt

Low fence fixture

Universal rip fence fixture

T-nut

Rip fence

Blade

PROFILE - PATTERN FENCE

latter procedure is preferable if you intend to make a number of pieces to one curve.

With the template or batten affixed to the workpiece, the next step is to set up the pattern fence as described earlier for template-cutting. If the offcuts of the stock will be too big to fit between the blade and the rip fence, you must first trim any oversize areas.

Mark the location of the front of the blade on the top of the pattern fence as a visual reference. This is where you must keep the template or batten in contact with the fence as you proceed through the length of the cut. Feed the stock smoothly and steadily through the spinning blade, keeping the guide tight to the pattern fence at your mark, as shown in the photo

below.

Be sure to set an outfeed table to catch the stock. If you encounter resistance and/or see wisps of smoke, the curve is too tight for your blade. Stop feeding immediately, lower the blade and remove the board. Try another blade with greater tip clearance. If this isn't available or doesn't help, you'll have to use another cutting method.

THE RABBET FENCE

You can cut a rabbet quickly and accurately in a single pass by using a dado blade and this specialized rabbet fence that bolts securely to the universal fence fixture.

The fixture's T-slot accepts bolts

CURVE-CUTTING WITH THE PATTERN FENCE

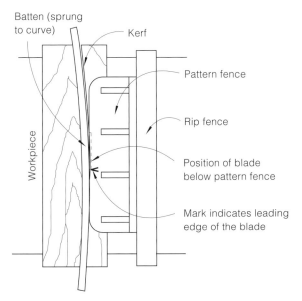

PLAN - PATTERN FENCE

Batten (sprung to curve)

Kerf

Pattern fence

Rip fence

Position of blade below pattern fence

Mark indicates leading edge of the blade

Workpiece

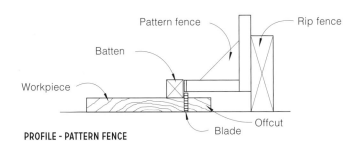

Pattern fence

Rip fence

Batten

Workpiece

Offcut

Blade

PROFILE - PATTERN FENCE

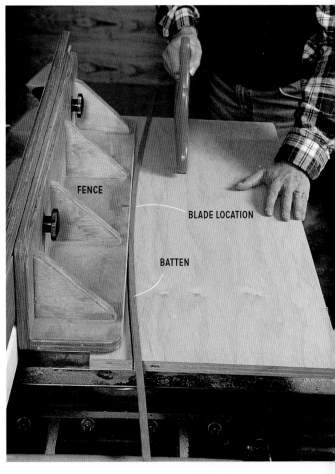

FENCE

BLADE LOCATION

BATTEN

A long, gentle curve cut can be made with the pattern fence by attaching a curved guide batten to the workpiece and running it carefully against the edge of the fence.

to secure my shop-made comb-type hold-downs as needed to hold the stock flat to the table. The cavity cut in the fence lets you "hide" a portion of the dado blade within the fence itself, allowing you to adjust the width of the dado simply by setting the position of the fence rather than changing the width of the dado blade by adding or subtracting cutters or shims.

With the cutter height adjusted to the depth of the rabbet, you need only to run the workpiece against the fence to produce the finished cut. Be sure the hold-downs are secured firmly in place, as any lifting of the stock up from the table will cause the rabbet to fluctuate in depth.

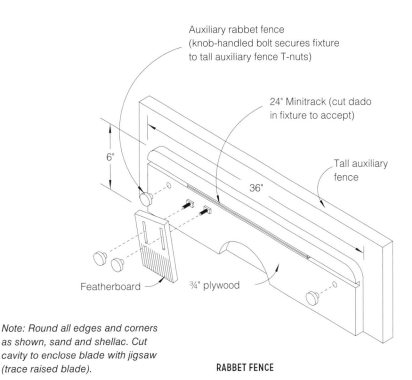

Auxiliary rabbet fence (knob-handled bolt secures fixture to tall auxiliary fence T-nuts)

24" Minitrack (cut dado in fixture to accept)

Tall auxiliary fence

6"

36"

Featherboard

¾" plywood

Note: Round all edges and corners as shown, sand and shellac. Cut cavity to enclose blade with jigsaw (trace raised blade).

RABBET FENCE

PANEL-CUTTING SLED

This jig carries its share of work while increasing the usefulness of your table saw. By Glen Huey

I've never been a fan of any jig that requires a degree from the Massachusetts Institute of Technology to build or use. So the Jig Journal column is a perfect fit for my shop jigs. This month's offering is a jig that has carried many of my furniture parts over the past 15 years – a panel-cutting sled.

THREE PARTS TO SQUARE PANELS

This jig is made up of three parts, all of which can likely be found in your scrap bin. The major player is the panel (3/4" x 18" x 24") that carries the workpiece. Attached to that panel is a straightedge fence (7/8" x 7/8" x 36") running perpendicular to the blade and a guide (3/8" x 3/4" x 27") that runs in the miter-gauge slot of the table saw. It's best to use quartersawn hardwood for the fence and guide. Small pieces of plywood tend to delaminate – or if you hit a void it's trouble.

However, plywood is the best choice for the panel. There's greater stability in plywood over a hardwood panel, because there is no seasonal movement. And plywood is better than MDF because it's tougher to ding as you move it around the shop and it's more resistant to moisture.

To locate the guide bar, measure the distance from the right edge of the left-hand miter-gauge slot to the saw blade, then add 1/4" – this jig rides to the left of the blade. Once the guide bar is attached, the additional 1/4" allows you to trim a straight edge that's aligned with the table-saw blade.

Transfer that distance to the underside of the panel. Hold one end of the guide bar flush with the leading edge of the panel as shown in the center picture atop the next page, and

attach the 3/8"-thick hardwood, snugly fit to the saw's slot, with four #6 x 1/2" flathead wood screws. The guide bar attaches at the line, away from the blade.

By allowing the guide to extend beyond the back edge of the panel (the edge nearest the operator), you gain additional panel-cutting width. But don't go overboard. You need to have the majority of the panel resting on your saw's top after the cut is complete. Push too far and the sled tumbles off the saw.

Place the guide bar into the saw slot so it's well behind the saw blade. Start the saw and push the sled into the blade. The edge of the sled's panel is now parallel to the guide and the saw blade.

SQUARING THE IMPORTANT PIECE

Aligning the sled's fence is the most important step in building the jig. To accurately set the fence, use geometry. The calculation is a 3-4-5 triangle. Using multiples of three and four for the two legs sets any right triangle. Then, the hypotenuse is a multiple of five.

Measure down the cut edge marking at 1" from the front edge of the panel (this gives you a place to connect the fence) and again at 16". The 15" difference is a multiple of three – 3 x 5". Set a ruler across the panel holding the zero mark at the 1" line. Set a second ruler with the zero point at the 16" line while angling up toward the first rule. Where the 20" mark on the first rule and the 25" mark on the second overlap, is the second point of the straight line to which the fence is to fit (see the photo at the bottom of the next page).

Attach the fence to the panel with

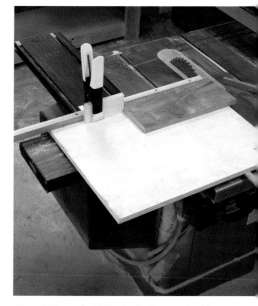

Repeatable, perfect 90° cuts. Cutting panels with a standard issue miter gauge is "iffy" at best. While the degree of difficulty to build and use this panel-cutting sled is near zero, the results are a 10.

#8 x 1 1/4" wood screws directly along that layout line allowing the end to extend slightly past the edge closest to the saw blade. Make a second cut with the guide in the miter slot to cut the fence exactly at the blade. Now the fence shows you the exact cut of the blade and is great for a reference point while aligning your cuts.

PROPERLY CUT PANELS

Using the sled is a simple and effective process. The design allows you to cut the end of a wide panel square to the edge that's placed against the fence.

Begin with a panel that is surfaced on three sides at a minimum. Position the panel flat on the sled, with the milled edge against the straightedge fence and the end hanging beyond the edge of the sled. Trim the end of the panel by sliding the jig and panel through the blade. That end is now

Follow the guide. The guide is a key component of the sled. The accuracy of the fit to the table slot is paramount in attaining a square cut. A sloppy fit equals a sloppy cut.

Guiding the sled. Countersink the screws for the guide. The quartersawn-hardwood guide should show no sign of sloppiness. Paste wax allows the pieces to slide easily.

Getting the accurate edge. Sawing the edge of the jig after the guide is attached to the panel ensures the edge is parallel to the blade as well as the guide.

square to the edge pushed against the fence.

Next, flip the panel end for end without changing the edge that is against the fence. This ensures that the two ends will be square to that one edge. If you switch the edge that's against the fence and the board's edges are not truly parallel, the end cuts won't be parallel to each other.

Mark the measurement, the exact cut line, on your panel along the fence edge then set that layout mark even with the end of the straightedge fence closest to the saw blade. Because the end of the fence is the exact cut line of the jig, it will also be the exact cut line of the panel.

It's possible to nick the fence with a turning saw blade as you position the jig, so be careful. If that happens you'll be unable to use the fence to set your cut into position. If that occurs,

you can relocate the guide and create a new edge or match the exact cut line with the blade each time you use the sled.

This jig works with different sized panels, both wide and narrow. I've used it to square cut the ends of drawer dividers and pieces as small as 1" in width.

OTHER OPERATIONS

Need a few pieces cut to the same length? Another woodworking operation at which the sled excels is making multiple pieces using a stop block. I used this setup for years before bringing a miter saw into my shop.

Find your length by nudging your rule tight to the saw blade and mark the location on the jig. Clamp a secondary piece, the stop block, to

the fence at that location. Remember to slide the table saw's fence out of the way before making any cuts.

Place a squared end of stock against the stop block allowing extra material to hang past the sled's edge nearest the blade. Make the cut. The second end is now square and the piece is cut to the correct length. Slide the leftover material, which also has a freshly cut, squared end, toward the stop block to make another piece that matches the previous one. Repeat the operation until the desired number of pieces is reached or the stock runs out.

The panel-cutting jig is one of a handful of jigs that get a tremendous amount of work in my shop. The sled extends the total amount of work that you're able to complete with the table saw. It's a real woodworking timesaver.

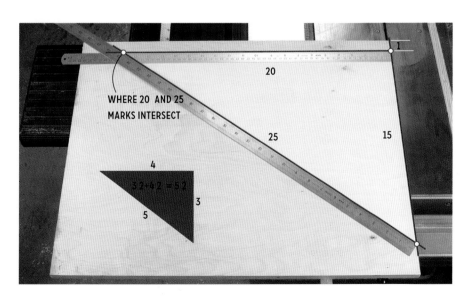

WHERE 20 AND 25 MARKS INTERSECT

20

25   15

4

3²+4²=5²

3

5

Caution — geometry ahead. Come down 1" from the edge of the plywood to leave room for the fence. Using the 3-4-5 triangle formula guarantees the jig's fence is perpendicular to the blade and that the resulting cut will be square. Use 15", 20" and 25" to set the fence line.

DOVETAIL FIXTURE FOR THE TABLE SAW

This dovetail fixture isn't for the birds. It really works.

By Jim Stack

The table saw is a great tool to use to cut dovetails. You can create the look of hand-cut dovetails and take advantage of what the table saw does well — cutting straight and square. To make the fixture, first cut the parts as shown in the materials list. Then attach the miter guide to the bottom center of the base, using three No. 6 × ¾" wood screws.

Attach the mounting cleats to their respective fences. Then attach the long fence assembly to the base, using one No. 8 × 1½" wood screw at the end of the mounting cleat. Put the base on the table saw with the miter guide in either of the two miter slots in the top of the saw. Locate where the saw blade will be cutting into the sled. Mount a blade guard block on the back of the fence assembly, then move the sled so the miter guide is in the other slot in the table saw top. Mark and mount another blade guard

block where the blade will cut into the sled.

Unplug the saw and raise the table saw blade to its full height. Keep the sled in one of the slots on the tabletop. Lay a framing square on the top of the sled and rest one arm of the square against the fence. Let the other arm of the square stick out toward the saw blade. Align the edge of this arm along the side of the saw blade and move the fence until it is square to the saw blade. Put another screw at the other end of the fence mounting cleat.

Cut a 10° angle on the left end of one of the angled fences and on the right end of the other fence. You can do this on the table saw. Use a miter gauge set to 80° to the left and make the cut on one fence. Set the miter gauge 80° to the right and cut the opposite end of the other angled fence.

Turn the sled around 180° and put the miter guide in the tabletop slot to the left of the saw blade. Put the right-hand angled fence on the sled as shown in the illustration. Using a sliding T-bevel set to 10°, and holding the bevel against the side of the saw blade, attach the fence to the sled. Move the sled to the slot to the right of the saw blade and attach the other fence in the same manner.

Mark where the saw blade will cut into the sled on each of the angled fences and attach the remaining two blade guard blocks, one on each fence.

Plug in the saw and make test-cuts to double-check all the angles. Make adjustments if necessary.

Apply paste wax to the bottom of the slide and miter-guide strip. This will allow the sled to slide easily on the table saw top.

I usually cut the pins of the dovetails first, but it's just fine to cut the tails first if you like. Try it both ways and see which works best for you. Start by laying out the dovetails on your stock, spacing them to your personal tastes. Cut one edge of the pins freehand, using the sled to cut to your marks. Move the sled to the other tabletop slot, move the stock to the other fence and cut the other side of the pins. Nibble the waste between the pins by moving the stock a little at a time across the saw blade. If there is any variation in the pins, or if they aren't exactly the same width, don't worry. You're going to use these pins as a template to lay out the tails on the other parts. Be sure to mark each end with its mate.

After marking the tails using the pins as your template, set the table saw blade at a 10° angle and cut the cheeks of the tails. Cut the left cheek, flip the stock face for face and cut the right cheek. Then, set the saw blade back to vertical and cut as much of the waste as you can between the tails. You can clean up the inside corners of the cutout with a chisel. If you plan to cut a lot of dovetails and want to make this process go even smooth-er, have all the teeth on a saw blade ground to a 10° angle so that the tilted saw blade will cut the corners cleanly between the tails. Be sure to double-check the tilt of your saw blade so you can tell your saw sharpener which way to grind the 10° angle!

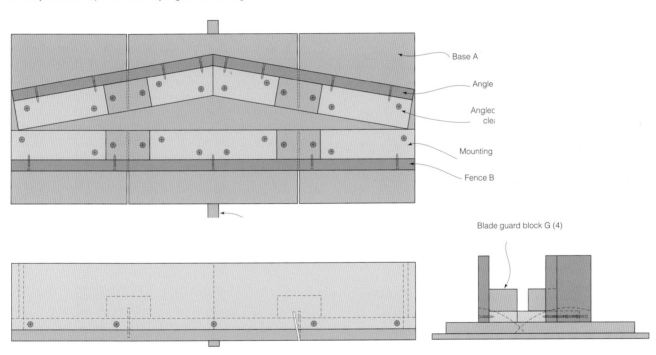

Base A

Angle

Angled
cle:

Mounting

Fence B

Blade guard block G (4)

INCHES (MILLIMETERS)						
REFERENCE	QUANTITY	PART	STOCK	THICKNESS (MM)	WIDTH (MM)	LENGTH (MM)
A	1	base	plywood	¾ (19)	11½ (292)	28 (711)
B	1	fence	plywood	¾ (19)	4½ (114)	28 (711)
C	2	angled fences	plywood	¾(19)	4½ (114)	14 (356)
D	1	mounting cleat	plywood	¾ (19)	2 (51)	28 (711)
E	2	angled mounting cleats	plywood	¾ (19)	2 (51)	14 (356)
F	1	miter guide	hardwood	³/₈ (10)	¾ (19)	13½ (343)
G	4	blade guard blocks	hardwood	1½ (38)	2 (51)	3 (76)

HARDWARE

29 No. 8 × 1½" (No. 8 × 38mm) flathead wood screws
3 No. 6 × ¾" (No. 6 × 19mm) flathead wood screws

TAPERING FIXTURE

You'll have the right slant on things using this fixture.

By Jim Stack

Tapering fixtures come in many different sizes and shapes. This fixture incorporates a couple of features that make it safer. Begin by cutting out all the parts as shown in the materials list. Join the two arms using a butt hinge, and attach the stop block to the adjustable arm. Then, attach the fixed arm to the bottom plate. Install the hanger bolt in the fixed arm, attach the slotted metal strap to the adjustable arm and hook it over the hanger bolt. Install the knob and attach the two toggle clamps to the adjustable arm.

This fixture is safe to use because the toggle clamps hold the part being cut securely to the bottom plate.

Lay the two arms flat on a bench and install the hinge. The space between the ends of the arms is equal to the diameter of the hinge barrel.

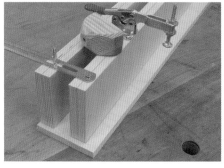

Install the hanger bolt in the fixed arm, put the slotted strap over it and put the pivot screw in place.

HARDWARE

1   3" × 3½" (76mm × 89mm) butt hinge
2   toggle clamps
1   metal strap with ¼"-wide (6mm-wide) slot
1   No. 8 × ¾" (No. 8 × 19mm) wood screw
1   1½" × ¼"–20 (38mm × 6mm–20) hanger bolt

INCHES (MILLIMETERS)

REFERENCE	QUANTITY	PART	STOCK	THICKNESS (MM)	WIDTH (MM)	LENGTH (MM)
A	1	fixed arm	plywood	1 (25)	3½ (89)	32 (813)
B	1	adjustable arm	plywood	1 (25)	3½ (89)	32 (813)
C	1	bottom plate	plywood	½ (13)	7½ (191)	32 (813)
D	1	stop block	hardwood	3½ (89)	2¼ (57)	3 (76)
E	1	knob	hardwood	1½ (38)	2 (51)	2½ (64)

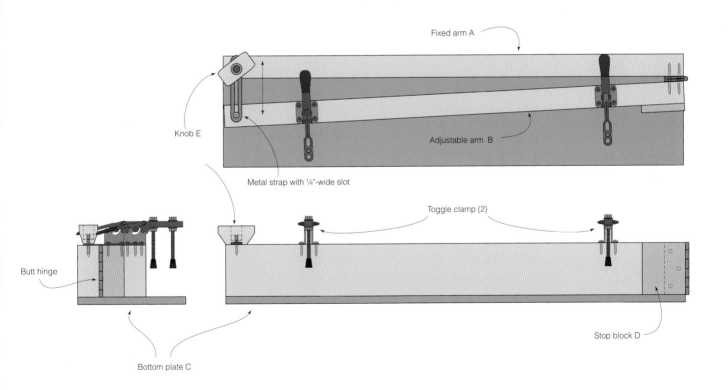

Fixed arm A

Knob E

Metal strap with ¼"-wide slot

Adjustable arm B

Toggle clamp (2)

Butt hinge

Bottom plate C

Stop block D

SECTION 5

JIGS & FIXTURES

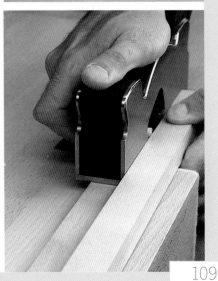

FLUSH-CUTTING JIG

An end to the troublesome task of trimming solid-wood edging.

By Christopher Schwarz

Adding a solid-wood edge to plywood is a necessary but evil task for most woodworkers. And while clamps and cleverness go a long way toward getting the edging stuck to the plywood, the real trouble begins when you trim the edging flush to the plywood.

Thanks to the ever-shrinking thickness of plywood's exterior skin, it seems to get harder every year to work the stuff without cutting through the face veneer and exposing the ugly plies below. So you have to be careful any time you deal with the stuff.

There are lots of ways to trim the edging, and I've tried just about every one of them. Here's what I've found:

Scraping or sanding. If you can get your edging on just right so that it's only about $1/64$" proud of the plywood, then it's a simple thing to sand or scrape it flush as you prepare your parts for finishing.

Unfortunately, to work to this tolerance generally requires great skill or special router bits that create an interlocking joint between the edging and the plywood. You also can add splines to the edging and the plywood to create this interlock – which is an extra step.

Just a little off the bottom. When you add solid-wood edging to plywood, trimming the solid wood flush to the plywood can be tricky or tedious. This simple jig (two bits of wood that are nailed and glued together) makes it simple and quick.

PLANNING

If you don't have the special router bits or don't want to cut splines, you can make your edging just a little wider and simply use glue and clamps to apply the edging. The edging will slip around a bit, but that's why you give yourself a little extra meat on the edging – usually $1/32$" to $1/16$" on each face. This is too much to easily sand or scrape, and so one solution is to plane it, then scrape or sand it. Planing it (I use a block plane) is OK if you have only a few shelves to do. When you are building an entire

run of shelves, it's more work than necessary.

ROUTING OR SAWING OFF THE WASTE

Other solutions include removing the waste with a router with a flush-trim bit, or sawing off the waste with the cut being limited by some sort of accessory fence. Every one of these solutions involves balancing the work on its skinny edge and pushing it past the cutter. This can be a tippy situation – one false move and your plywood or edging is toast. Plus, it can be difficult to keep the workpiece against your fence with enough force to get the edging truly flush to the plywood.

SOLUTION: WORK FLAT

My solution came to me a few years ago when trimming all the edging for the built-ins in a home addition.

I needed something that could run hundreds of feet of plywood with little chance of spoiling the work. And I didn't want to buy some fancy tooling.

So here's how it works: You need a couple scraps of plywood (their size will vary depending on your work), a stack dado set and your table saw. The two pieces of scrap are screwed together to form an "L" shape: One part sits flat on the top of the saw, the other hooks over the rail of your saw's fence (don't forget to clamp it there). Then you install the dado stack. Put enough chippers on the arbor so that it will make a cut that is slightly wider than your edging. Then raise the saw's arbor so the dado stack is exactly as high as the scrap plywood piece on your saw's table. (One note on dado stacks: This jig won't work well if you have a cheap dado stack where the chippers are shorter than the outside blades.)

Now set your table saw's rip fence.

An overgrown bench hook. This jig works on the same principle as a bench hook, but it's essential to clamp the hook to your table saw's rail to be safe. You don't want it to move.

Safe and accurate. One of the things I really like about this jig is that you can push the work flat over the blades, plus you can use your basket guard for added safety.

A brush with flushness. To set the dado stack so it is exactly as high as the top of the jig, rub a piece of your work over the knives. The knives should just brush the work.

Results. Here you can see how the jig cut this edging flush (the small ridge is actually the glue squeeze-out left behind). Above it is an example of the shelf's finished and profiled edge.

Lock down the fence so that when you push your workpiece over the jig and against the fence, the edging will pass over the dado stack.

This jig and technique have a number of advantages:

•The work remains stable during the cut. The more you press the work against the jig, the cleaner the resulting cut. Plus, it works fine even if the plywood has a little waviness to it.

• You don't have to balance the work on edge, so you won't gouge the plywood or the edging by accident.

• You can easily use a basket-style table saw guard with this jig.

• Feeding the stock is a natural and easy motion – like ripping a board.

• The jig is so simple you can just recycle it at the end of the project.

As you get more confident with the technique, you will be able to easily set the fence so that the outside teeth of your dado stack are positioned exactly where the seam is between your plywood and the attached edging. When you hit this sweet spot, it's almost impossible to cut through the plywood skin.

And while this jig removes a major source of anxiety with a project, it's still not enough to make me enjoy working with these plywoods with paper-thin veneers.

SAWING PARTICLE BOARD AND PLYWOOD

Precision cutting with a hand-held circular saw.

By Nick Engler

I'd like to know who it was that decided that plywood was best sold in 4-foot by 8-foot sheets. I've always thought that it was a practical joke in questionable taste to take such a wonderfully useful woodworking material and manufacture it in sheets that are bigger than most woodworkers.

More to the point, sheet materials are larger than the capacity of most woodworking machines. You can't cut them safely on a garden-variety table saw without first chopping them into smaller pieces. Consequently,

making precise cuts in sheet goods is a two-step process for most woodworkers. First you cut the sheets into manageable sizes with a circular saw, then you trim the pieces to precise dimensions on a table saw. You can buy a panel saw or a sliding table for high-end table saws, but these are expensive pieces of equipment. And even if you can afford them, do you have space to use them? A panel saw, for example, takes up an enormous amount of wall space that most of us don't have. I would much rather preserve the walls of

my workshop as God intended – hung floor to ceiling with unfinished projects.

MAKING A CIRCULAR SAW GUIDE

Fortunately, there is an inexpensive, space-saving and ridiculously simple solution to this problem. You can make precision cuts in plywood and other sheet materials with an ordinary circular saw using a jig that that relies on the straightness of the outside edges that come with every piece of plywood.

The outside edges of a sheet of plywood as it comes from the manufacturer are commonly called factory edges. They are too rough to use in assembly, but they are usually dead straight. Consequently when you buck up a sheet of plywood to trim on a table saw, it's a good idea to make sure each piece has a factory edge. Most craftsmen begin trimming operations by guiding this factory edge along the table saw rip fence – this creates another straight edge.

Instead of using the factory edge as a guide to trim the plywood on a table saw, I skip the trimming altogether and use a factory edge to guide a circular saw. To do this, you must make a circular saw guide.

Select a sheet of cabinet-grade ½" or ¾" hardwood plywood. With a circular saw, trim a 3"-wide strip from one of the 8'-long edges – this is the guide. To make the base, trim another strip 8½" wide from a sheet of ¼" plywood. Glue the guide and the base together with the sawed edge (not the factory edge) of the guide aligned with one of the edges of the base. Tip: The 3"-wide guide is narrow enough to bend, so check the assembly as you glue the parts together. Sight along the factory edge (or better yet, stretch a string along it) to make sure the guide remains straight.

When the glue dries, clamp the saw guide to a long board. Mount a high-quality carbide-tipped combination

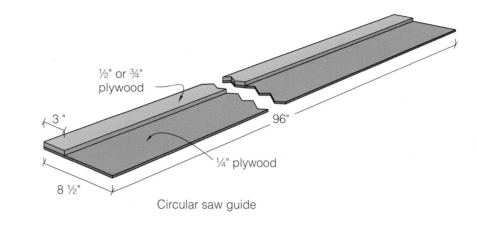

½" or ¾" plywood

3 "

96"

8 ½"

¼" plywood

Circular saw guide

After measuring the plywood and marking the beginning and end of the cut, align the base of the saw guide with the marks. The saw guide should be on the "save" side of the cutting path, and the tommy bars of the clamps must point down. If the bars stick up, they may interfere with the circular saw.

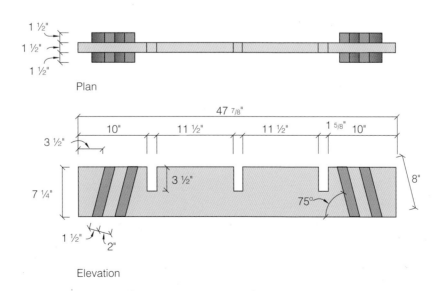

1 ½"

1 ½"

1 ½"

Plan

47 ⁷/₈"

10"   11 ½"   11 ½"   1 ⁵/₈" 10"

3 ½"

3 ½"

7 ¼"

75°

8"

1 ½"

2"

Elevation

The cutting grid breaks down when you're not using it and stores against a wall, along with the circular saw guide. The grid is so useful however, that mine is set up more often than not.

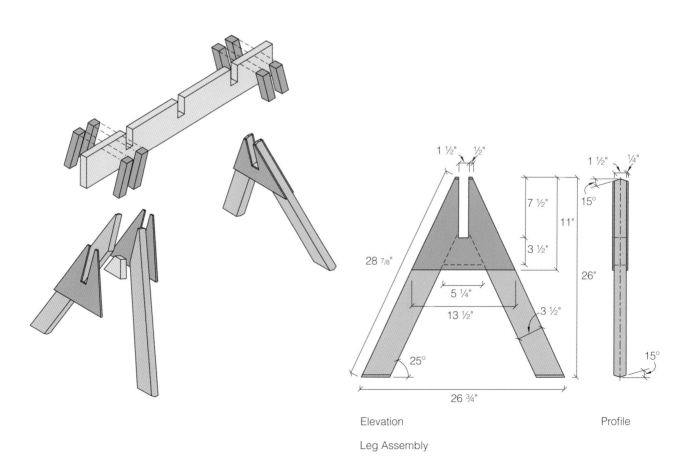

Elevation

Profile

Leg Assembly

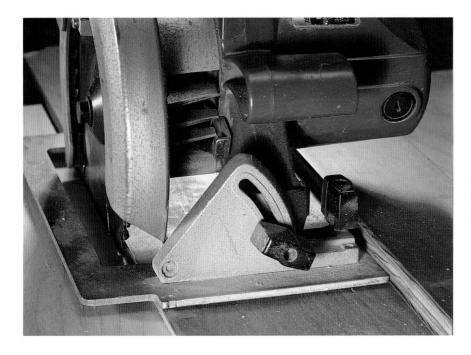

Make the cut with the circular saw motor hanging over the guide – this arrangement provides the most support for the saw and keeps it from tipping.

blade on your circular saw. This is important! For you to make precision cuts with any saw, you need a precision blade. Place the shoe of the saw on the base with the edge against the guide. The saw motor should overhang the guide. Trim the base so the distance from the guiding edge to the base edge is exactly the same as the distance from the edge of the shoe to the saw blade. This makes it a cinch to set up for a cut, as you'll see in a minute.

MAKING A CUTTING GRID

Before you get to the cutting, however, I suggest you make one more jig – a cutting grid to properly support the plywood while you're laying out the parts and sawing them. My "grid" consists of two knock-down sawhorses. The horizontal beams of these sawhorses are notched to hold ordinary 8'-long 2 x 4s. When set up, the top edges of the beams are flush with the top edges of the 2 x 4s. This arrangement supports a sheet of plywood of any size edge-to-edge and end-to-end to keep it from

sagging.

This grid is one of those truly indispensable jigs. Once I made one, I couldn't imagine how I did without it. Not only is it useful for sawing, it also makes a great assembly table for large projects. On occasion, I've used it as a clamping grid for odd-shaped assemblies. And I always seem to employ it as a drying rack when I'm finishing a project. Even though I made the cutting grid to break down, it spends most of its time set up.

MAKING A CUT

Place the plywood on the cutting grid. If it's a small piece, rest it over a sawhorse beam and a stringer so it's supported in both directions. Measure the plywood and make two marks to indicate the beginning and end of the cut. If you were to draw a line through these marks, there is a "save" side of the line (the piece you're going to save) and a "waste" side. Place the saw guide on the plywood over the "save" side and align the trimmed edge of the base

with the marks. Clamp the guide to the plywood with two small (2") C-clamps.

Adjust the depth of cut of the circular saw so the blade protrudes just $1/16$" to $1/8$" below the underside of the plywood as you make the cut. The saw will bite into the top surfaces of the cutting grid; this can't be avoided. But it won't weaken the supporting structure as long as the cuts are shallow. Tip: When cutting across the surface grain of a sheet of plywood, you can prevent the veneer from splintering or "feathering" by scoring along the edge of the base with a utility knife before you make the cut.

Just how accurate is this system? Very, which some folks will find surprising given the simplicity of the jigs and tools involved. I have now built the cabinets for two complete kitchens and scores of shelving systems using a circular saw as my primary cutting tool. I'm convinced that I couldn't do any better with a sliding table or a panel saw.

PLYWOOD CARRIER

Don't break your back whilemoving sheetgoods. Take a couple of minutes and build this plywood carrier that turns on a dime.

By Christopher Schwarz

The big problem in a one-man shop is there's only two hands and one back. And that one back gets tired after years of lugging sheets of plywood around (or worse, particleboard). I was flipping through an industrial material handling catalog (I really need to get a life) when I saw a metal cart designed to carry sheet goods. The light bulb went off, and I headed to the shop.

After two tries I came up with this design that moves sheet goods easily, has a tight turning radius (for small shops) and a kickstand to hold the sheet in place while I get into a non-back-injuring position to throw it up on the saw.

The idea is simple, made from shop scraps and glued and screwed together. It all rolls on one fixed caster and one swivel caster for super maneuverability. I purchased the casters from a home center store right off the rack. They shouldn't set you back more than $10. To make the swivel caster swing properly, the entire rack is canted 10 degrees, so you only need to tip the carrier a degree or so to make movement possible.

Begin construction by cutting the mounting block and support block to size, beveling one edge to 10 degrees on each piece. In gluing and screwing the pieces together, I recommend pre-drilling clearance holes to avoid splitting the wood, and to generally make things easier. Screw the two pieces together, centering the support block on the mounting block as shown in the diagram. Next, attach the carrier lip to the support block. You will find that beveling or rounding over the back edge of the carrier lip will keep it from dragging while the carrier is in motion. Use a router or block plane to soften this edge.

Now mount the casters to the mounting block as shown. The closer to the back edge, the easier the "tip" will be. Next I trimmed 6" x 6" corners off the top of the back panel to reduce the weight. You're now ready to screw the back panel in place to both the support and mounting blocks. It's not a bad idea to run a couple of nails up through the carrier lip into the back panel as well.

With the back panel in place, cut a 10-degree bevel on the bottom end of

the handle and, if you choose, round over the top to match the shape of the dowel-stock grip. Attach the handle to the center of the back panel, then mount the grip to the top of the handle. Use a long and heavy screw to support the grip, as this is where much of the stress occurs.

You're almost ready for a test drive, but first, add the little spacing block to the front side of the handle at the top. This will keep a full 4' x 8' sheet from trying to "walk" off the leading edge of the carrier lip.

The last step is to add the kickstand. This is simply a piece of poplar radiused at one end and bolted to the underside of the mounting block. A small "handle" is attached to the opposite end of the stand so the stand can be reached and extended easily.

You're ready to roll. It might take a little practice to get the feel of the proper "tip" angle for best performance, but after a sheet or two you'll get a handle on it — get it? The handle. Sorry. Anyway, enjoy your project and save your back.

INCHES (MILLIMETERS)

SCHEDULE OF MATERIALS : PLYWOOD CARRIER

NO.	LET.	ITEM	DIMENSIONS T W L	MATERIAL
1	A	Back panel	½" x 24" x 24"	P
1	B	Carrier lip	½" x 3½" x 18"	P
1	C	Spacing block	½" x 1½" x 2"	P
1	D	Support block	1½" x 2" x 18"	S
1	E	Mounting block	1" x 3½" x 24"	S
1	F	Handle	1½" x 1½" x 32"	S
1	G	Grip	1½" dia x 4"	S
1	H	Kick stand	1" x 1½" x 9"	S
1	I	Kick handle	½" x 1½" x 2½"	S

P=plywood • S=solid wood

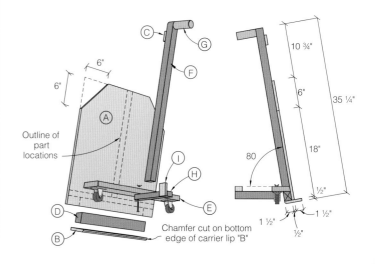

Outline of part locations

6"
6"
6"

Chamfer cut on bottom edge of carrier lip "B"

10 ¾"
6"
18"
35 ¼"
80
½"
1 ½"
1 ½"
½"

PORTABLE CHISEL RACK

Keep your tools right where you need them.

By Christopher Schwarz

I've seen, used and built a number of chisel racks, but none has ever seemed to suit me. Most of them are just a bit awkward. And don't even get me started on the alternatives to a chisel rack: Chisel boxes and rolls take up too much valuable space on your bench, and keeping the chisels in the bench's tool tray just adds to the clutter that collects there. What most woodworkers need is a rack that holds all their chisels upright where they can grab them.

They need a rack that protects the sharp tips. And they need to be able to move the rack off the bench when they're assembling big projects there.

After months of sketches, we're sure we've got the perfect rack. It does everything we want it to do and it can be hung anywhere in the shop (on a bench, a wall or even a cabinet side) thanks to a clever cleat.

And best of all, it's easy and fast to build with shop scraps.

HOW DOES YOUR STEEL MEASURE UP?

The first thing to do is to measure a few dimensions on your chisels with a ruler and a dial caliper.

Find the thickest part of your thickest blade. Add $^1/_{32}$" to that measurement and that will be the thickness of all the spacers between the chisels.

Next measure the length of all of your chisels' blades and find the longest one. That length is the width

of all of your spacers. (Yes, I do mean width. You want the grain of the spacers to run in the same direction as the front and back pieces.)

Then measure the width of each chisel (don't assume that what is marked on the tool is correct). Add $^1/_{16}$" to each measurement and that will determine the distance between each spacer. Take these measurements to the saw and rip a small piece of scrap to each of these widths. Mark them with their width. These scraps will help you place your spacers during assembly.

The spacers between each tool are $2^3/_8$" long. This might seem like a lot, but it allows you to grab any chisel without rapping your knuckles against its neighbor. Most chisel racks I've seen place the tools' handles too close together so you're always fishing out the specimen you need.

A CHISEL LASAGNA

This rack is essentially four layers of wood sandwiched together. You glue

the spacers between the front and back pieces, then you screw a cleat to the back of the rack to hang it.

The stop piece, which is located below the spacers, accomplishes two things: First, it keeps all the chisels at the same height. Second, it prevents you from destroying your rack.

Let's say you built the rack without the stop. Someday, you're going to accidentally drop something on one of your chisels in the rack. The chisel's socket will then wedge into the rack, splitting apart all your work. So spend the extra five minutes to cut and install the stop.

Now that you know the size of the spacers, the space that needs to go between them and the lengths of the blades, you can calculate the dimensions of your front and back pieces (don't forget to add some width for the stop piece). You are ready to begin milling your wood.

Plane down all the pieces you'll need for the rack, then rip and crosscut

all your pieces to size. The first step is to attach the stop piece to the back. But before you attach the stop, cut a 45° chamfer on one long edge that measures $\frac{3}{8}$" x $\frac{3}{8}$". The chamfer makes it easier for dust that gets into the rack to fall out. Then glue the stop in place on the back.

Now nail one of the end spacers in place. Remember those scraps you ripped to width after you measured the width of your chisels? Get them. Place them between your spacers and make sure everything fits to your satisfaction. Now glue and nail the spacers (but not the scraps) in place using $\frac{1}{2}$"-long brads.

When that's complete, glue the front piece to the spacers. You're almost done. Clean up all four edges of the assembled rack. Run the bottom edge over your jointer (or clean it up with a hand plane), then rip the rack to width

on your table saw to clean up the top edge. Finally, crosscut the ends to tidy things up.

A CLEVER CLEAT

This rack hangs anywhere using two cleats that interlock thanks to a $\frac{3}{8}$"-deep x 1"-wide rabbet on each part. You want the fit between the two cleats to be firm. Here's how to do it right: Cut the rabbet on one long edge of each cleat so it's just a touch shy of $\frac{3}{8}$" deep, maybe by a few thousandths.

Screw one of the cleats to your bench, shop wall or cabinet. With the other cleat, plane or sand the rabbet at the ends so that the surface is a very gentle and subtle curve. Break the sharp corners of the joint using a block plane or sandpaper, which will make nesting the two cleats easier.

Now screw (but don't glue) this cleat to your rack and give it a try. If the fit

is too tight, remove the cleat and thin down the rabbet a bit more. If the fit is too loose, remove the cleat and make a few passes with a plane on the area where the cleat attaches to the rack. This will tighten up the fit.

Once you're satisfied, glue and nail the two side stops on either end of the cleat that's attached to the rack. The side stops will prevent you from pushing the rack off its cleat.

Sand, plane or scrape the surfaces of the rack and add a clear finish. Finish your rack with whatever you used on your workbench. For me it's a wiping varnish comprised of three parts varnish and one part paint thinner.

Since I've installed this rack I've been astonished at how many trips it has saved me to hunt down the chisel I'm looking for. This rack's a keeper.

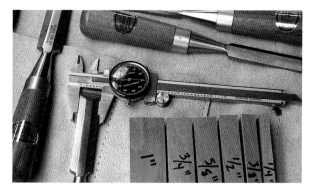

A dial caliper is handy for checking your chisels' dimensions. Measure the width of each blade, add $\frac{1}{16}$" to each measurement, then rip a scrap piece to that width, which will come in handy during assembly.

Use those scrap pieces to lay out the location of the spacers on your back piece. When everything fits, glue and nail the spacers in place.

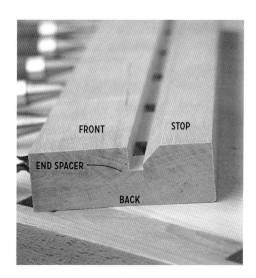

The chamfer on the stop piece and the slightly narrow front piece allow dust to escape the rack easily.

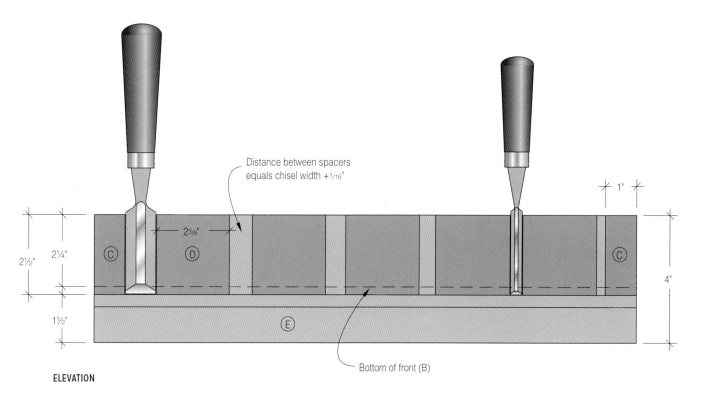

Distance between spacers equals chisel width +$\frac{1}{16}$"

2$\frac{3}{8}$"

1"

2$\frac{1}{2}$"

2$\frac{1}{4}$"

4"

1$\frac{1}{2}$"

Ⓒ   Ⓓ   Ⓔ   Ⓒ

Bottom of front (B)

ELEVATION

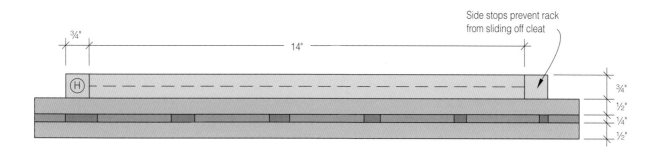

Side stops prevent rack from sliding off cleat

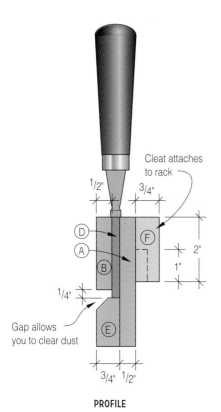

PROFILE

Cleat attaches to rack

Gap allows you to clear dust

A rabbet plane or shoulder plane makes quick work of fitting the cleats together. You want the cleat to fit tightly in the middle and a bit looser on the ends. This will allow you to pivot the chisel rack on and off its mating cleat.

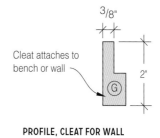

Cleat attaches to bench or wall

PROFILE, CLEAT FOR WALL

PORTABLE CHISEL BACK

NO.	LET.	ITEM	DIMENSIONS (INCHES)			MATERIAL
			T	W	L	
1	A	Back	$\frac{1}{2}$	4	$17\frac{3}{4}$*	Birch
1	B	Front	$\frac{1}{2}$	$2\frac{1}{4}$	$17\frac{3}{4}$*	Birch
2	C	End spacers	$\frac{1}{4}$	$2\frac{1}{2}$†	1	Birch
5**	D	Spacers	$\frac{1}{4}$	$2\frac{1}{2}$†	$2\frac{3}{8}$	Birch
1	E	Stop	$\frac{3}{4}$	$1\frac{1}{2}$	$17\frac{3}{4}$*	Birch
1	F	Cleat for rack	$\frac{3}{4}$	2	14*	Birch
1	G	Cleat for wall or bench	$\frac{3}{4}$	2	$13\frac{1}{2}$*	Birch
2	H	Side stops	$\frac{3}{4}$	$\frac{3}{4}$	2	Birch

KEY: * Actual measurement depends on how many tools go in the rack.
   ** Number of spacers depends on the number of tools.
   † Thickness of spacers depends on thickness of tools.

CLAMP ASSIST

Simple solutions to three perplexing assembly problems.

By Nick Engler

Most woodworkers operate under the theory that you can't have too many clamps and stock them by the dozens, even the hundreds. I'm one of those, I admit. My clamp inventory takes up a whole corner of my shop — when my shop is straightened up, that is. On most days, my clamp collection is spread out over the entire shop so I can enjoy it properly.

For all my clamps, however, I frequently run across assembly tasks that I can't do properly with store-bought clamping equipment alone. For these tasks, I've developed several simple "clamp assists" that extend the capabilities of ordinary clamps to help accomplish extraordinary clamping jobs.

HOLDING ASSEMBLED PARTS SQUARE

When assembling projects, you frequently need to hold the parts square to one another. Miter clamps have their place, but they aren't as versatile or as easy to use as corner squares. These simple jigs are triangular pieces of plywood with cleats along the edges at right angles to one another. You clamp the cleats to the parts you are assembling and the corner squares hold them at 90°.

To make the corner squares, first cut right triangles from ¾"-inch plywood. Note that I put a little notch in the right corner. When you glue the parts together, sometimes a little glue squeezes out of the joint. The notch prevents the glue from sticking the jig to the assembly. Attach cleats to the right sides, then trim the cleats on a table saw to make sure the outside edges are

precisely 90° from one another.

These jigs are useful for dozens of shop chores. They also will hold temporary assemblies together while you test the fit of the parts. They hold boards together while you drill holes for fasteners, or hold the parts of a frame or a box square to one another while the glue dries. I have even used them to hold large boards — too large to fit in a vise — while I worked the ends or edges.

CLAMPING FACE-TO-FACE

Occasionally, I need to clamp two boards face to face. This is a simple chore when the boards are narrow, but it becomes more difficult as the boards grow wider. Even deep-throated clamps have a limited capacity that may not reach to the center of wide boards. Consequently you won't get an even clamping pressure all across the width, and the assembly will be weak in the center. You run into a similar problem when trying to attach veneer or marquetry to a wide panel. How do you clamp the center area?

For years, I solved the problem by keeping a stack of concrete blocks outside the shop. When I needed pressure in the center of a wide assembly, I stacked blocks on it. It works, but it's inconvenient and somewhat limited.

A better solution is to make a set of crowned bars. These are hardwood bars, 24" to 36" long, with one convex edge. This edge is crowned only slightly, about ¹⁄₁₆" to ⅛" wider in the center than it is at the ends. I cut a crown by raising the outfeed table of my jointer a few thousandths of an inch above the knives and jointing the edge.

You can also create a crown with a band saw, hand plane or a disc sander.

To use the crowned bars, lay the assembly on a flat workbench and lay the bars across the assembly with the crowned edge down. (I label the opposite edge with the word "Up" to help me orient the bars properly.) Then clamp the ends of the bars to the workbench. The bars will flex slightly, evenly distributing the pressure from the middle out to the edges of the assembly.

APPLYING TENSION

Clamps are designed, by and large, to generate compression to squeeze two boards together. But every now and then, you need some tension either to pull an assembled joint apart or to clamp a part inside a larger assembly. When I need a little tension, I rely on a set of grooved wedges.

I cut the wedges from a hardwood with a slope of about 10°. If the slope is any steeper than that, you run the risk of the wedges slipping when you use them. Make grooves in the sloping edges by cutting shallow saw kerfs down the center. Finally, make a spline to fit the kerfs. The spline should be as thick as the kerf is wide and twice as wide as the kerf is deep.

To use the wedges, position them slope-to-slope with the spline in the grooves. Use a bar clamp to slide the wedges together so each wedge climbs the other's slope. As this happens, the outside edges of the wedges will push against the parts of the assembly, applying tension.

When using the corner squares, clamp the cleats to the parts of the assembly. You can make fine adjustments by loosening a clamp until it's just snug and tapping the clamped part with a mallet until it shifts a fraction of an inch. At right, I'm trimming the corner square on the saw.

For the crowned bars to work properly, the assembly must rest on a flat, rigid surface such as a workbench. Be careful not to over-tighten the clamps. If the middle of a bar lifts off the assembly, the clamps are too tight.

Grooved wedges are useful not only for putting projects together but also for taking them apart. Here I'm using the wedges to pop the joints of a wobbly chair as I prepare to restore it.

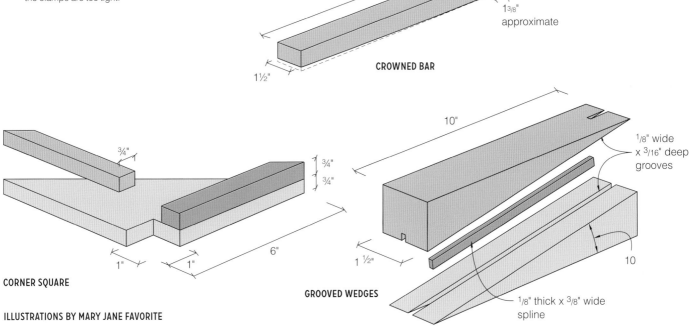

24" - 36"

1¼"

1³⁄₈"
approximate

1½"

CROWNED BAR

¾"

¾"
¾"

6"

1"   1"

CORNER SQUARE

ILLUSTRATIONS BY MARY JANE FAVORITE

10"

1/8" wide
x 3/16" deep
grooves

1 ½"

10

1/8" thick x 3/8" wide
spline

GROOVED WEDGES

SECTION 6
STORAGE & STANDS

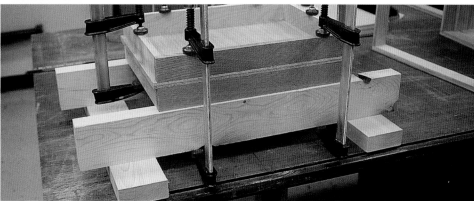

A BETTER MITER SAW STAND

Is it the saw or where the saw lives that increases your accuracy?

By Robert W. Lang

There are two types of miter saws. The first can be a mainstay in the woodshop, dependably making accurate crosscuts day in and day out. Or it can be a cantankerous helper, needing constant attention and delivering inconsistent results. The difference usually isn't in the saw; it is where the saw lives in the shop – how it is set up, the table it sits on and the fence and stop.

All messed up and nowhere to go. Our old stand had lots of bells and whistles, but it lacked a way to deal with scraps and debris.

Miter saws were designed to be portable, taken to a job site and moved often. In many shops, the miter saw is still treated as a visitor, not a permanent resident. This makes sense if you're just setting up shop, or often move your tools to share space. If, however, you have the room, a fixed location is preferred.

In our shop, our miter saw has floated around for several years on a mobile cart with folding tables. We still have a limited amount of space, but we assessed our needs, the way we work and the way we share our shop, and a permanent miter saw workstation was at the top of our list of shop upgrades.

MEETING OF THE MINDS

I met with the other editors and we talked about how we use the saw and what our expectations were. And we listed the things we didn't like about the old setup. We planned a new stand and decided to concentrate on the important things, leave the bells and the whistles for someone else to add, and keep to a tight budget.

The two main tasks our saw faces are breaking down rough lumber at the beginning of a project and then making precise, repeated cuts after the lumber has been milled. Most saws on the market today are capable of being very precise with one big "if." Tossing rough lumber around can knock a wimpy saw stand out of whack with the first piece of 8/4 hardwood that comes its way, so the first requirement is strength and stability.

But this strength needs to be focused and refined. The alignment of tables and fences needs to be right on – and stay that way – or the saw is useless for precise work.

At least nine out of 10 cuts we make are with the bulk of the material to the left of the saw blade. We decided to trade some flexibility for precision and build a solid stand to the left of the saw. To the right of the blade is a rolling stand that's the same height as the saw to hold material and to give some support when we need it.

Right at home. This miter saw workstation is compact and inexpensive to build. As a bonus, our crosscuts are more accurate, and our shop is cleaner.

PULLING OUT THE STOPS

The final point we agreed on was a stop system. We use stops on a regular basis to cut multiple parts to an exact length. We needed a simple and easy way to add a stop when we needed one. We also decided that it's hard to beat a block of wood and a clamp (especially on the price).

We've seen more than our fair share of systems with T-track and fancy stops that flip up and down and decided that for us the time, expense and chance of a stop moving or slipping weren't worth it.

One of my pet peeves is the buildup of offcuts and sawdust around the saw, so we left the saw table open on top, with a trash can directly below the saw.

We also borrowed a trick from the zero-clearance insert on our table saw. The kerf in the insert shows the exact location of the blade, and is an excellent aid to cutting right to a layout line. It sure beats trying to line up a cut to a tooth on the saw blade, especially if you're trying to cut to one side of your line, or trying to split the line.

We added a sacrificial insert that sits outside of the saw's metal fence. It won't last forever, and it will get trashed as soon as we bevel the saw, but nearly all of the cuts we make are

at 90°. The additional accuracy we get from having the insert makes moving or changing it on occasion no big deal.

LITTLE THINGS MEAN A LOT

The saw we chose to use, the DeWalt DW781, has a lot going for it. It is capable of wide crosscuts in thick material. The detents lock in place without wiggling around, it's simple to change the settings and it is solid overall. One of the things we like most is the small footprint and short length of the saw's slide bars. This saves space, of course, but more important, short bars reduce the leverage that works against precision in this type of saw.

Many saws we have used work fine on a narrow piece, but get sloppy when the bars extend to make a wide cut. The guide tubes still take up space behind the saw, but much less than other saws in this category. The thing we like the least is the dust-collection bag, but with the way we mounted the saw, most of the debris falls into the trash can below.

The saw has a flat, level table and a straight fence, but most of the wood you are going to cut will sit off the table. If it isn't properly supported, the quality of cuts will suffer. If we

can extend the machine's surfaces, we can cut confidently. What may seem like a tiny error can turn into a woodworker's worst nightmare.

A quarter of a degree, caused by a sagging outfeed table may not seem worth worrying about, but when you assemble four table legs and four aprons all with that error, there will be a lot more to be concerned with. Little errors are a social bunch. They like to gather in one corner of a project and have a party. And when they party, they like to cause trouble. That insignificant deviation can now become a racked carcase, a twisted drawer, or an out-of-square door.

DESIGN AROUND THE SAW

What we came up with works well for us, is adaptable to nearly any saw and shop, and you won't spend a lot of time or money making your own. The first part of designing your stand is establishing the footprint of your miter saw. I set ours on a piece of plywood to mark the layout. Put the front edge of the saw on the edge of the plywood, and push the head of the saw as far back as it will go (if it has a sliding carriage).

Hold one leg of a framing square against the back of the guide tubes and mark the plywood. Swing the

Sow's ear. Construction lumber is so wet that it will twist and warp as it reaches equilibrium with the shop environment. If used in this state, your work won't come out straight.

Silk purse. After drying, jointing and planing, this common material is now fit to use.

table to its right and left extents and make marks both at the back of the guide bars and at the control handle at the front of the saw. Extend the fences out from the saw and mark the distance at full extension. These marks will determine the size of the stand that the saw sits on. When the saw stand is complete, you want it to be tight against the wall, and the saw should be able to move to any position without interference.

Our stand fits in a limited space between an existing lumber rack and a corner of the room. The integral lumber rack we added holds the back of the saw stand away from the wall by 3¼". Taking this into account with the footprint of the saw, this stand would be 3¼" deeper if we omitted the lumber rack.

We also made this stand a little narrower than the actual width of the saw with the fences extended. This puts the end of the left-hand fence over the end of the fence assembly. This means cutting a notch in the right end of the fence, but makes it easier to line up the end of the fence assembly with the saw's fence.

The final parameter is the height above the floor. We chose 42⅛" – which might seem tall, but it makes it much easier to see our work and line things up without an awkward bend.

CHEAP IS GOOD, WITH PATIENCE

The construction of the tables makes use of a common, cheap material and an assembly method that gives a solid and sturdy surface with basic joinery. All of the solid-wood parts began as spruce, pine or fir 2x4s from the home center. In our neighborhood, the least-expensive hardwood available is poplar, and in 6/4 material, it costs about $2 a board foot.

I paid $2.38 each for "pre-cut" studs, slightly less than 8' long; this works out to about 70 cents a board foot. The drawback is that this stuff can be soaking wet when you buy it. This can be overcome, but it requires time and effort.

Construction lumber is kiln-dried, but it comes out of the kiln at 18-20 percent moisture content. Similar material that has been in our shop for a year is between 8-10 percent moisture content. As the 2x4s reach equilibrium with the shop's environment there will be some shrinkage, warping and twisting.

I've found some ways to work around this. The most important thing to do is wait. The drying process can be assisted, but it still takes time. When the wood gets to equilibrium, I mill it on the jointer and planer and obtain straight and flat material. Even though I am a procrastinator, I wanted to speed the process so I cut the studs to rough lengths.

Most of the moisture exits the board through the end grain, so this opens up the middle of the board and lessens the distance the water in the wood needs to move. Then I cut a bunch of scraps into ¼"-square strips and stacked the rough-length 2x4s with spaces between the edges of the boards and my ¼" stickers between each layer of the stack. I scanned a few boards with a pinless moisture meter every few days, and in about

MITER SAW STAND						
NO.	ITEM	DIMENSIONS (INCHES)			MATERIAL	COMMENTS
		T	W	L		
16	Fixed table legs	1¼	3¼	37¾	SPF*	
8	Rolling table legs	1¼	3¼	34⅝	SPF	Adjust to wheel diameter
12	Table frame side rails	1¼	3¼	19½	SPF	
8	Left & right table frame rails	1¼	3¼	27	SPF	
4	Saw table frame rails	1¼	3¼	28¾	SPF	
1	Saw table front rail	1¼	3¼	27¼	SPF	
4	Rack uprights	1¼	3¼	80	SPF	
1	Rack cross piece	1¼	3¼	71⅞	SPF	
1	Lower brace between tables	1¼	3¼	50⅛	SPF	
8	Lumber supports	1¼	3¼	12	SPF	
16	Support brackets	¾	6½	9¾	Plywood	
2	Saw supports	¾	7	20¾	Plywood	
2	Tabletops	¾	20¾	32	Plywood	
2	Table shelves	¾	19½	29½	Plywood	
1	Saw table shelf	¾	19½	31¼	Plywood	
2	Fence top & bottom	¾	6⅞	72	Plywood	
2	Fence front & back	¾	6	72	Plywood	Notch back for saw fence
2	Fence strips	¾	2⅛	72	Plywood	Match height of saw table
1	Fixed fence	½	4¾	60	Plywood	
2	Sacrificial fence	½	4¾	47½	Plywood	Make extras
1	Cut-off stop	½	4¾	9	Plywood	

*SPF = Spruce, pine or fir

a month the wood was dry enough to use.

Without a moisture meter, it's still possible to tell when the material is dry enough to use. If you have a piece of similar material that has been in your shop for several months, you can use that as a comparison to the new material. Wet wood will be heavier, and noticeably damp and cool to the touch.

The length of time it takes for the wood to acclimate will vary depending on where you live, and the environment of your shop. A month in our air-conditioned shop is the best-case scenario, but it could take two or three months in a damp basement shop. If you live in the desert, it could dry on the way home from the lumberyard.

PRETEND IT'S ROUGH LUMBER

When the wood was dry, I milled it down to 1¼" x 3¼" on the jointer and planer. This may seem like a lot of waste, but in my experience, this is what it takes to get straight material from 2x4s. With a pile of now-straight and square stock, I cut the parts to final length and assembled the benches.

There are two subassemblies to the benches: "L"-shaped legs, and butt-joined frames. Glued and screwed together, the jointed edges of the leg components hold each other straight, resisting warping and twisting. The legs are far stronger than just a 2x4, and the shape allows solid attachment of the frame. This method can be used to make sturdy benches of nearly any size.

The legs are held together with #8 x 2½" screws and glue. Set one of the leg parts on edge on the bench, and apply glue to the top surface. Put the other part on top, using a piece of scrap to support it while you align the edge with the face of the vertical piece. With the parts aligned, drill countersunk holes and drive three or four screws to connect the two parts of each leg. The frames are glued and butt-joined and these joints are also screwed together.

The frames fit in the inside corner of the leg assemblies. Lay two legs on the bench with the inside of the "L" facing up. Put some glue on the inside faces of the legs and put a frame unit in place with one of the long pieces down. Drill holes and connect the frame to the legs with #8 x 2" screws. With a combination square, mark the location of the lower frame 20" up from the bottom of the leg and glue and screw it in place. When the three tables are assembled, attach the plywood shelves and tops to the frames with glue and #8 x 1¼" screws.

The right-hand table has shorter legs so that it can roll on swivel casters. A block of scrap leg material is glued into the inside corner at the bottom of each leg, providing a place to mount the wheels with #10 x ¾" panhead sheet-metal screws. A simple plywood box, the same height as the fence beam, can be placed on top of this rolling table to provide support for material to the right of the saw when needed.

ILLUSTRATIONS BY MARY JANE FAVORITE

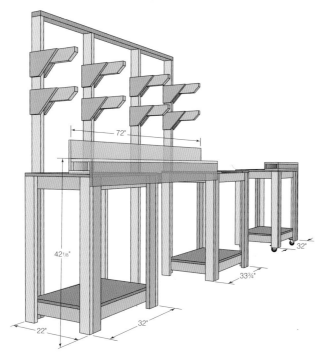

3-D VIEW

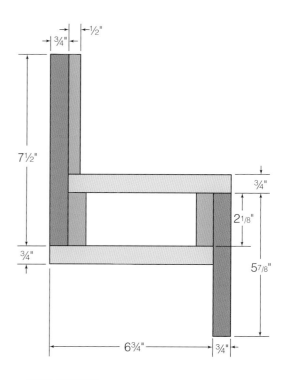

FENCE, END VIEW

LEAVE YOURSELF AN OPENING

The front upper rail of the saw table is reinforced with a second piece of wood that fits between the legs. I didn't bother with screws; I just glued it on, holding it to the existing frame's front with clamps while the glue dried. The plywood on the top of this unit isn't a solid piece; it is two 7"-wide strips going front to back at the right and left ends. The lower shelf on this unit may need to be slightly lower than the other units to ensure that the trash can fits. I used a Rubbermaid 32-gallon "Brute" that I purchased from the home center, but you'll need to adjust the opening size if you opt for a different container, or if you change the height of the saw table.

ON THE FENCE

The fence assembly is a plywood box-beam. The extended front and back pieces of the beam are held to the top

and bottom with strips of plywood. This beefs up the beam, and the width of the strips helps to level the surface to the surface of the saw table. In this entire project, the width of the strips is the only dimension that is important to hit exactly. This dimension will depend on the exact thickness of the plywood, and on the distance from the top of the saw's table to the base of the saw.

Because ¾" plywood is notorious for being undersized, I took two scraps and placed them on top of each other, next to the base of the saw. To get a precise measurement I took my combination square and set the head on the saw table and slid the blade down until the end of the blade rested on the plywood scraps. After cutting a test strip, I put it on top of the scraps and used the blade of the square as a straightedge to check the width. If the strips are a bit too narrow, that won't cause any problems, as the fence beam can be shimmed up to match the saw table.

One strip is attached to the long edge of each of the front and back pieces. I used 1¼"-long narrow crown staples and glue, but the strip can also be held in place with nails or screws. Be careful to keep the long edges of the two pieces of plywood flush during assembly. Attach the beam bottom to the edges of the front and back, then attach the top of the fence beam. If you need to notch the end of the fence, you can cut the notch with a jigsaw, either before or after assembly.

The box that sits on the rolling table is made from the same size parts as the box beam fence, minus the wider pieces that extend up and down. I glued and screwed the parts together and considered attaching it to the rolling tabletop, but it does its job, supporting long pieces to the right of the saw just as well if left loose.

A material rack is built into the back of the saw stand. It isn't designed to hold a lot of material; it is more of a temporary place to put

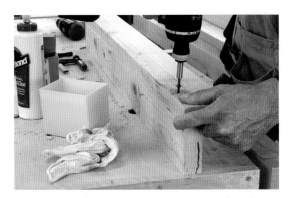

Dynamic tension. The jointed edge of one part helps keep the face of an adjacent part straight. Held together with glue and long screws, these legs are strong and straight.

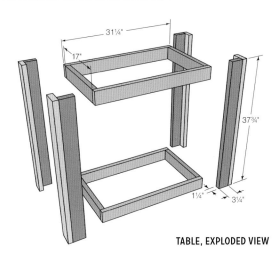

TABLE, EXPLODED VIEW

All together now. With the frames inside the leg assemblies, this table is ready for a plywood shelf and top.

to length. Three 80"-long uprights are screwed to the back legs on the left-hand table, and the back left leg of the saw table. A cross piece connects the two tables at the back, keeping the entire assembly from racking, and this provides a place for a fourth upright. The supports are short pieces of 1¼" x 3¼" material, held in place with simple plywood brackets.

With the tables and fence assembled, the complete saw station can be put in place and assembled. Start with screwing or bolting the saw to its table, then level the table with shims under the legs as needed. The left table is set in place, and the fence beam is set across the two tables. Check to see that the fence beam is sitting level, and that the fence itself is in line with the metal fence on the saw.

When everything is level and in line, attach the fence assembly to the two tables with a couple screws. Attach the ½"-thick secondary fence to the thicker back fence with #6 x ¾" screws. We used Baltic birch plywood, which comes in sheets that are 60" square. The permanent portion of the secondary fence is one rip from the sheet.

MAKING SACRIFICES FOR ACCURACY

Rip some extra pieces from the sheet for the replaceable fence sections. Hold one of these against the right-hand edge of the permanent piece and mark the length directly from the right edge of the metal fence on the saw. To provide clearance for the saw carriage, you'll need to trim the upper portion of the replaceable fence in the middle. Hold it in place, trace the outline of the saw's fence on the back, then make the cut on the band saw or jigsaw.

Gauge the distance. Stacking two pieces of plywood next to the saw table will give you a precise distance without measuring.

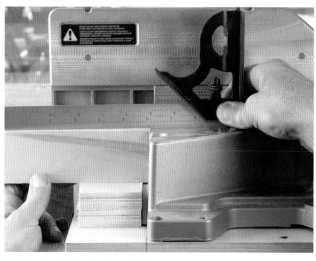

Double check. Checking the width of the strips with a straightedge will help keep the fence beam at the same height as the saw table.

Keep the edges flush. The thin plywood strip reinforces the front and back of the fence assembly, and locates the top and bottom correctly.

Quick and strong. The box beam construction keeps the fence assembly straight, and the narrow strips of plywood make it easy to put together.

The sacrificial fence is held in place with #6 x ¾" screws. Most saws have a few holes in the metal fence that will allow you to run a few screws in from behind, and you can run a couple screws from the face of the fence into the thicker plywood back fence. With the saw set at 90°, make a cut through the plywood fence.

This cut through the fence gives a convenient and accurate way to line up a cut line on your work with the saw blade. When you need to renew this kerf line, you don't need to replace the entire piece.

Remove the sacrificial fence, cut the edge back to square and put it back, pushing the freshly cut end against the edge of the remaining right-hand fence. This will leave a gap on the other end, but that won't hurt anything.

The only remaining part is the stop, which is a cut-off piece of ½" plywood. I nicked off the end at a 45° angle to keep sawdust from building up between the end of the stop and the material being cut.

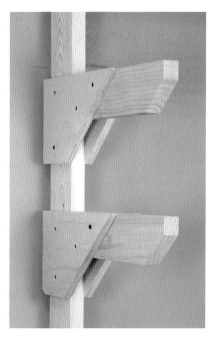

A place to put your stuff. Adding brackets to the back of the stand is a convenient way to store material about to be cut and parts that have just been cut.

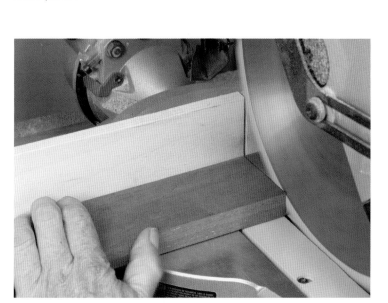

Zero clearance equals accurate cuts. A replaceable sub fence indicates exactly where the saw blade will be during the cut.

Right where you want it. Using the kerf in the subfence allows you to cut inside or outside a pencil line, or split it down the middle.

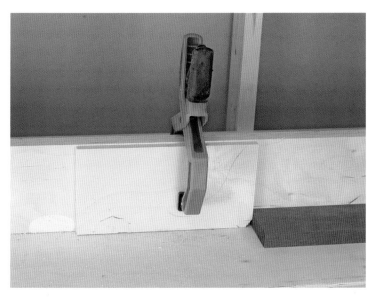

Keeping it simple. An offcut of plywood and a clamp make an effective stop system.

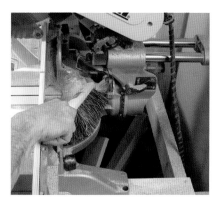

Dealing with the trash. Miter saws can make a mess, but leaving the top open below the saw lets dust and scraps fall into the trash can below.

ULTIMATE MITER SAW STAND

Built from two sheets of plywood, this rolling cart makes surgical crosscuts, automatically collects its dust and folds up to fit in a small corner.

By Jim Stuard

When I worked in professional shops, there was always a chop saw on some kind of cart. The less organized shops put the saw on the nearest work cart. It didn't take up much space, but it wasn't as useful as it should be. The better shops mounted the miter saw to a rolling cart and attached permanent wings to support long pieces and to hold a fence with stops for doing repetitive cuts. This setup was useful, but it took up a lot of space.

What I had in mind for Popular Woodworking's shop would have a dead-on stop system and collapsible wings so the stand would take up less space. The top of this stand adjusts up and down so you can line up the saw's table with the wings. (In fact, the adjustable table allows you to use a drill press or a mortiser on this stand.) It's got on-board dust collection that turns itself on and off. And the kicker to the whole

thing is that the cart is made from one sheet each of ¾" and ½" plywood, with some solid wood trim.

Begin construction by cutting the parts out according to the Schedule of Materials and using the optimization diagram. You'll notice that the case top is in two pieces on the optimization diagram. That's because you have to edge glue the plywood together, then cut it to size. There isn't much scrap on this project.

ONE QUICK CABINET

Begin by building the cabinet. To join the sides to the top, first cut ½" x ¾" rabbets in the top and bottom edges of the sides. To hold the back, cut ½" x ½" rabbets in the back edges of the sides, top and bottom pieces. Now assemble the case. An old trade secret is to assemble the case with it face down

on your assembly bench. This way you can ensure the joint at the inside of the rabbet is flush all around. Set each joint with a couple nails, then screw the case together. Check your cabinet for square and make sure the back fits snugly. Attach the back with screws. Flush up the front edges of the cabinet with a plane and apply iron-on birch veneer tape. File the tape flush, sand the cabinet and mount the casters.

AN ADJUSTABLE SAW PLATFORM

Now is a good time to mount the leveling riser (or platform) to your cabinet and get the miter saw set up. First cut a 1½" radius on the corners of the riser. Make sure this cut is square so that you can apply veneer tape without too much trouble. Ironing on veneer tape to the riser in one piece

is a real challenge, but it looks great. When the riser is ready, center it on top of the case and clamp it in place. Place your miter saw in the center of the riser. With a pencil trace the locations of your saw's feet onto the riser. Also trace the holes in the machine's feet that you'll use to mount the saw to the riser. This is important because the riser floats over the case on four bolts, which allows you to adjust the saw up and down. Now mark locations for the bolts that attach the riser to the case. Be sure to keep the bolts as close as you can to the feet without them interfering with each other.

When you've marked the locations for the riser bolts, drill your holes completely through the riser and the top of the case. Hold a piece of scrap inside the case where the drill will come out to minimize tearout. Ream out the holes a little to ease the riser adjustment.

Remove the riser from the case and drill the holes for mounting the saw. Now you can mount the riser to the case (see

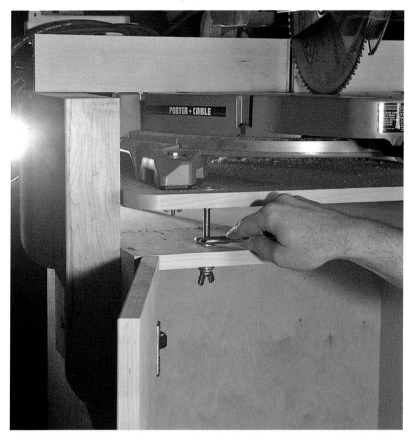

Adjusting the height of the saw is as easy as loosening the wing nuts inside the cabinet and using the jam nuts on top of the cabinet to raise or lower the saw until it's flush with the wing assemblies.

HARDWARE LIST

LEVELING RISER
4-4$\frac{1}{2}$" x $\frac{3}{8}$" stove bolts (coarse thread)
4-$\frac{1}{2}$"x1$\frac{1}{2}$" fender washers
12-$\frac{3}{8}$" flat washers
4-$\frac{3}{8}$" lock washers
4-$\frac{3}{8}$" wing nuts (coarse thread)
8-$\frac{3}{8}$" jam nuts (coarse thread)

CASE
4-4"casters w/locking wheels
16-$\frac{1}{2}$" x #10 panhead-sheetmetal screws
16-$\frac{1}{4}$" lock washers
1-Six outlet plug strip

DOORS
4-130° European-style cup hinges

WING SUPPORTS AND FENCE
8-2"x$\frac{1}{4}$"-20 hex head bolts
16-$\frac{1}{4}$" flat washers
8-$\frac{1}{4}$" lock washers
8-$\frac{1}{4}$"-20 wing nuts
2-36" continuous hinge
3-36" sliding track
1-L to R reading tape (72")
1-R to L reading tape (72")
2-2" square sets of Velcro (hooks and loops)

STOP
1-$\frac{1}{4}$"-20 star knob
1-1$\frac{1}{2}$"x$\frac{1}{4}$"-20 hex-head bolt
1-$\frac{1}{4}$" flat washer

SAW (FASTENING TO LEVELING SUPPORT)
4-2$\frac{1}{2}$"x$\frac{1}{4}$"-20 hex head bolts
8-$\frac{1}{4}$" flat washers
4-$\frac{1}{4}$" lock washers
4-$\frac{1}{4}$"-20 wing nuts

the list of hardware you need at left). Put the bolt through the fender washer, then into the hole in the riser. Put another flat washer on the other side of the riser with a jam nut to set the bolt in place. Run a jam nut up the bolt, leaving a 2" gap between the riser and the loose jam nut. Place flat washers over the holes in the case and set the riser in place on the case.

On the underside of the case, put a flat washer on the bolt, followed by a lock washer and wing nut. When you want to adjust the riser height, simply loosen the wing nuts and adjust the jam nut against the case top to raise or lower the riser.

To complete the case, build and hang the doors. Make the doors from plywood and nail a $\frac{13}{16}$" solid maple edge with a bullnose profile to the edges.

Use European hinges on your doors. I'm fond of a $30 jig that easily locates the holes for the hinges and the mounting plates (Jig-It System from Rockler item #31077). Drill the hinges' cup holes about 4" in from the top and bottom of the case.

AUTOMATIC VACUUM

Now mount the saw and outfit the cabinet with the vacuum and electrical parts. When the saw and vacuum are hooked up properly, the vacuum will come on automatically when you turn the saw on (thanks to Craftsman's "Automatic Power Switch" #24031, $16.99), and it will turn off a few seconds after you finish your cut.

Start by drilling two 2" holes in the back near the bottom of the case. One hole is for the vacuum hose (locate it according to your vacuum). The other is for the wiring. I enclosed the vacuum in a partition made from two pieces of plywood and the shelf. The shelf height in the drawing works for a small shop vaccum. Lay out the height of the bottom edge of the shelf. Mount a pair of cleats to these lines. Screw the shelf in from the top.

Now screw cleats to the inside of the case to make the partition and false front that conceals the vacuum. Notch your plywood pieces to wrap around the shelf cleat and the power cord for the vacuum. Turn the vacuum's switch to "on," place it in the new cubby and hook up the hose going through the back. Screw an outlet strip to the bottom of the case and run its cord through a hole in the back. Plug Craftsman's Automatic Power Switch into the outlet strip. Screw the partition and false front in place.

HUGE WINGS

The wings are the last thing to do. Begin by gluing and nailing a $\frac{1}{4}$"-thick solid wood edge to one end of the wings. This edging gives the piano hinge some meat to bite into. Finish the wings by applying the $\frac{1}{2}$" x 1$\frac{1}{2}$" trim to the other three edges.

Study the diagram to see how the wings are supported. First apply the upright ledges to the uprights. Cut the side of the wings using a 10" piece of continuous hinge, with the notched end of the swing arm $\frac{1}{4}$" in from the point where the wing meets the case. To keep everything from flopping around when the arms are down, use adhesive-backed Velcro between the swing arms and wings. Reinforce the Velcro's adhesive with staples.

Finish the wings by cutting a $\frac{3}{8}$" x $\frac{3}{4}$" dado down the middle of the wing for the extruded aluminum channel for the stop. Next to that dado, cut a second shallow dado that's $\frac{1}{2}$" wide and as deep as your tape is thick. Cut the channel to length and screw it in place.

Now concentrate on the flip-out supports. After cutting out the mating notches for the swing arms, cut a $\frac{3}{16}$" x $\frac{5}{8}$" rabbet into the end of the support to accept a 4$\frac{3}{4}$"-long piece of continuous hinge. Lay out and mount the support to the upright, centered and flush to the bottom edge.

The last step on the wings is to attach the wing assembly to the upright. Do this carefully so that the surface of the wing is flush with the upright ledge.

Now, if everything's OK, your wings should lock flush and square to the upright. If you didn't get it right the first time, add a flat-head screw to the inside of each notch to adjust the height of the wing.

To attach the wing assemblies, temporarily remove the saw/riser assembly and remove the wing from the upright assembly. Cut a spacer that's 2$\frac{3}{4}$" plus the height of the saw's table. Clamp the spacer flush to the upright ledge. Lay the wing assembly on the edge of the case. On the saw/riser assembly, measure from the front edge of the riser to the saw fence. Subtract 1$\frac{3}{4}$" from that number and mark it on the case, measuring from the front. This is where the upright should be mounted. It accounts for the thickness of the $\frac{3}{4}$" saw fence and the distance from the center of the stop to the fence. Mount the upright with the hardware listed. Make sure to counterbore the bolt heads and washers.

SCHEDULE OF MATERIALS: MITER SAW STAND

CABINET

NO.	LTR.	ITEM	DIMENSIONS	MATERIAL
			T W L	
2	A	Top & bottom	$\frac{3}{4}$" x 20" x 24$\frac{1}{2}$"	Ply.
2	B	Sides	$\frac{3}{4}$" x 20" x 27$\frac{3}{4}$"	Ply.
1	C	Back	$\frac{1}{2}$" x 23$\frac{3}{4}$" x 27$\frac{1}{4}$"	Ply.
1	D	Leveling riser	$\frac{3}{4}$" x 20" x 24$\frac{3}{4}$"	Ply.
2	E	Doors*	$\frac{3}{4}$" x 12$\frac{1}{16}$" x 27$\frac{3}{8}$"	Ply.
1	F	Door trim	$\frac{3}{16}$" x $\frac{13}{16}$" x 16'	Solid wood
1	G	Shelf	$\frac{1}{2}$" x 19$\frac{1}{2}$" x 23$\frac{1}{2}$"	Ply.
2	H	Shelf cleats	$\frac{3}{4}$" x $\frac{3}{4}$" x 19"	Solid wood
1	I	Partition	$\frac{1}{4}$" x 15" x 14"	Ply
1	J	False front	$\frac{1}{4}$" x 15" x 11$\frac{1}{2}$"	Ply.
2	K	Cleats	$\frac{3}{4}$" x $\frac{3}{4}$" x 13$\frac{3}{4}$"	Solid wood
1	L	Cleat	$\frac{3}{4}$" x $\frac{3}{4}$" x 5"	Solid wood

WINGS

NO.	LTR.	ITEM	DIMENSIONS	MATERIAL
2	M	Wings	$\frac{3}{4}$" x 10$\frac{1}{2}$" x 30"	Ply.
2	N	Uprights	$\frac{3}{4}$" x 11$\frac{1}{2}$" x 14$\frac{1}{4}$"	Ply.
2	O	Upright ledges	$\frac{3}{4}$" x 2$\frac{3}{4}$" x 11$\frac{1}{2}$"	Solid wood
2	P	Swingarm braces	$\frac{3}{4}$" x 4" x 10$\frac{1}{2}$"	Solid wood
2	Q	Swingarms	$\frac{3}{4}$" x 3" x 20"	Solid wood
2	R	Flip-out supports	$\frac{3}{4}$" x 4$\frac{7}{8}$" x 7$\frac{3}{4}$"	Solid wood
2	S	Front brackets	$\frac{1}{2}$" x 2$\frac{3}{4}$" x 15$\frac{3}{4}$"	Solid wood
2	T	Rear brackets	$\frac{1}{2}$" x 2$\frac{3}{4}$" x 10"	Solid wood
1	U	Wing trim	$\frac{1}{2}$" x 1$\frac{1}{2}$" x 15'	Solid wood
1	V	Edge trim	$\frac{1}{4}$" x $\frac{13}{16}$" x 24"	Solid wood
2	W	Fences	$\frac{3}{4}$" x 3" x 16$\frac{1}{4}$"	Ply
1	X	Stop block	$\frac{3}{4}$" x 2" x 3"	Solid wood

* Size before applying door trim.

The easiest way to assemble the wing is to attach the hinge to the upright assembly. Then remove it and attach it to the wing. Clamp the upright in a vise and reattach everything. Make sure to mark each hinge's location. Otherwise you'll mess up how some parts go together.

There is a lot of aluminum channel out there these days, but I chose this kind because a $1/4$"-20 bolt head will fit in the channel. It comes predrilled and countersunk from Woodcraft and machines nicely. You'll probably have to file down some screws that pop out from the other side.

This allows the flip-out support to fold flat against the upright. Re-attach the wings and flush the saw table up to the wings using a straight piece of lumber.

The last step is to make the fences and the stop and to attach the tapes. Rip a couple of $3^1/2$"-wide sections of plywood from your scrap. Cut them to 1" longer than the distance from the blade to the outside edge of the upright. That should be about $16^1/4$" if everything was centered correctly. Cut $3/8$" x $3/4$" dadoes 1" to the center from one edge. The

edge that the dado is closest to is the bottom edge. Repeat the $1/2$" dado for the tape so it's above the dado. Glue in a 4"-long filler into the groove at the end next to the blade and attach a length of aluminum channel to fill the remaining length. Make a mirror part for the other side. This keeps your hands at least 4" away from the blade. Attach the fences by lowering the saw (as if you were making a cut) and butting each fence against the blade. Clamp the fence pieces there and screw them in place.

Cut the measuring tape to 16" and stick it in place. Use a square block to index off the 16" marks and, after cutting the tapes to length (around 46"), stick them in place, butting the end up against the block on each side.

The stop is a simple 2" x 3" block with a $1/4$" hole in it. Make a guide strip that's about $5/16$" x $1/16$". It's easier if you make the strip a little thick and plane it down to the $1/16$" thickness. Drill the $1/4$" hole through and test it with a bolt and star knob.

OPTIMIZATION DIAGRAM

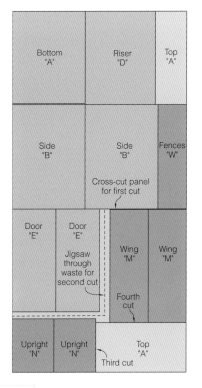

Here you can see how the stop works with the fence system. Note the thin guide strip that prevents your stop from wobbling as you set it.

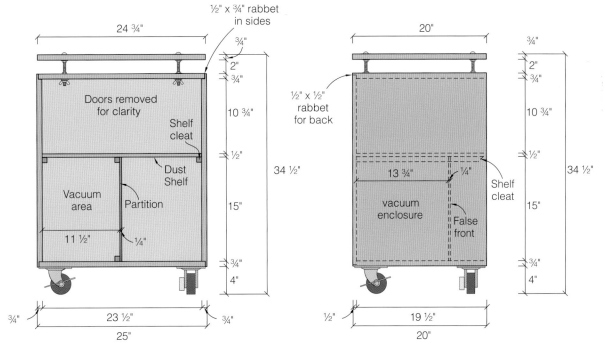

½" x ¾" rabbet
in sides

24 ¾"

¾"
2"
¾"

Doors removed
for clarity

Shelf
cleat

10 ¾"

½"

Dust
Shelf

34 ½"

Vacuum
area

Partition

15"

11 ½"

¼"

¾"
4"

¾"
23 ½"
¾"
25"

20"

¾"
2"
¾"

½" x ½"
rabbet
for back

10 ¾"

½"

13 ¾"
¼"
Shelf
cleat

vacuum
enclosure

15"

False
front

34 ½"

¾"
4"

½"
19 ½"
20"

PROFILE

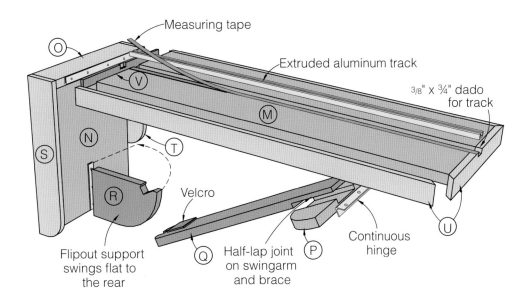

Measuring tape

O

V

Extruded aluminum track

3/8" x ¾" dado
for track

M

N

T

S

R

U

Velcro

Flipout support
swings flat to
the rear

Q

Half-lap joint
on swingarm
and brace

P

Continuous
hinge

ELEVATION

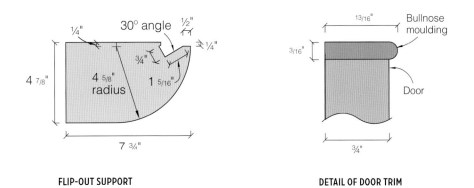

30° angle

½"

¼"

¼"

¾"

4 ⅞"

4 ⅝"
radius

1 5/16"

7 ¾"

FLIP-OUT SUPPORT

13/16"

Bullnose
moulding

3/16"

Door

¾"

DETAIL OF DOOR TRIM

GERMAN WORK BOX

A fold-out, carry-anything
tool chest on wheels.

By David Thiel

During a recent trip to Germany, our publisher, Steve Shanesy, snapped some pictures of a utilitarian, but also clever, rolling tool cart used in one of the woodworking shops he visited.

The cart was designed to hold your tools so your bench or assembly platform remained tidy. It had doors and drawers on the lower section, plus wings that opened on top to reveal three tool wells that kept things orderly and prevented items from falling onto the floor. When not in use, the cart closed to a nice size and could even be locked.

The staff agreed that the idea was a good one, but we decided to put a Popular Woodworking spin on it. We divided and detailed the lower drawer space some more and added a tool till inside the center well with magnetic tool holders.

Plus we made sure the construction was simple. Mechanical fasteners do all the hard work. You could easily build this cart with a circular saw, a drill and a router, making it a great project for beginners or even a professional cabinetmaker in a production shop.

AFFORDABLE SPACE

While we didn't start out worrying about price, the finished bill is worth talking about. Using two sheets of good-quality ¾" shop-grade plywood and one sheet of ½" Baltic birch ply for the drawers, wood costs came in at about $125. The necessary hardware (there's a lot more than you might think imagine) comes in around $200 if you build it exactly as we have. So for $325, you're still getting a lot of storage for the price and the space is arranged to be exactly what you need, unlike a store-bought toolbox.

THE BASICS

While this is a utilitarian work cart for the shop, we expended a little extra effort (veneer tape on the plywood edges and no exposed screw heads) to make it a more finished-looking project while maintaining the solid, simple construction details.

The cart joinery is a collection of butt joints. We used a new product on the market, Miller Dowels, to assemble all the butt joints. This is a stepped wood dowel that replaces the screws and plugs the holes left by the drill bit at the same time.

The back is ¾" plywood (plywood offers great gluing strength on edge because of the long grain part of the plywood core). This size back offers excellent stability and the opportunity to square-up the case without worrying about wood expansion because of changes in humidity.

On the interior plywood drawers we used simple rabbet joints to add some extra strength. The bottoms of three of the drawers are screwed to the drawer boxes and stick out past the drawer sides to serve as effective drawer guides, emulating the metal drawers used on the right side of the case.

BEGIN WITH THE BIG BOX

First cut the plywood panels to size according to the cutting list below.

To allow the three smaller drawers to slide in and out of the case, you

need to cut $\frac{1}{2}$"-wide x $\frac{3}{8}$"-deep dados in the left side of the case and in the left side of the center divider. Lay out the dado locations – according to the illustrations – then cut them using either a dado stack in your saw, repeated cuts with a circular saw, or with a straight bit, using two passes to achieve the full depth. There is $\frac{1}{2}$" of space between each of the drawers and we worked from the bottom up, leaving a larger gap above the top drawer to allow clearance for the door catches.

DOWELS AND GLUE

As mentioned, we used veneer tape to dress up the edges of the plywood. We had been using iron-on veneer

tape for years, but recently discovered a self-adhesive veneer tape that is much simpler to use, takes the concern out of the glue melting evenly and sticks very well to the work.

After veneering all the exposed edges, sand the interior surfaces through #150 grit. Now you're ready to assemble the case.

Start by clamping the divider between the upper and middle shelves, holding the front edges flush. We used regular #8 x 1$\frac{1}{4}$" screws here because they would be hidden inside the case. Drill and countersink $\frac{3}{16}$"-diameter clearance holes through the shelves and drill $\frac{3}{32}$"-diameter pilot holes in the divider. Add glue and screw the assembly together.

Next use either screws or Miller Dowels to attach the back to the center assembly. Check the spaces to ensure they are square, then add the bottom shelf to the back, holding the back flush to the bottom side of the shelf.

Clamp your center assembly between the two sides, drill the appropriate holes, add glue and assemble the rest of the case. It's a good idea to trim the dowels flush to the case side before flipping the case onto that face: It's more stable and there's less chance of messing something up.

Add the front piece to the front edges of the sides, holding it flush to the top edge. The front will overlap the top shelf, leaving $\frac{1}{4}$" of the shelf edge exposed. This allows room to attach the front to the shelf with brad nails. The exposed edge will act as a door stop once hinges are installed.

The wings go together like simple versions of the case. The side closest to the cabinet on each wing is $\frac{3}{16}$" narrower than the other. This creates a recess to house the hinge to mount the wings to the cabinet.

We recessed the captured panels $\frac{1}{4}$" in from the outside edges to avoid any alignment problems. Using the stepped dowels, attach the wing sides to the wing panels. Attach the fronts and backs to complete the assembly.

STORAGE DETAILS

Start by adding the till lid to the back with a length of continuous (or piano) hinge. Because of the way the hinge needs to mount inside the cabinet (so the wings can close) we added a $\frac{3}{4}$" x $\frac{3}{4}$" maple strip to the back $\frac{1}{8}$" down from the top edge. This allows the till lid to open to about 110°. Mount the lid to the strip with a length of piano hinge. Carefully check it for clearance between the two sides as it closes.

Next, attach the till support to the top shelf by screwing into the support

SOURCES
LEE VALLEY TOOLS
800-871-8158 OR
LEEVALLEY.COM
4 • 2"metal drawers
 #05K98.20, $12.80 each
4 • 1" metal drawers
 #05K98.10, $10.80 each
2 • gripper mats
 #88K18.05, $8.80 ea.
3 • 12" magnetic bars
 #93K75.12, $11.50 ea.
WOODWORKER'S HARDWARE
800-383-0130 OR
WWHARDWARE.COM
3 • 1$\frac{1}{2}$" x 48" nickel piano hinges
 #C11248 14A, $6.66 ea.
2 • 2$\frac{1}{2}$" swivel casters
 #JH25 S, $2.73 ea.
2 • 2$\frac{1}{2}$" swivel casters w/brake
 #JH25 SB, $2.73 ea.
1 • lid stay
 #KV0472, $3.04
2 • 4" chrome pull
 #UFWP4 SS, $1.46 ea.
4 • 1" pull screws
 #SC832 1SS, $.48 ea.
2 • roller catches
 #A09714 A2G, $1.73 ea.
1 • 18" 100# full extension slide
 #KV8417 B18, $14.51 pr.
WOODCRAFT
800-535-4482 OR WOODCRAFT.COM
2 • Miller Dowel 1X walnut packs (40)
 #827526, $14.59 ea.
1 • stepped dowel kit 1X
 #827532, $25.59
WOODWORKER'S SUPPLY
800-645-9292 OR
WOODWORKER.COM
1 • $\frac{13}{16}$"x 50' PSA birch edge tape
 #934-960, $23.69
Prices as of publication deadline.

Cut the drawer dados in the case sides prior to assembly. We used a router to make the dados and a store-bought guide that clamps across the plywood to guide the router. You could just as easily clamp a straight board to the side to serve as a guide. Use two passes on each dado to achieve the full depth. This puts less strain on the router and the bit.

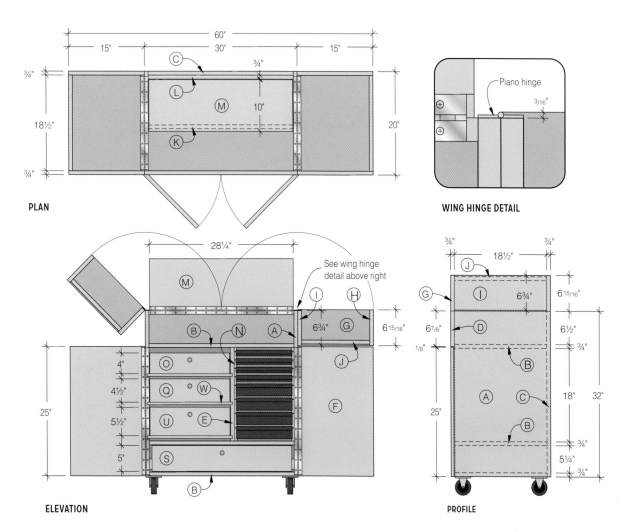

PLAN

WING HINGE DETAIL

ELEVATION

PROFILE

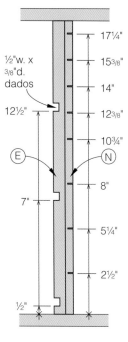

DRAWER DADO LAYOUT

GERMAN WORK BOX						
NO.	LET.	ITEM	DIMENSIONS (INCHES)			MATERIAL
			T	W	L	
CASE						
2	A	Sides	3/4	19 1/4	32	Shop plywood
3	B	Shelves and bottom	3/4	18 1/2	28 1/2	Shop plywood
1	C	Back	3/4	28 1/2	32	Shop plywood
1	D	Front	3/4	6 7/8	30	Shop plywood
1	E	Divider	3/4	18	18	Shop plywood
2	F	Doors	3/4.	14 15/16	25	Shop plywood
4	G	Wing front and back	3/4	6 15/16	15	Shop plywood
2	H	Wing sides	3/4	6 15/16	18 1/2	Shop plywood
2	I	Wing sides	3/4	6 3/4	18 1/2	Shop plywood
2	J	Wing panels	3/4	13 1/2	18 1/2	Shop plywood
1	K	Till support	3/4	5 1/2	28 1/2	Shop plywood
1	L	Till lid spacer	3/4	3/4	28 1/4	Maple
1	M	Till lid	3/4	10	28 1/4	Shop plywood
2	N	Drawer section sides	1/2	12	18	Shop plywood
DRAWERS						
2	O	Drawer front and back	1/2	4	15 3/4	Baltic birch
2	P	Drawer sides	1/2	4	17 1/2	Baltic birch
2	Q	Drawer front and back	1/2	4 1/2	15 3/4	Baltic birch
2	R	Drawer sides	1/2	4 1/2	17 1/2	Baltic birch
2	S	Drawer front and back	1/2	5	27 1/2	Baltic birch
2	T	Drawer sides	1/2	5	17 1/2	Baltic birch
2	U	Drawer front and back	1/2	5 1/2	15 3/4	Baltic birch
2	V	Drawer sides	1/2	5 1/2	17 1/2	Baltic birch
3	W	Drawer bottoms	1/2	16 3/4	18	Baltic birch
1	X	Drawer bottom	1/2	17 1/2	27	Baltic birch

through the shelf. The support is set back ½" from the front edge of the till lid to allow you to get your fingers under it to lift the lid. Add some glue and a couple of stepped dowels through the sides to hold everything in place.

Now you need to attach the two wings to the case with more piano hinge. Clamp the wings to the case in the open position (flush to the front) while attaching the hinges to ensure even and well-supported wings.

Lastly, attach the doors to the case (use a piano hinge again). To get the doors to seat flush against the cabinet front, cut a shallow rabbet (³⁄₁₆" deep,

the thickness of the hinge) the width of the closed hinge on the back of the door on the hinge side. This cut can be done with your router or table saw.

When attaching the doors, pay careful attention to the height. Preferably they will be about ⅛" below the wings when open to keep things from bumping.

You'll also notice that the left-hand door's hinge covers the dados for the drawers. Rather than place the hinge on the outside of the cabinet (making it too visible), we opted to simply file out the hinge to match the dado locations, as shown below.

DRAWER SPACE
Ultimately you'll decide how the interior space in your cart is used. We've used drawers because our experience has shown that low shelving just collects junk at the back of the case that you can never see or reach easily.

We've used a selection of drawer types for this project, both shop-made and purchased. You can follow our lead or choose whatever style you prefer.

The lower shop-made drawer is simply a Baltic birch box drawer mounted on full-extension, 100-lb.

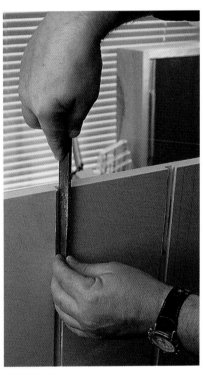

The veneer edge tape is easy to use and quickly adds a finished appearance to the cabinet. Even though we ended up painting the exterior, the paint still applied better to the veneer tape than on a bare plywood edge. You'll need to notch the tape with a file at the dado locations in the left case side.

Screw the divider between the top and middle shelves by first drilling a pilot hole for the screws and countersinking the flathead screws to the shelf surfaces.

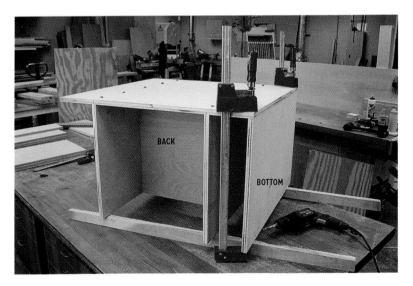

Attach the back to the center assembly using the Miller Dowels. Put glue on the back edges of the center pieces, then position the back and clamp it in place. After using the proprietary stepped drill bit to make the holes, add glue to the dowel and then tap it into place in the hole. Lastly, attach the bottom to the back with stepped dowels.

drawer slides. This is a fine heavy-duty drawer joined at the corners with simple rabbet joints. We used a ½" bottom fit into a rabbet in the sides. While we usually would have recommended a ¼" bottom, we had the ½" material and didn't feel like buying a whole sheet of ¼" for just one drawer.

The store-bought drawers are metal, lighter-duty drawers of 1" and 2" depths and have metal flanges that ride on dados cut into the sides of the case. With these, the front of the drawer overlaps the case sides to both hide the dados and serve as a drawer stop. As this would interfere with the door hinge, we added two drawer section sides made of ½" Baltic birch and set them back 1" from the front of the case. This also made it possible to cut the dados in the section sides after the case was assembled.

The three drawers to the left use the best of both worlds, finishing off some of the wood at hand and avoiding the cost of more drawer slides by using the "lip and groove" concept of the metal drawers. On all the wood drawers, a simple 1" hole drilled in the front serves as an adequate drawer pull.

FINISHING TOUCHES

The last steps are adding a finish (we opted for two coats of dark green latex paint on the outside; the inside was left as-is) and then some sturdy 2½" casters to the case and placing and organizing your tools. The photos will show you a couple of storage tricks and items available for sale to help keep things neat and tidy.

Before attaching the second side, it makes sense to cut the dowels on the first side flush to the surface. I used a Japanese flush-cutting pull saw that has teeth with very little set to them, reducing the chance of scratching the cabinet side. By applying pressure on the blade to keep it flat to the cabinet surface, I further reduced the chance of scratches. Do a little sanding, then flip the cabinet over and attach the second side, then the front.

The next step is to attach the first side (which side doesn't really matter). Carry your location lines from the back around to the side and use them to lay out the dowel locations. Add glue, clamp, drill and dowel the joint.

TILL LID

TILL SUPPORT

After attaching the till lid, the wings are ready. The wings are held flush to the front and are tight against the cabinet side. The recessed wing side is the attachment point for the piano hinge, allowing the lid to close flush against the top of the cabinet.

MILLER DOWELS

Miller Dowels are a clever concept that can make some types of assembly faster and easier. Essentially, the stepped-dowel idea offers the strength of a standard dowel with the ease of a tapered dowel. Alignment and splitting difficulties often associated with standard dowels are reduced, while the strength offered is actually better than with a standard dowel thanks to the ribbed design (increasing glue coverage).

These stepped dowels can be used in place of screws (as we've shown in this project) – think of them as self-plugging screws.

We're going to stop short of advocating Miller Dowels as a replacement for all screws, though. While the strength is good, they still won't pull up an ill-fitting joint, and if the glue is not allowed to cure before removing the clamps, there is the potential for the joint opening slightly after removing the clamps. So proper clamping and glue-curing time is still essential.

Then there is the economic consideration. A pack of 50 dowels (2 3⁄4" or 3 1⁄2" long) and the necessary bit cost about $30. Packs of 25 dowels cost about $7. That's about 28 cents per dowel versus 4 cents per #20 biscuit or about 8 cents per premium screw.

All things considered, we like the idea of an all-wood, strong and simple joint – but we'd recommend choosing your application carefully.

The dowels are available in birch, red oak, cherry and black walnut, and more weather-resistant species are on the drawing board. For details, contact Miller Dowel at 866-WOODPEG (866-966-3734) or millerdowel.com.

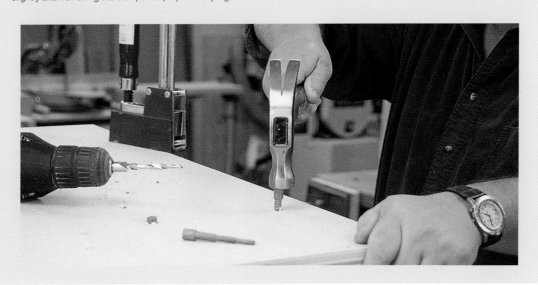

You can see the two sets of dados for the drawers with a few drawers removed. Also, notice the notched piano hinge to allow the drawers to slide in and out.

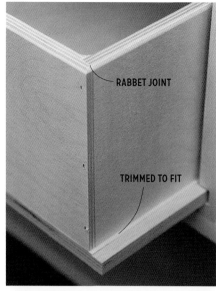

RABBET JOINT

TRIMMED TO FIT

This shot of one of the drawers shows the rabbet joinery used. Also note that the bottom was trimmed slightly in width to allow the drawer to move more smoothly in the dados.

Pads line the bottoms of the wing and till sections to keep tools from rolling and to help trap dust. Dividers in the till section can be customized to fit the tools you need. The magnetic bars on the till lid provide secure storage for small ferrous tools. Small-parts storage is easily accomplished with a couple of plastic storage bins held in place in one of the metal drawers with some hook-and-loop fasteners.

10-DRAWER TOOL CHEST

Store your smaller tools in style with a tool chest that's surprisingly simple to build.

By Jim Stack

Most woodworkers have dozens of tools that are small, such as screwdrivers, files, chisels, pliers, dividers and compasses. All these can be stored in shallow drawers, which is where this chest comes into the picture.

The design for the chest came from two inspirations. One was a Craftsman-style bookcase plan. The sides and top are shaped like the bookcase, and the chest is made of quartersawn white oak. The other inspiration came from multi-drawer chests that were made years ago to store sheet music.

This chest was assembled with butt joints and screws. I countersunk the screws and plugged the holes with $\frac{3}{8}$" redheart plugs. The drawer pulls also are redheart, which I cut using a $\frac{1}{2}$" plug cutter.

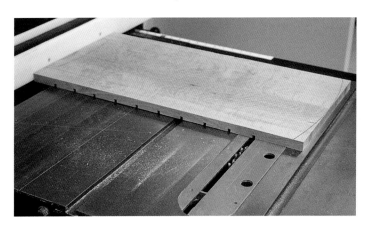

1 The first step is to cut the sides $\frac{3}{8}$" narrower than the finished dimension. Then cut the $\frac{1}{4}$" x $\frac{1}{4}$" dados for the drawers. Glue a $\frac{3}{8}$" x $\frac{3}{4}$" strip to the back of each side. This strip covers where the dados exit the sides, creating a stopped dado.

2 Now draw the top arc on each of the sides. Trammel points mounted on a stick are great for drawing arcs. A little trial and error is involved here unless you can figure the radius using math. I try connecting the dots, moving the pencil up or down the stick until I find the radius that works. If you don't have trammel points, drive a nail through a stick at one end. This is your fixed point. Use a small clamp or rubber band to hold a pencil anywhere you need along the length of the stick to draw your arc.

149

3 Now you need to draw the arc at the bottom of each side. When laying out the radii at the bottom of the sides, use a small, round object to draw the small radius that defines each foot.

4 Connect these two small radii with an arc that is 1" high from the bottom of the side.

6 Smooth and shape the arcs with a rat-tail file or curved rasp.

5 Drill holes with the same radius as the small arcs and connect them by cutting the larger arc with a jigsaw or band saw.

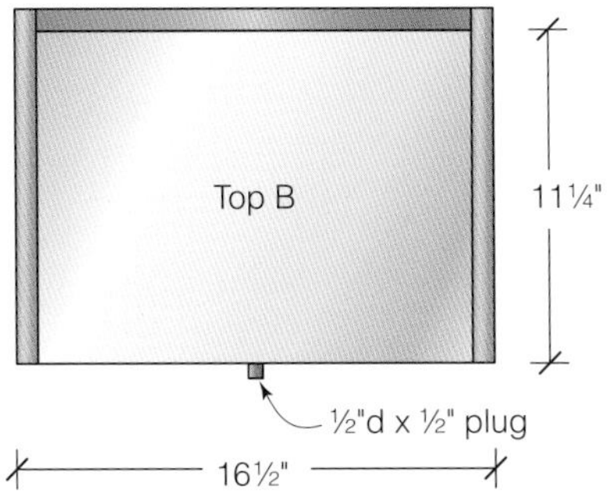
Top B
11¼"
½"d x ½" plug
16½"

PLAN

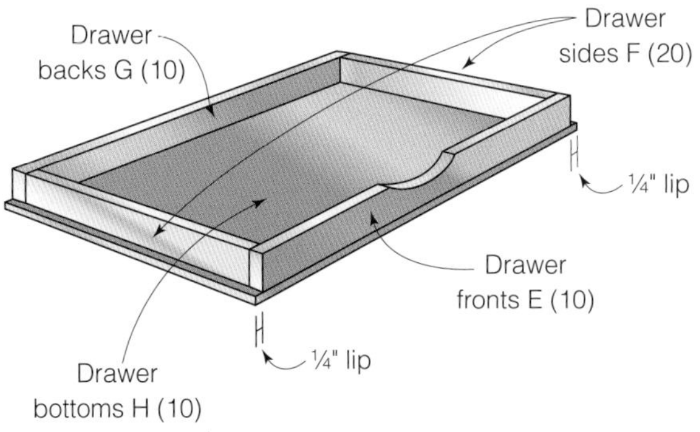
Drawer backs G (10)
Drawer sides F (20)
¼" lip
Drawer fronts E (10)
¼" lip
Drawer bottoms H (10)

DRAWER ASSEMBLY

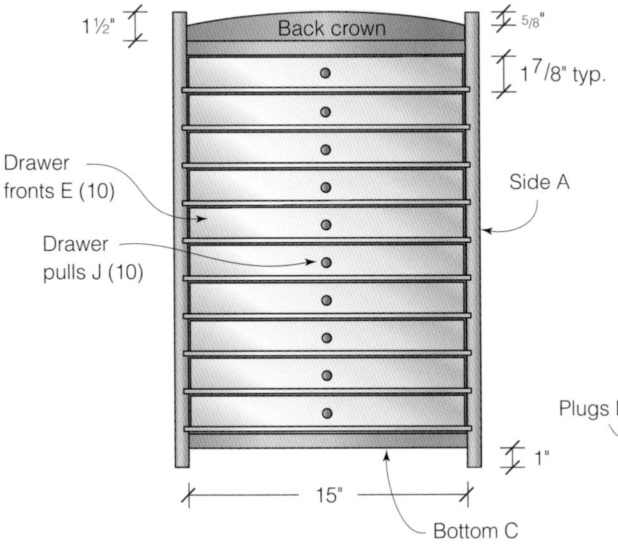
1½"
Back crown
5/8"
1 7/8" typ.
Drawer fronts E (10)
Side A
Drawer pulls J (10)
1"
15"
Bottom C

ELEVATION

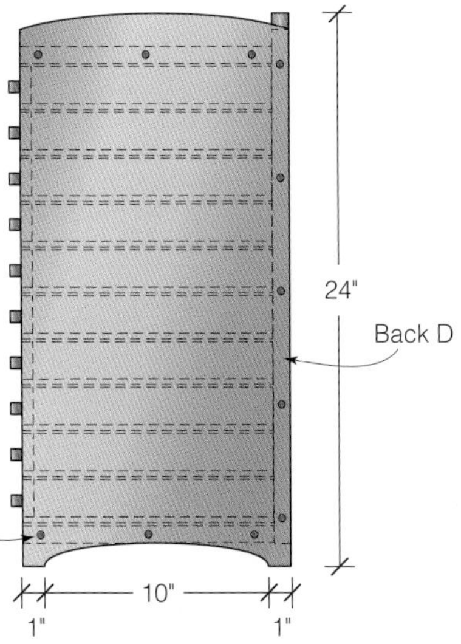
24"
Back D
Plugs K
10"
1"
1"

PROFILE

10-DRAWER TOOL CHEST

NO.	LET.	ITEM	DIMENSIONS (INCHES) T	W	L	MATERIAL	COMMENTS
2	A	Sides	3/4	12*	24	White oak	Width includes 3/8" edging
1	B	Top	3/4	11 1/4	15	White oak	
1	C	Bottom	3/4	11 1/4*	15	Plywood	Width includes 3/8" edging
1	D	Back	3/4	15	23*	Ply/oak	Top crown is 2 1/4" wide, glued to ply
10	E	Drawer fronts	1/2	1 5/8	14 15/16	White oak	
20	F	Drawer sides	1/2	1 5/8	10 1/4	Poplar	
10	G	Drawer backs	1/2	1 5/8	14 15/16	Poplar	
10	H	Drawer bottoms	1/4	11 1/4	15 1/2	Plywood	Trim sides to fit after drawers are assembled
10	J	Drawer pulls	1/2-dia.		1/2	Redheart	Cut with 1/2" plug cutter
22	K	Plugs	3/8-dia.		1/4+/-	Redheart	Cut with 3/8" plug cutter
2		Side strips	3/8	3/4	24	White oak	Glued to back edge of sides
1		Bottom strip	3/8	3/4	15	White oak	Glued to front edge of bottom
1		Back crown	3/4	2 1/4	15	White oak	Glued to top edge of back
10		Dowel rods	1/8-dia.		3/4	Hardwood	

*Measurement is finished dimension and includes solid-wood edging

7 Glue the back crown on top of the plywood back panel. Make the arc on the crown as you did for the sides. Cut the top and bottom panels to size, then glue a $^3/_8$" x $^3/_4$" strip on the front of the bottom panel. Assemble the chest using 2" screws. Cut the plugs and glue them in place to cover the screw heads.

8 Here you can see how the two arcs meet nicely at the back corner of the case. These little details will make the sides and back flow together nicely.

9 Cut all the drawer parts to size. The sides are captured between the front and back parts, so glue-up can be done with two clamps. I just used glue on these butt joints. I know what you're thinking: Why would he use just glue and no fasteners or other joinery to strengthen this joint? Well, after the plywood bottoms are glued in place, the drawers are quite strong. (If you would like to use fasteners, please do so. Screws or dowels would work well.)

10 I use bench horses all the time to hold parts for gluing. Several drawers can be glued at one time. After applying glue to the bottoms, hold them in place with a few small brads or nails. Then stack up a few drawers and clamp them while the glue dries. This also helps keep the drawers flat.

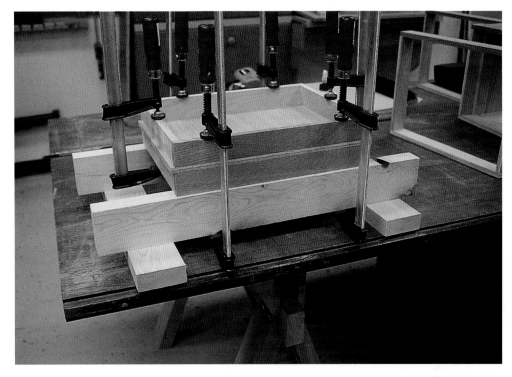

11 When the glue has dried on the drawers, rout the ¼" bead on the top and bottom of the drawer fronts. The drawer bottoms are the perfect thickness to accept the radius of the bead. (See below.)

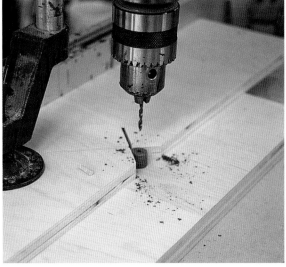

12 If necessary, fit the drawers by planing or sanding the sides of the bottoms that fit into the grooves to ensure the drawers slide smoothly. Then cut the plugs for the drawer pulls. I attached the pulls with an ⅛" dowel rod. Drill a hole in the center of the plug, and a matching hole in the drawer front. Glue the pulls in place, then sand and finish the chest and drawers.

After drawer is assembled, rout bead

½"

½"-thick sides

1 5/8"

¼"

DRAWER PROFILE DETAIL

ALL-IN-ONE CABINET
For the Small Shop

This shop cabinet squeezes 13 cubic feet of tool storage into less than 3 square feet of floor space.

By Jim Stuard

If you're like most woodworkers, your shop is packed to the gills with tools, tooling and accessories. Storing power tools on open shelves is no good; dust will get into the windings and shorten the life of your motors. You need an enclosed cabinet, and you need one that takes up less floor space than a band saw. This cabinet has a place to store routers, all the bits a woodworker could need and other accessories such as edge guides, bases and template guides. There's also room for other tools such as jigsaws, sanders, biscuit joiners and even a portable planer.

BUILD THE CASE

All the plywood pieces can be cut from two sheets of plywood, so start by deterim ing the best way to cut the pieces for best yield. After the parts are cut to size, cut $\frac{1}{2}$" x $\frac{3}{4}$" rabbets on the ends of the sides to hold the top and bottom pieces. Unless your shop has high ceilings, you'll need to cut the rabbets with a plunge router, straight bit and an edge guide. First set the router for the finished depth using your turret depth stop. Now raise the bit halfway and make a pass that defines the shoulder of the rabbet. Now climb cut (which is basically routing in reverse, moving the router backwards) the waste out to the edge of the board. Finally, plunge to the full depth of your rabbet and repeat the above procedure.

The next step is to cut the $\frac{1}{4}$" x $\frac{3}{4}$" dadoes in the sides. Mark the location of the dado and make a simple jig to rout it. The jig uses a bearing-on-top straight bit to guide against the edges of the jig. To make the jig, take the fixed shelf and place two strips of plywood against it on a flat surface. Place all this on top of two cross pieces on either end of the strips and glue and nail them in place. Leave a little room (about $\frac{1}{2}$") across the length of the dado cut to adjust the jig. Clamp the jig on the marked lines and rout the dado in two passes. Finish machining the sides by cutting the $\frac{1}{2}$" x $\frac{1}{4}$" rabbet for the back on the back edge of both sides, top and bottom. (If the cabinet won't be attached to the wall, use a thicker back for stability.) Check the top, bottom and fixed shelf for a good fit, then glue and nail or screw the cabinet together. Fit the back and set it aside. Place the case on a flat work surface and add iron-on edging. Finish the case by gluing and nailing the hanging rail into the top of the case, flush with the rabbet in the back.

Here's the simple jig to rout the dadoes. It uses a bearing-on-top straight bit to guide against the edges of the jig. Clamp the jig right on the marked lines and rout the dado.

PHOTO BY AL PARRISH

Use screws and glue to attach the levelers to the inside corners of the base frame. The top of the block (the end opposite the foot) should be flush with the top edge of the base frame.

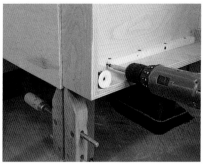

With the case on its back, take two hand screws and attach them to the back lip of the case, ¼" in from the back. This provides a little offset for the moulding on our walls. If you have larger base moulding where you are, make the base a little taller or less deep to accommodate the larger moulding. Place the base up against the case bottom. Center it on the bottom and temporarily screw it into place with four 1¼" screws.

After making the stock according to the diagram, take a piece and cut a miter on one end. Be sure to make the first cut with the bullnose up. This isn't important for the first two edges, but it's very important for the last two. Use a piece of scrap with a miter cut on both ends to test the fit of the miters.

BUILD THE BASE

Now comes the adjustable base. When I made custom cabinetry, we often added an adjustable-height base to cabinets so we could compensate for uneven floors or walls. The base is a simple plywood rectangle. You attach the adjustable feet to the inside corners and drill holes in the case above the feet. This allows you to adjust the base with a screwdriver while the cabinet is in place.

The base itself is a simple mitered frame, with biscuits added at the miters. Cut the miters, then glue and clamp the base together. Make sure the base is square by measuring across the corners.

While the glue dries, cut out the blocks that hold the adjustable feet. They're just 1½" x 1½" x 3¼" blocks. Drill a centered, ⁷⁄₁₆" hole through the length of the block for a T-nut. Drill holes at right angles to one another in the block that will be used to screw the blocks to the base. Hammer in the T-nuts. With the feet threaded into the blocks, the entire assembly is about 4" long. It should flush up with the top and bottom of the base frame.

Now it's time to attach the base. Cut out four ¾" x ¾" cleats that fit between the levelers and drill mounting holes in the cleats for attaching the case bottom. Screw them in place about 1⁄₃₂" down from the top edge of the base. Make sure

to Position the base on the bottom. Temporarily screw the base in place with four 1¼" screws. Take out all the feet and use a pencil to mark the location of the top of the leveler hole. Drill the holes using a piece of scrap to back up the hole or you'll tear out the veneer on the inside of the case bottom. When you re-attach the base, you'll be able to adjust the levelers using a straight-bladed screwdriver.

BUILD THE DOORS

The doors are plywood slabs with a mitered moulding nailed to the edges. The moulding is a ³⁄₁₆" x ¹³⁄₁₆" solid wood edge with a bullnose routed on the front (see diagram). The bullnose is referred to as a cockbead, which is

When fitting the second set of edges, start by cutting the miter on one end. Flip the edge over and place what will be the bottom edge of the miter into the miter on the right. Gently press the flat edge up against the other miter. Mark the location of the miter and make the cut.

Drill the holes for the hinge cups on your drill press. Always make a test piece with a hinge and mounting plate to test your setup.

Take out all the feet and use a pencil to mark the location of the top of the leveler hole. Remove the base and drill ½" holes into the case bottom.

SUPPLIES

LEE VALLEY TOOLS

800-871-8158 - WWW.LEEVALLEY.COM

4 - 107° Full overlay hinges,
   #00B10.01, $5.95 ea.
1 - 14" Full ext. drawer slides,
   #02K30.14, $12.20 pr.
4 - 4" Swivel leveler,
   #01S06.04, $2.80 ea.
4 - $\frac{3}{8}$"-16 T-nuts (10 pc.),
   #00N22.24, $2.10
5 - 4" Wire pulls,
   #01W78.04, $2.40 ea.
1 - Coat hook,
   #00W80.01, $6.90
24 - Shelf pins (50pc.),
   #94Z03.12, $3.60
1 - 25' Maple edge banding,
   #41A05.01, $6.50
2 - 25mm x 15mm hinges,
   #00D30.08, $1.50 ea.
8 - #1 x $\frac{3}{8}$" screws (10pc.),
   #91Z01.02X, $0.80/pack

Note: The screws supplied with the hinges
use a #1 (square) drive. You'll need a small
#1 square drive bit.

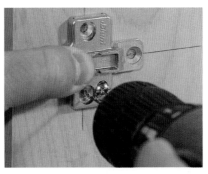

Lay the plate on the marks and drill pilot holes
into the cabinet.

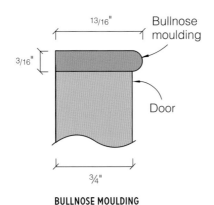

BULLNOSE MOULDING

13/16"

3/16"

Bullnose
moulding

Door

3/4"

a common detail on period furniture
from the 18th and 19th centuries. It's
an easy way to dress up a door or
drawer front.

After the edging's been applied,
it's impossible to sand into the
corners, so begin making the doors
by finish sanding the fronts of the
doors and drawer fronts. Next,
attach the moulding. First apply two
opposite pieces, then fit and attach
the last two pieces.

Use a sharp pencil to mark the
location of the miter cuts. Place the
piece on the miter saw and cut to the
line. You don't always get the cut right
the first time. Make your cut a little
long and nibble away at the miter until
you get a snug fit, then glue and nail
the edges in place. We use Accuset's
micropinner to attach the mouldings.
The 23-gauge pins don't split the
edge, and they leave a hole about
the size of a period on this page.
Putty the holes if you like. Rout off

any overhang on the back side with
a router and straight bit. Finish sand
the backs.

You're ready to hang the doors.
The cups for European cabinet
hinges are usually 35mm or really
close to 1⅜".

Using the instructions supplied
with the hinges, derive a drilling
location for the hinge cup. I've always
drilled hinge cups about 3" or 4" in
from the top and bottom of the door.
This leaves enough room to adjust the
hinge when mounted. The first thing
is to drill the hinge cup holes. Set
your drill press to drill the holes a little
deeper than the cup.

Now transfer the layout holes to
the door on the cabinet. Attach the
mounting plate and screw the hinges
in place. European hinges can be
adjusted in three dimensions: in-out,
up-down and left-right. When the
cabinet is level and plumb, adjust the
hinges to make the doors even.

BUILD THE ROUTER BIT DRAWER

The drawer uses standard
construction. Cut ¼" x ½" rabbets on
the ends of the sides. Cut a ¼" x ¼"
groove in the bottom inside edges of
all the parts to hold the bottom. Glue
and nail the drawer together with the
bottom set into the groove.

After the glue is dry, take apart
the commercial drawer slides, scribe
a line on the sides and attach the
small part of the slide to the drawer
box. Make sure it's flush to the front
of the drawer box. Measure from the
mounting line and add ¾" to that for
the lid, hinges and gap. Measure
that distance down from the inside,
underneath the fixed shelf. Mark the
location and mount the slide. The
slides have two different mounting
holes. The drawer has slots that allow
up and down adjustment, and the
cabinet parts have slots that allow

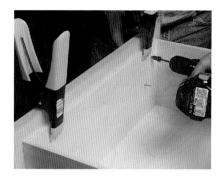

Position the drawer front and place a couple of clamps on the drawer box to hold it in place. Drill countersunk clearance holes into the drawer box and attach the front with 1" screws.

Drill the $\frac{1}{2}$" and $\frac{1}{4}$" holes. Nail in a couple of rails on the inside of the drawer and simply drop the panels in place. The panel for $\frac{1}{2}$"-shank bits is drilled all the way through and the panel for $\frac{1}{4}$"-shank bits is drilled down $\frac{5}{8}$".

Use a stop collar on your drill bit when drilling holes for the shelf pins. I made this drilling jig from shop scrap.

forward/backward adjustment. Insert the drawer into the slides on the cabinet.

Before mounting the front on the drawer box, nail two finish nails through the front of the drawer box until they just protrude from the outside. Place the front against the drawer box and space it so the gaps on the top and bottom are equal. Push the front against the nails in the drawer box and gently push the drawer out. Drill some clearance holes and attach the front.

Now nail on the drawer lid's back rail and attach the lid with two hinges. Drill a 1" hole in the lid so you can lift it easily. Cut out, drill and attach the two router storage inserts.

Finish up the project by drilling a series of 7mm holes for the shelf pins. Make a template from scrap for this. Lee Valley sells metal sleeves for the shelf pins, but I deemed them unnecessary. You could probably get away with using a $\frac{1}{4}$" bit to make these holes, but it makes the pins fit a little sloppy. Attach the back with #6 x $\frac{1}{2}$" flathead screws. Check the fit of all the doors, drawer and shelves, then disassemble all the loose parts for sanding. Apply three coats of clear finish and reassemble all the parts.

SHOP STORAGE CABINET

NO.	ITEM	DIMENSIONS T W L	MATERIAL
2	Sides	$\frac{3}{4}$" x 16" x 68"	Birch ply
2	Top and bottom	$\frac{3}{4}$" x 16" x 23$\frac{1}{2}$"	Birch ply
1	Fixed shelf	$\frac{3}{4}$" x 15$\frac{3}{4}$" x 23"	Birch ply
4	Shelves	$\frac{3}{4}$" x 15$\frac{1}{2}$" x 22$\frac{1}{2}$"	Birch ply
1	Back	$\frac{1}{4}$" x 23$\frac{1}{2}$" x 67$\frac{1}{2}$"	Birch ply
4	Doors*	$\frac{3}{4}$" x 12" x 29$\frac{1}{4}$"	Birch ply
2	Base front and back	$\frac{3}{4}$" x 4" x 23$\frac{1}{2}$"	Birch ply
2	Base sides	$\frac{3}{4}$" x 4" x 14"	Birch ply
1	Cleats for base	$\frac{3}{4}$" x $\frac{3}{4}$" x 96"	Solid wood
4	Leveler blocks	1$\frac{1}{2}$" x 1$\frac{1}{2}$" x 3$\frac{1}{4}$"	Solid wood
1	Support cleat	$\frac{3}{4}$" x 3" x 23$\frac{1}{2}$"	Birch ply
1	Drawer front*	$\frac{3}{4}$" x 9$\frac{3}{8}$" x 24"	Birch ply
2	Drawer sides	$\frac{1}{2}$" x 8" x 15$\frac{1}{2}$"	Baltic birch
2	Drawer front and back	$\frac{1}{2}$" x 8" x 21"	Baltic birch
1	Drawer bottom	$\frac{1}{4}$" x 15" x 21"	Baltic birch
2	Drawer rails	$\frac{1}{2}$" x 1" x 20$\frac{1}{2}$"	Baltic birch
1	Drawer insert slider	$\frac{3}{4}$" x 14$\frac{1}{2}$" x 12"	Birch ply
1	Drawer lid	$\frac{1}{2}$" x 12$\frac{1}{2}$" x 21$\frac{1}{2}$"	Baltic birch
1	Lid back rail	$\frac{1}{2}$" x 3" x 21$\frac{1}{2}$"	Baltic birch

* Finished size with bullnose edging attached

After attaching the slide to the drawer, mark the location of the cabinet part of the slide on the cabinet side. Use a framing square to run a line back from this mark and mount the slide $\frac{1}{16}$" back from the front of the cabinet.

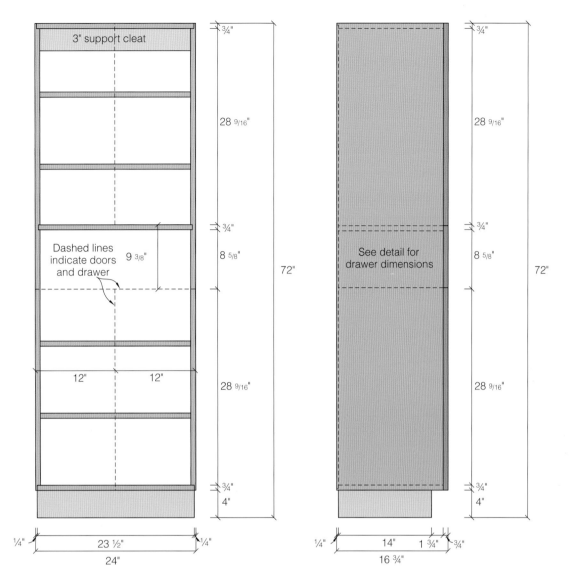

ELEVATION

PROFILE

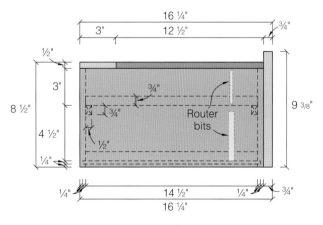

PROFILE OF DRAWER

$30 LUMBER RACK

It doesn't take a lot of time or money
to build a flexible and sturdy rack
for your rough lumber and offcuts.

By Christopher Schwarz

In my family, we still remember the day my old lumber rack collapsed. I was upstairs with the kids when there was a sudden and horrible crash. The two cats ran in four directions; the baby started to wail. It was that loud.

When I went down the steps to the shop it looked like a giant box of toothpicks had spilled everywhere. It seems the metal brackets I had bolted to the walls had reached their limit. One of the brackets gave way and everything came tumbling down.

So when I went to rebuild, I wanted something stout, simple and cheap. I pored over books and magazines for ideas, borrowed a few and made some changes. Here's what I came up with:

PIPE AND 2X4S

Essentially, the backbones of this rack are 2x4s bolted on edge to the double top plate and the bottom plate of my shop wall. The bottom edges of your 2x4s should rest on something solid. In most shops, that means running them to the floor. In my shop, the lower half of my wall is cinder block, so I set the 2x4s on those. To hold the lumber, I drilled $7/8$"-diameter holes through the 2x4s at 4" intervals and at a 5° angle. Then I inserted 12" lengths of $1/2$" galvanized pipe in the holes. The $1/2$" pipe, available in the plumbing section, actually has an exterior diameter of just under $7/8$", so it fits nicely.

Before you get started, there are a couple things to consider when building this rack for your shop. First, I used 12" lengths of pipe because I rarely have anything in my rack wider than 8". Wider lumber needs longer pipes. Plus, this rack is right over my jointer, so I didn't want the pipes to stick out any more than necessary.

PREP YOUR LUMBER

I bought a single Southern yellow pine 2x8 that was 8' long for this project. By ripping it down the middle and crosscutting it into 4' lengths, I got four 4'-long 2x4s. If you don't have Southern yellow pine in your area, try vertical-grade fir or any other tough construction timber.

I ran the parts over my jointer and through my thickness planer to get them straight and true. They finished out at $13/8$" thick and 3" wide.

CLEARANCE HOLES

The first thing to do is taper the ends of the boards and drill the clearance holes to bolt them to your wall. I used $41/2$"-long lag screws and $13/8$"-diameter washers. You want the holes in your boards to be clearance holes — that is, you want the threads on the lag bolt biting only into the wood in the wall.

Examine the diagrams and you'll see that the easiest way to accomplish this is to taper the ends as shown. I used a band saw to cut the taper and cleaned up the cut with a hand plane.

The holes for the lag screws should be located so the screws enter into the top plate and bottom plate of your stud wall. The location of the hole in the diagram is for a stud wall with a double top plate. Your wall may be different.

Now drill a $13/8$"-diameter recess for the washer — it only needs to be deep enough to seat the washer. Then drill a $1/2$"-diameter hole in the middle of the recess. Repeat this process on the other end of the board and on the other boards.

EVEN MORE DRILL PRESS WORK

Now, drill the holes for the galvanized pipe. Chuck a $7/8$" Forstner bit in your drill press and set the table at a 5° angle. This slight angle will use gravity to keep your lumber in the rack.

Because the table is at a 5° angle, it's easier to align your holes using the rim of the Forstner bit instead of the center spur.

PHOTO BY AL PARRISH

Clamp all the pieces of wood together with the ends aligned and make a mark every 4" across all four boards.

Now drill the holes through the boards. Because the table is at 5°, it's difficult to get the center of the bit to hit your line. So don't. Instead, align your holes so the edge of the Forstner bit touches the line instead of the center. It's much easier.

PIPES AND INSTALLATION

I bought galvanized pipe and cut it to length using a hack saw. Dress the ends using a grinder or file to remove the rough spots. Now get ready to install your rack.

Use a level to ensure your layout lines are plumb and parallel. Mark where the bolts will go and drill pilot holes for the lag screws. Fasten the

lag screws to the wall using a ratchet.

I think you'll see quickly how nice it is to have a flexible rack like this. You can reserve a couple pipes for short scraps, and add more pipes or braces as your lumber pile expands.

Clamp all your pieces together when laying out the holes. This is faster and more accurate.

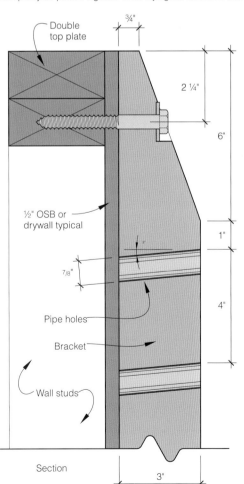

Double top plate

¾"

2 ¼"

6"

½" OSB or drywall typical

1"

⅛"

⅞"

Pipe holes

4"

Bracket

Wall studs

Section

3"

$30 LUMBER RACK					
NO.	**ITEM**	**DIMENSIONS (INCHES)**			**NOTES**
		T	**W**	**L**	
4	Vertical braces	1⅜	3	48	Yellow pine
16	Pipes	½ID	12		Galvanized pipe
8	Lag screws	4½			
8	Washers	1⅜ dia.			

ID=interior diameter; the exterior diameter of this pipe is just under ⅞".

I-BEAM WORK ISLAND

By Nick Engler

This bit of plywood engineering can serve as a stout base for almost any kind of workbench or shop table.

I seem to be setting up a lot of workshops lately. So far, our little band of pioneer aviators have set up two shops in Dayton, Ohio, where we are manufacturing the parts of Wright airplanes and assembling them, and a third shop in Kitty Hawk, N.C., which serves as a repair station to take care of the inevitable wing-dings these primitive aircraft suffer when you fly them. And because the heart of any good shop is its workbench, I seem to be building a lot of benches as well.

With time and materials at a premium, I've developed a simple and economical design for a bench that

we use in these shops. It's strong, true, offers loads of storage and with the addition of a few casters, can serve as a movable work island. We find this last feature especially important, because we must constantly reconfigure the shops as the Wright airplanes grow during construction.

A SANDWICH OF I-BEAMS

The base of the bench is made entirely of ¾" plywood. The plywood parts form three "I-beams," each beam consisting of two caps and a center beam. The shelves and dividers in the

bench make up two small I-beams – the shelves become the caps and the dividers are the beams. These are sandwiched together inside a large I-beam that consists of the two workbench ends (the caps) and a center divider (the beam). The resulting structure is very strong.

It's also very true, another important characteristic of a good bench. The benchtop should be flat if you are going to use it for precision work. I cut up the plywood sheets so the factory edge – the outside edge of the plywood as it comes from the factory – is the top of the center divider

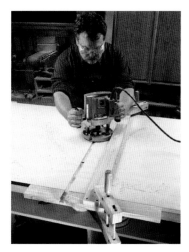

I make utility benchtops by laminating two layers of particleboard between two sheets of tempered hardboard. This doubles the life of the benchtop. When the hardboard surface facing up becomes dirty and stained, remove the screws from the cleats, turn the top over and replace the screws.

and the top of the two ends. As a rule, factory edges are pretty straight even if they appear a bit rough. When I attach the benchtop to the base and draw it down tight, the factory edges brace the top perfectly flat.

MAKING THE SANDWICH

The bench can be made almost any size – it's only limited by the size of the sheet materials you use. The dimensions shown in the plans are just suggestions – make the bench whatever size you need. Most craftsmen, I know, will immediately want to make the top a bit higher – 34" is somewhat low for a work surface for most people. But it works for me because I'm a short guy.

Once you've decided on the overall dimensions of the bench, cut the plywood parts and rout a few dados to help you assemble and align the parts. Cut the bench ends with three intersecting dados in each – one vertical dado to hold the center divider and two horizontal dadoes to hold the shelves. Make each of these dadoes $\frac{3}{4}$" wide and $\frac{1}{4}$" deep. Also make $\frac{1}{4}$"-deep dados in the shelves to hold the shelving dividers. Then rout horizontal dadoes in the center divider, $\frac{3}{4}$" wide and $\frac{1}{8}$" deep. You must make these dados on both sides of the center divider – that's why they're only $\frac{1}{8}$" deep.

Assemble the base parts with glue and screws (use pocket screws to attach the shelves to the center divider). To make sure that the top edges of the ends and center divider remain true to one another while the glue dries, stretch two strings diagonally from the outside corner of one cap to the outside corner of the other.

The two strings should cross the base, forming a large "X." The strings should just kiss each other where they cross over the center divider, and they should rest lightly on the edge of the divider. If the strings aren't laying properly, level the parts of the workbench's base with small wedges and shims before the glue dries.

TOPPING THE SANDWICH

You can put a variety of tops on this base – I've used both butcher-block tops made from rock maple and less-expensive tops laminated from particleboard and hardboard. Any hard material about 1 $\frac{1}{2}$" thick will do. To attach the top, screw wooden cleats to the center divider and the ends, flush with the top edges. Position the top over the base and drive screws through the cleats and up into your top piece.

You can customize this work island to serve your own needs with vises, work lamps and other workbench accessories. The first thing I usually add are swivel casters to make the bench easy to move. If you want more shelves, drill $\frac{1}{4}$"-diameter holes in the ends and shelving dividers for shelving support pins, then rest the shelves on the pins. To add drawers, mount guide rails to the ends and divider, then build wooden boxes to slide on the rails.

Rout the dados using a T-square jig. The one shown here is designed to cut 3/4"-wide dados. First mark on your work the location of the dados. Line up the dado that's plowed in the T-square jig with your lines. Clamp the jig in place, set the depth of the cut on your router and make the dado.

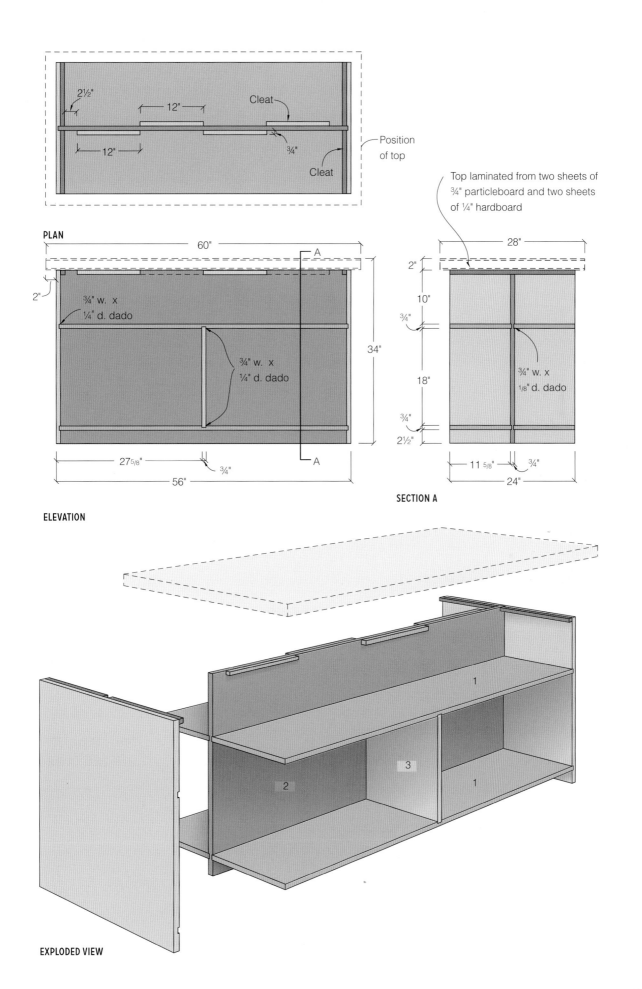

2½"

12"

Cleat

12"

¾"

Cleat

Position
of top

PLAN

Top laminated from two sheets of
¾" particleboard and two sheets
of ¼" hardboard

60"

A

28"

2"

2"

10"

¾"

¾" w. x
¼" d. dado

34"

18"

¾" w. x
¼" d. dado

¾" w. x
⅛" d. dado

¾"

2½"

27⅝"

¾"

56"

A

11⅝"

¾"

24"

SECTION A

ELEVATION

1

2

3

1

EXPLODED VIEW

SECTION 7

OTHER IDEAS

AUXILIARY BAND SAW TABLE

The cure for the incredible shrinking work surface isn't a new band saw.

By Nick Engler

There I was, perfectly content with my miniscule14"-square band saw table, not even aware that there was something far, far better. Then I took a job teaching wood craftsmanship at the University of Cincinnati, and life was never the same. I walked into class and was smitten by a classic Tannewitz band saw. This industrial-sized baby had 20" wheels, more cast iron than an armory and—best of all—a table that was bigger than most workshops. I was seduced by the ease with which you could handle workpieces of all sizes on that expansive surface.

If you've never worked on a large band saw, you'd be surprised and delighted by how it supports and balances the work. It also adds to the safety and accuracy of operations that involve large boards. If you use your band saw for ripping and resawing, the large table mounts a longer fence, making those chores easier.

No longer satisfied with a small work surface, I studied my own band saw and was amazed to find it has room for a much larger table. Fact is, almost all band saws that are made for small workshops will accommodate bigger tables. In most cases you can easily triple the size of your work surface—I expanded my table from 196 square inches to 576 square inches!

To expand the work surface on a band saw, make an auxiliary table. The simplest way to do this is to cut a piece of plywood or particleboard to the size you want. Drill a hole for the blade no more than 10" from the front edge. Cut a saw kerf from an outside edge to the hole. Attach this fixture to the saw by bolting it to the fence rails, if your machine has them. If not, fashion wooden clamps to hook over the bottom edge of the metal table and screw them to the underside of the auxiliary table.

While this design works well, it has a drawback. It decreases the vertical capacity of the saw by the thickness of the auxiliary table. You'll find yourself removing the fixture when sawing thick stock or resawing wide boards—the very occasions when an expanded table is most needed.

To solve this problem, I made the auxiliary band saw table you see here to extend the existing table, rather than cover it. The extension is made from medium density fiberboard (MDF) and edged with

hardwood. I covered the surfaces with plastic laminate to make them more durable, although this isn't absolutely necessary. The cutout in the middle of the extension is made to the same size and shape as the band saw's table, so the extension rests on the old fence rails. If your band saw doesn't have rails, bolt hardwood cleats to the edges. Rabbet the extension so the top surface will be flush with the table. I cut my rabbets a little deeper than they needed to be, then shimmed the extension with strips of masking tape to get it dead even with the table. Secure the extension by bolting it to the rails (or cleats).

You can make this extension any size you want, but don't extend the table more than 4" at the front. Any more, and it may become difficult to reach the blade while you're working. Don't make the table rectangular—knock off the corners to prevent painful bumps and scrapes. To mount a fence and other jigs, rout slots in the extension at the front and the back.

I've gotten so fond of this extended work surface that I can't imagine how I ever did without it. It's not exactly a Tannewitz, but it's the next best thing.

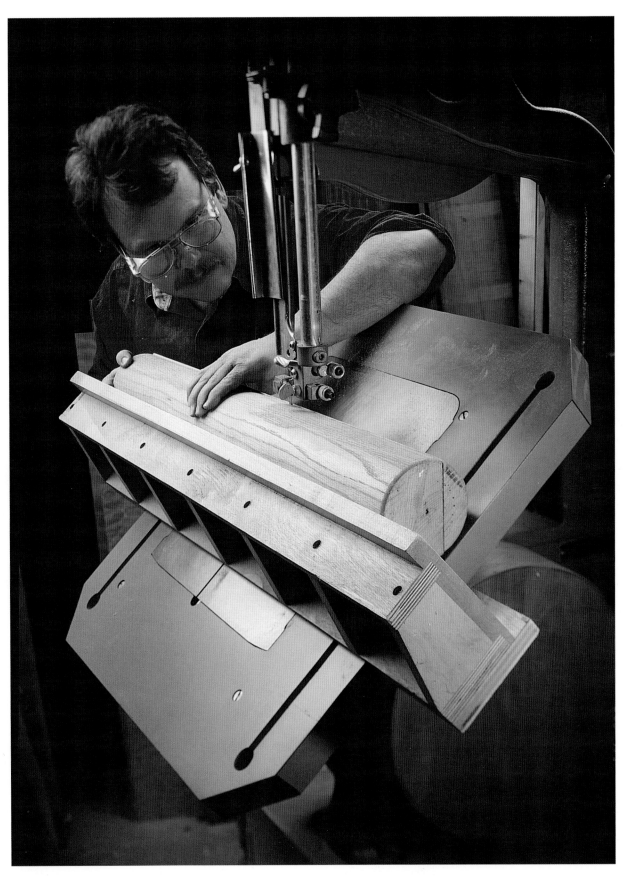

PHOTOS BY AL PARRISH

The tie bar holds the auxiliary table rigid after allowing space for the fixture to be slipped over the blade. Use a wooden clamp to hold the fixture's surface flat while you tighten the tie bar.

The expansive surface of the band saw table gives you extra support when you need it, such as when cutting large ovals.

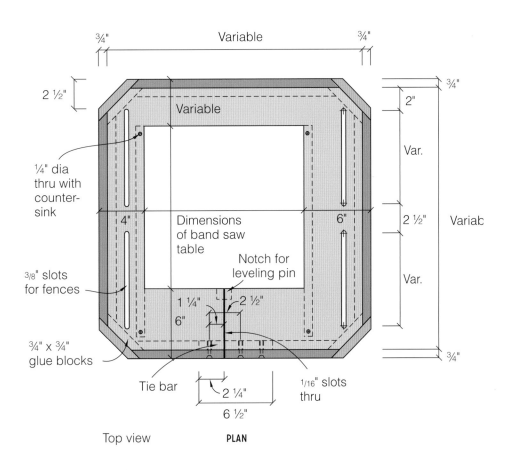

¾" Variable ¾"

2 ½"

¼" dia
thru with
counter-
sink

Variable

4"

Dimensions
of band saw
table

Notch for
leveling pin

6"

¾" ¾"

2"

Var.

2 ½"

Var.

¾"

Variab

3/8" slots
for fences

¾" x ¾"
glue blocks

1 ¼"
6"

2 ½"

Tie bar

2 ¼"

6 ½"

1/16" slots
thru

Top view   **PLAN**

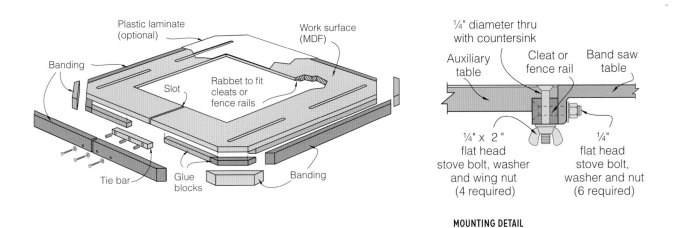

Plastic laminate
(optional)

Work surface
(MDF)

Banding

Slot

Rabbet to fit
cleats or
fence rails

Tie bar

Glue
blocks

Banding

¼" diameter thru
with countersink

Auxiliary
table

Cleat or
fence rail

Band saw
table

¼" x 2 "
flat head
stove bolt, washer
and wing nut
(4 required)

¼"
flat head
stove bolt,
washer and nut
(6 required)

MOUNTING DETAIL

DRILL PRESS TABLE

Turn your metalworking drill press table into
a woodworking table in just a few hours and with only
a few dollars worth of materials.

By David Thiel

Despite the fact that your drill press is designed mostly for poking holes in sheet metal, it has many uses in a woodshop. It's a mortiser, a spindle sander, it bores huge holes and – of course – drills holes at perfect right angles to the table. Because the table on most drill presses is designed for metalworking, it's hardly suited for these tasks. So I built this add-on table with features that will turn your drill press into a far friendlier machine:

• First, it has a fence that slides forwards and backwards as well as left and right on either side of the drill press's column. This last feature also uses the drill press's tilting table feature with the auxiliary table for angled drilling.

• Built-in stops (both left and right) that attach to the fence for procedures that need to be replicated, such as doweling or chain-drilling mortises.

• Hold-downs that can be used on the fence or on the table for any procedure.

The sizes given in the cutting list are for a 14" drill press, with the center falling 9" from the rear edge of the

table, with a 2" notch in the back to straddle the column. Adjust the center location and overall size of the table to match your particular machine.

BUILD THE BASE

The base platform for the table is made from ¾" plywood, which should be void-free. Again, adjust the size as necessary to fit your drill press. First

you need to get the table ready for the T-track, which is what holds the fence and hold-downs in place. Start by locating the four recessed holes that allow the T-slot mechanism to slip into the track without disassembling the mechanism. Each hole is 1½" in diameter and ⅜" deep.

Next, locate the grooves in the center of the holes and use a router with a ¾"-wide straight bit to cut the

The grooves for the T-slot track allow the fence to be used left-to-right and front-to-back on the table to take advantage of the tilting feature of the existing table.

After cutting the hole with a jigsaw, the opening is rabbeted using a bearing-piloted router bit. Then chisel the corners square and fit the replaceable insert plates tightly into the rabbet. Make a couple extra insert plates.

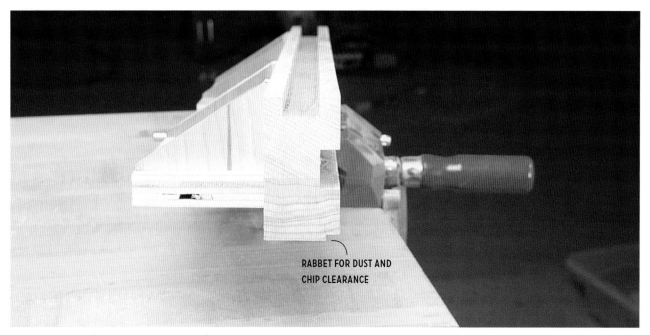

RABBET FOR DUST AND
CHIP CLEARANCE

The fence is made of a sturdy, stable hardwood. Cut a groove the length of the top and face of the fence. The grooves hold T-slot tracks, which can be used for stops, hold-downs and other accessories.

grooves to a ³⁄₈" depth. The T-slot track should fit into the grooves with the top surface just below that of the plywood table. The grooves should be as parallel as possible to one another to allow smooth movement of the fence.

Now cut the hole for the 4" x 4" replaceable insert plate. First mark its location on your table, then mark in from that line by ³⁄₈" to locate your cutting line. Drill clearance holes in two corners of the inner square, then use a jigsaw to cut out the center piece. Next, determine the thickness of the material you will use for your insert plate (the ³⁄₈"-thick Baltic birch we used is actually metric and shy of ³⁄₈"). We used a ³⁄₈" piloted rabbeting bit in a router set to a height to hold the insert flush to the top surface of the table.

While your jigsaw is still out, locate, mark and cut out the notch in the back of the table. This allows the table to move closer to the drill press' post and also to tilt without interference.

As a final friendly touch on the table, I used a ³⁄₈" roundover bit in my router to soften all the edges on the table, both top and bottom. You'll get fewer splinters if you do this.

A FLEXIBLE FENCE

The fence is the heart of the table, and the wood should be chosen for durability and straightness. Quartersawn hardwood, carefully surfaced and planed, will do nicely. After cutting the fence to size, use a dado stack to mill two ³⁄₈"-deep by ³⁄₄"-wide grooves in the fence. The first is centered on the top surface of the fence, and as in the grooves in the base platform, a piece of T-slot track should be used to confirm that the groove is deep enough to allow the track to fit just below the surface of the wood. The second groove is then cut centered on the face of the fence.

One other bit of table saw work is a ¹⁄₈" x ¹⁄₄"-wide rabbet on the inside bottom edge of the fence. The rabbet keeps debris away from the fence, so your work will fit tightly against it.

One option that I considered was adding an indexing tape measure on the fence. Every time the table is moved, the tape would need to be readjusted to zero, and for the infrequent use the tape would see I decided against it. A stick-on tape can easily be added to the fence face if that's more to your personal taste and needs.

Unlike the fence on a router table, the fence on a drill press table won't see a lot of lateral pressure. So the

DRILL PRESS TABLE						
NO.	LET	ITEM	DIMENSIONS (INCHES)			MATERIAL
			T	W	L	
1	A	Platform	³⁄₄	20	29	Plywood
1	B	Fence	1½	2³⁄₄	30	Hardwood
2	C	Fence base plates	³⁄₄	3	9	Plywood
4	D	Base plate braces	³⁄₄	3	1⁷⁄₈	Hardwood
2	E	Stops	³⁄₄	2½	2½	Hardwood
2	F	Hold-down plates	³⁄₄	1½	3	Hardwood
1	G	Insert plate	³⁄₈	4	4	Plywood
2		Part #88F05.02, DeStaCo clamps – $21.50 ea.				
6		Part #12K79.22 24" T-slot track – $9.30 ea.				
8		Part #00M51.02 1¹⁄₈" 3-wing knobs – $1.80 ea.				
8		Part #05J21.15 T-nuts – $3.10 for 10				

All hardware available from Lee Valley 800-871-8158 or www.leevalley.com

ILLUSTRATION BY JIM STUARD

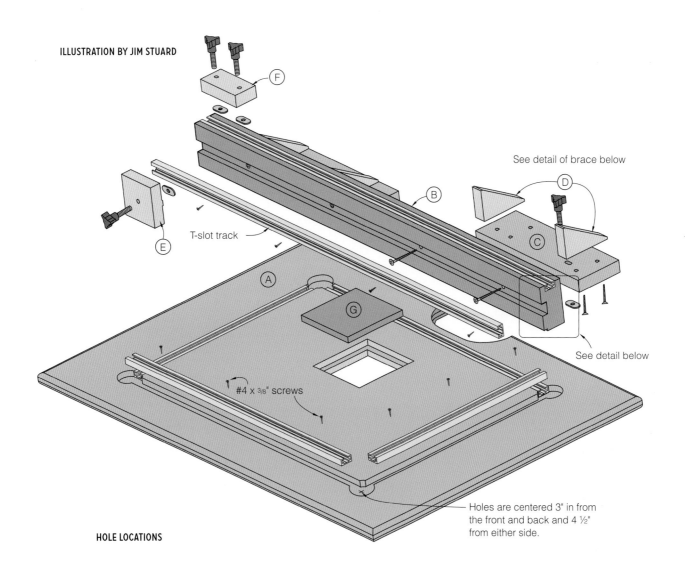

See detail of brace below

T-slot track

#4 x 3/8" screws

Holes are centered 3" in from the front and back and 4 ½" from either side.

See detail below

HOLE LOCATIONS

Location of base plate braces
Right side shown, left is mirror image

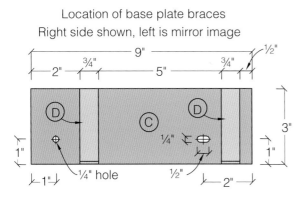

¼" hole

PLAN DETAIL OF HOLE LOCATIONS FOR BASE PLATE

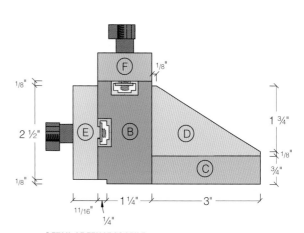

DETAIL OF FENCE PROFILE

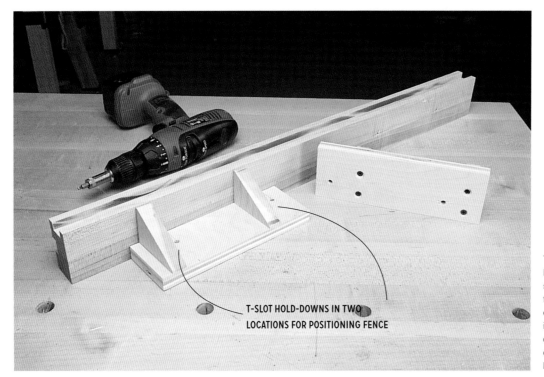

T-SLOT HOLD-DOWNS IN TWO
LOCATIONS FOR POSITIONING FENCE

The fence is supported by two simple brackets screwed to the rear of the fence. The location of the triangular braces is important to the track orientation, so follow the diagrams carefully for location.

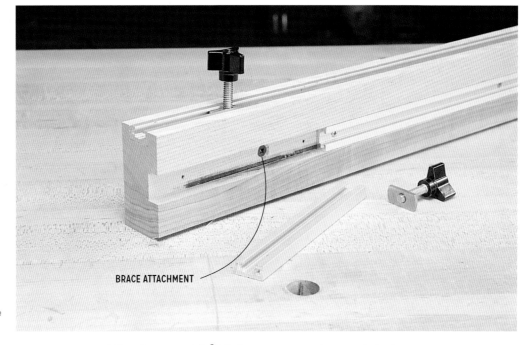

Install the T-slot tracks in the grooves with flat head screws countersunk into the track. The braces are attached to the fence by screwing through the face groove prior to attaching the T-slot track.

BRACE ATTACHMENT

main purpose of the braces is to hold the fence square to the table at the drilling point. In my case I've also given the braces the job of mounting the fence to the table.

Start by cutting the two base plates and the four braces to size. The braces are triangles with the bottom edge 3" long and the adjoining right angle edge 1⅞" long. The third side is determined by simply connecting the corners. Locate the braces on the base plates according to the diagrams and pre-drill and countersink ³⁄₁₆"-diameter holes in the base plates to attach the braces to the plates.

To mount the support braces to the fence, again refer to the diagrams to locate the proper spacing on the fence. Then drill and countersink screw holes through the face groove in the fence. Clamp the brace to the fence and screw the brace in place.

With the braces attached to the fence, use the T-slot fastener locations on the diagrams as a starting point for drilling the holes in the base plates, but check the location against your table for the best fit. Two holes are drilled in each plate to allow the fence to be moved to the perpendicular position (either to the right or left of the quill), by simply relocating one of the T-slot fasteners. Check each hole in relationship to that position.

ADD THE TRACK

Assuming you purchased the 24" lengths of track listed in the cutting list, you should be able to cut the tracks for the table first, leaving

T-SLOT GUIDES ALLOW HOLD-DOWNS TO BE USED ANYWHERE ON THE T-TRACK.

The hold-downs and stops are made from ³⁄₄" hardwood. To make the guide that holds the stops squarely on the fence, cut a ¹⁄₁₆" x 1¹⁄₈" rabbet on both sides of the inside face using your table saw.

fall-off that can be added to the two remaining full length tracks to give you the necessary 30" lengths of track for the fence. When attaching the track, first pilot drill the hole in the center of the track (a groove is provided in the track to simplify that operation), then use a countersink to widen the hole to accommodate a #4 x ⁵⁄₈" flat-head screw. Keeping the screw heads flush to the inner surface of the track will make the stops and hold-downs move much easier.

Stops and hold-downs designed for use in T-tracks make the drill press most useful. The stops are square blocks of wood with one face milled to leave an indexing strip that fits into the slot on the T-slot track. By using the saw to cut tall but shallow rabbets on two edges of each block, the stops are completed fairly easily. For safety, cut the rabbet on a longer 2¹⁄₂" wide piece of wood, then crosscut the stops afterward. The T-slot fasteners are simply inserted into a ¹⁄₄" hole drilled in the center of each stop block.

The hold-downs are blocks of wood with DeStaCo clamps screwed to the top. Each block is drilled for two T-slot fasteners. While the DeStaCos are good for this application, they

aren't as versatile as I wanted. I replaced the threaded-rod plunger with longer all-thread (¹⁄₄" x 36) to provide maximum benefit from the clamps. The rubber tip of the plunger is important to the function of the clamp, and if you can manage to reuse the existing tip, do so. If not, I found rubber stoppers in a variety of sizes in the local Sears hardware store.

To install the stopper, carefully drill

a ¹⁄₄"-diameter hole two-thirds of the way into the stopper and then you should be able to screw it to the rod easily.

The table should attach easily to your existing drill press table using four lag bolts countersunk flush into the surface of the auxiliary table. Once attached, you should find that the auxiliary table gives you more support and versatility than the metal one.

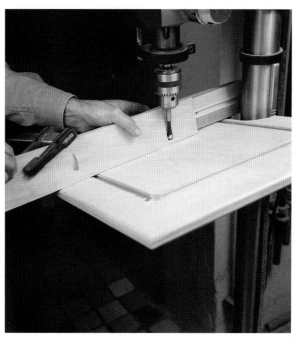

By utilizing the tilting action of the drill-presses' original table, drill angles holes is fairly simple.

DOWNDRAFT SANDING TABLE

This project can turn a dust-filled shopinto a pleasant work area, and the cardboard ducting is a snap to build.

By Jim Stuard

If you've ever sanded without dust collection in an enclosed space, you've probably seen the "cloud" that forms in your shop as you work. And if your shop is in a basement, you've probably heard from the person who does the dusting that the central air system has evenly distributed your sawdust throughout the entire house. Take heart, you can nix these two problems with one project.

A downdraft sanding table connected to a small dust collector will give you a place to sand small- to medium-sized parts and will eliminate virtually all your sanding dust.

The table is essentially a two-foot square box with a bottom and some ribs. On top of that is a sheet of strategically cut and folded cardboard with sloping sides that directs dust to a hole in the center and

in turn out a coffee can port to your collector. The work surface is made from a lighting grid (called diffuser) for a florescent ceiling fixture (cost: about $2) that is covered by an open-mesh carpet pad. The grid is reinforced by two steel bars underneath.

These grids are tougher than they look. As long as you don't abuse them all day, they can take a pounding. However, because of the way they are made, you can't cut them into a perfect square. To remedy this, I simply cut the box sides to suit the odd size. That's why the box is a little longer one way than the other.

Begin construction by ripping out the 6"-wide side material. Cut the sides to length with miters on the ends. Use a biscuit joiner to cut one slot in the center of each miter. Cut a $\frac{3}{8}$" x $\frac{3}{8}$" rabbet in the top edge of

the sides. Cut a $\frac{1}{4}$" x $\frac{1}{2}$" rabbet in the bottom edge of the sides for the box bottom. Glue the box together with a band clamp. Set the bottom in place to square up the box while the glue dries. Cut the wooden bracing to size and then to shape as shown in the diagram. Then attach the bracing and bottom with screws. Cut the hole for the dust collection hose now. As an aside, my dust collector has 4" diameter hose. I also recently discovered that baby formula cans and most 14 and 16 ounce coffee cans are just under 4" in diameter. This makes perfect connections for a 4" dust collector hose. With a 4" hole cut in the side according to the diagram, it's a simple matter of cutting up a can with tin snips to leave tabs that can be screwed to the inside of the box. Leave at least 2" of can

protruding from the box to attach the dust collection hose.

With the box assembled, you can see that the rabbet in the top edge of the sides leaves about $\frac{1}{8}$" all the way around when the plastic grid is inserted. This accommodates the carpet pad that's later glued to the grid. Now cut notches for the steel bars that will reinforce your lighting grid. Mark out $\frac{1}{4}$" x $\frac{1}{4}$" x $\frac{1}{4}$" notches in the sides according to the diagram, just below the rabbet in the top edge.

Build the ducting from cardboard because it's lightweight, easy to

shape and strong enough for this application. Cut the three pieces of ducting according to the diagram. Mark and cut the bends in the large piece and cut a 4" hole in the center. Place it in the box and check the fit against the bracing. Now place the trapezoidal ducting in place and check the fit. If all works well, tape the small pieces in place. This effectively holds the ducting assembly together and provides great airflow. Hook up the dust collection and check to see that the ducting is seating down on the bracing properly. If you want, caulk

the joint around the opening in the cardboard.

Finish the project by cutting out a sheet of open-mesh carpet padding a couple inches bigger than the plastic grid. Apply contact cement to the pad and the grid. Carefully apply the pad to the grid and fold the overhang over the edge of the grid, for a snug fit into the rabbet. A snug fit dampens vibration from the sander and keeps small parts from moving around while being sanded.

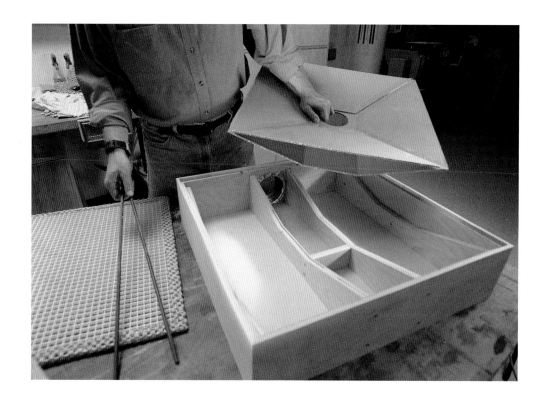

DOWNDRAFT SANDING TABLE			
NO.	ITEM	DIMENSIONS T W L	MATERIAL
2	Long sides	$\frac{3}{4}$" x 6" x 24$\frac{1}{2}$"	Plywood
2	Short sides	$\frac{3}{4}$" x 6" x 24$\frac{5}{8}$"	Plywood
1	Bottom	$\frac{1}{4}$" x 24" x 24$\frac{1}{8}$"	Plywood
4	Braces	$\frac{3}{4}$" x 4$\frac{13}{16}$" x 23$\frac{1}{8}$"	Plywood
1	Small bracing	$\frac{3}{4}$" x 2$\frac{1}{4}$" x 4$\frac{1}{2}$"	Plywood

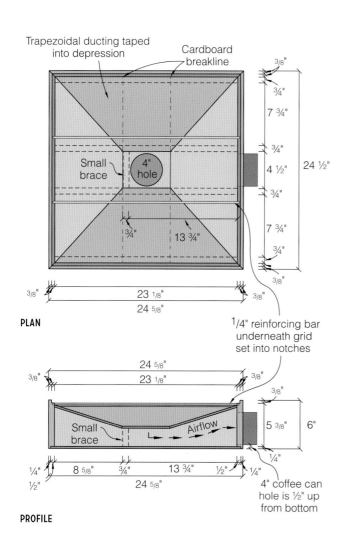

Trapezoidal ducting taped into depression

Cardboard breakline

3/8"
3/4"
7 3/4"
3/4"
4 1/2"
3/4"
7 3/4"
3/8"

24 1/2"

Small brace

4" hole

3/4"

13 3/4"

3/8"   23 1/8"   3/8"
24 5/8"

PLAN

1/4" reinforcing bar underneath grid set into notches

24 5/8"
3/8"   23 1/8"   3/8"

Small brace

Airflow

3/8"
5 3/8"   6"
1/4"

1/4"   8 5/8"   3/4"   13 3/4"   1/2"   1/4"
1/2"
24 5/8"

PROFILE

4" coffee can hole is 1/2" up from bottom

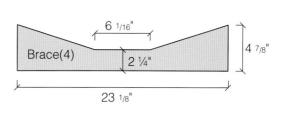

6 1/16"

Brace(4)   2 1/4"   4 7/8"

23 1/8"

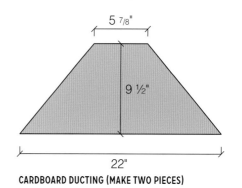

5 7/8"

9 1/2"

22"

CARDBOARD DUCTING (MAKE TWO PIECES)

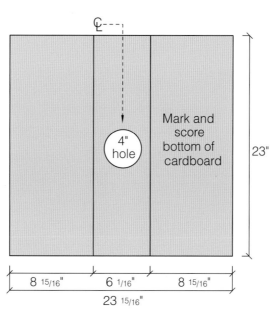

C̶L

4" hole

Mark and score bottom of cardboard

23"

8 15/16"   6 1/16"   8 15/16"
23 15/16"

CARDBOARD DUCTING (MAKE ONE PIECE)

DOVETAIL JIG

Save yourself years of practice with this incredible jig that helps you hand-cut

By Jim Stuard

Years ago when I first learned to cut dovetails, my first joints weren't things of beauty. Sometimes there were more shims than pins. Over time, my work got better and faster. But despite the improvement in my skills, I still had trouble cutting tails or pins consistently, especially if I got out of practice.

This jig allows you to make great dovetails on your first day. The idea came to me when I was building a Shaker step stool using hand-cut dovetails. I made a jig that fit over the end of a board to guide my saw through the cut and provide a perfect tail. The jig didn't cut pins and worked only on $^3/_4$"-thick boards. I guess I wasn't thinking big that day.

A few weeks later it came to me: Why not build a jig that cuts both tails and pins and is adjustable to a variety of thicknesses? So I made this jig. From the first joint I cut using it, I got airtight joints. It was very cool.

This jig uses a 9° cutting angle. Woodworking books say that 9° is intended more for softwoods than hardwoods (which use a 7° angle) but I thought it a good compromise. You can build this jig entirely by hand, but I cheated and used a table saw for a couple of the precise angle cuts. Let your conscience be your guide.

One of this jig's peculiarities is that you'll sometimes have to cut right on the pencil line. As designed, this jig works best with Japanese-style ryoba saws on material from $^3/_8$" to $^3/_4$" thick. Use the saw's ripping teeth when making your cuts. You could modify this jig to accommodate Western saws, but you'd have to take a lot of the set out of the teeth so as not to tear up the faces of the jig. The set of a saw's teeth basically allows you to "steer" a blade through a cut. This jig does all the steering. You just have to press the gas.

1 Begin by sandwiching three pieces of wood. This part is made from two pieces of $^3/_4$" × 6" × 36" plywood with a piece of 1" × 1" × 36" solid wood centered between. Use a spacer to index the center precisely in the middle of the larger panels. Glue and nail the sandwich together.

2 Set your saw's blade to 9° and crosscut the end of the sandwich while it's flat on the saw. Next, tilt the blade back to square and set the miter gauge to 9° as shown above. You can use the angled end of the sandwich to set your miter gauge. Lay out a center line down the middle of the sandwich and mark from the end of the line about 3½". Use a sliding T-bevel to transfer the angle to the flat side. This yields a jig that will let you cut dovetails in material as narrow as 3" wide. Any narrower and you'll have to shorten the jig. Lay the extrusion flat on the saw table and cut to the line. The jig will be a little narrower on the other side, but that's OK.

3 Attach the ½" × 4¼" × 6" faces to the ends of the jig with nails and glue. Use a ryoba saw to start the cuts to open up the channels in the jig. Use a coping saw to cut out the part of the ends that cover the little channels in the sandwich (see left and center figures below). Note, the blade is perpendicular to prevent binding on the jig itself. Clean up with a rasp and sandpaper.

4 Lay out and drill 5⁄16" holes as shown in the diagram. These accommodate the flanged insert nuts for the thumb screws. Attach the flanged inserts using a hex key.

5 Using contact cement, attach 120-grit sandpaper to the same side of the inside channel, on both sides of the jig.

6 Doctor up a couple of $1/4$"–20 T-nuts by pounding over the set tines and grinding off a little of the threaded barrels. With some two-part epoxy, attach some $1/8$"-thick wooden pads to the face of the T-nuts. When the epoxy is set, sand the pads to fit the T-nuts. Run your thumbscrews through the flanged inserts and attach the T-nut/pads to the thumbscrews with some thread-locking compound (available at any automotive parts store). Finish the jig by attaching something slick to the faces. I used some UHMW (ultra-high molecular weight) plastic self-stick sheeting. It's $1/16$" thick, and if you wear out the material on a face, you just peel off the old material and stick on some new. You could just as easily use some wax on the wood faces. You'll just have to sand them flat, eventually.

 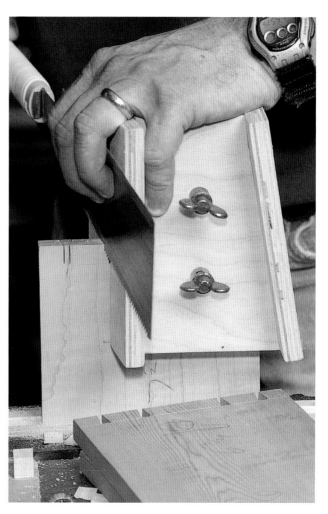

7 Using the jig couldn't be simpler. I cut tails first. That's a personal choice, but this jig will work well whether you're cutting tails or pins first. The layout is a little simpler than freehand. All you do is mark the depth of the cut with a cutting gauge and lay out the spacing for the tails on the end of the board. Use the pencil marks to cut out the tails, and when you get the waste cleaned out, use the tail end of the board to lay out the pins. Use a sharp pencil for marking, then cut out the pins. Check the fit of the pins to the tails, using a piece of scrap as a hammer block across the whole joint. If they're a little big, do some fitting with a four-in-hand rasp. The joint should be snug, but not so tight that it cracks the tail board when hammering the joint together.

INCHES (MILLIMETERS)

REFERENCE	QUANTITY	PART	STOCK	THICKNESS (MM)	WIDTH (MM)	LENGTH (MM)
A	2	sides	plywood	$^{3}/_{4}$ (19)	6 (152)	36 (914)
B	1	center piece	poplar	1 (25)	1 (25)	36 (914)
C	2	faces	plywood	$^{1}/_{2}$ (13)	$4^{1}/_{4}$ (108)	6 (152)
D	2	wooden pads		$^{1}/_{8}$ (3)		

HARDWARE

2	13mm flanged insert nuts	item #32025, $6.99/pack of 8	Rockler, www.rockler.com
2	$^{1}/_{4}$"–20 (6mm–20) thumbscrews		
	3"-wide (76mm-wide) UHMW self-stick tape	item #16L65, $22.99	Woodcraft, www.woodcraft.com
2	$^{1}/_{4}$"–20 (6mm–20) T-nuts	Item #130226, $250 for 10	Woodcraft, www.woodcraft.com

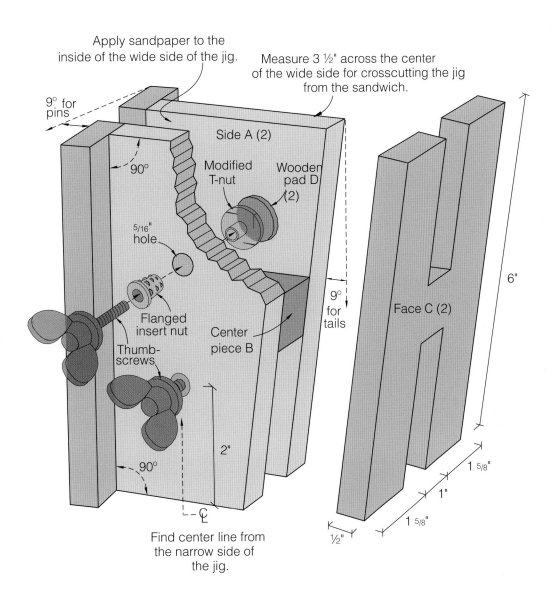

Apply sandpaper to the inside of the wide side of the jig.

Measure 3 ½" across the center of the wide side for crosscutting the jig from the sandwich.

9° for pins

90°

Side A (2)

Modified T-nut

Wooden pad D (2)

5/16" hole

Flanged insert nut

Thumb-screws

Center piece B

9° for tails

Face C (2)

6"

2"

90°

C̵L

Find center line from the narrow side of the jig.

1 5/8"

1"

1 5/8"

½"

CIRCLE-CUTTING FIXTURE FOR THE BAND SAW

If you've got a penny and some scrap wood, you can make this fixture in 30 minutes.

By Jim Stack

This fixture uses a sliding dovetail to hold the sliding arm in place. The arm is locked in place using a T-nut, a finger bolt and a penny.

Cut the parts as listed in the cutting bill. Cut the bevels on the top plates and the sliding arm. Set the top plates and the sliding arm on the base. Attach the plates to the base, making sure the arm slides easily between the top plates.

Set the fixture on the band saw and mark the locations of the runner and the bottom cleat. Then, attach the runner and the cleat to the base.

Drill a ³⁄₄"-diameter hole in the center of the dovetail groove in the base. Drill this hole deep enough to accept the thickness of the T-nut shoulder and the penny. Then bore the hole for the bolt. Insert the T-nut and seat it in place, put the penny on top of the T-nut, slide the sliding arm in place and insert the finger bolt.

Attach the fixture to the band saw and you're good to go.

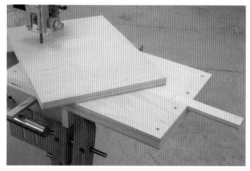

To use the fixture, measure from one edge of the blank and mark the radius. Drill a ¹⁄₄"-diameter hole just deep enough to accept the pivot pin. Set the blank on the fixture, inserting the pivot pin in the hole in the blank. Move the sliding arm until the edge that you marked is lightly touching the saw blade. Tighten the bolt to hold the arm in place. Turn on the saw and make the cut.

Set your table saw blade angle to 10°. Cut the bevel on one long edge of each top plate and both edges of the sliding arm.

Bore the clearance hole for the T-nut's shoulder and the penny. Then bore the hole for the bolt.

INCHES (MILLIMETERS)						
REFERENCE	QUANTITY	PART	STOCK	THICKNESS (MM)	WIDTH (MM)	LENGTH (MM)
A	1	base	plywood	³⁄₄ (19)	12 (305)	18 (457)
B	2	top plates	plywood	¹⁄₂ (13)	5³⁄₄ (146)	3 (76)
C	1	sliding arm	plywood	¹⁄₂ (13)	1³⁄₈ (35)	18 (457)
D	1	cleat	plywood	³⁄₄ (19)	2 (51)	12 (305)
E	1	runner	hardwood	³⁄₈ (10)	³⁄₄ (19)	15 (381)

HARDWARE

1	1½" × ¼"–20 (38mm x 6mm–20) finger bolt
1	¼"–20 (6mm–20) T-nut
1	¼" × 1" (6mm × 25mm) dowel
1	penny (any minting date will work!)

Top plate B (2)

Sliding arm C

Detail of Sliding-Arm Lock

Penny

T-nut

Finger bolt

Runner E

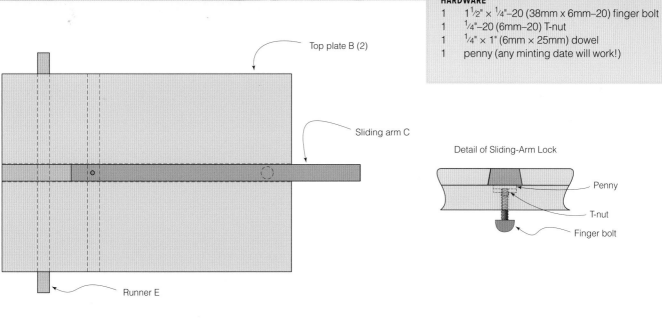

¼"-diameter dowel

Top plate B (2)

Cleat D

Base A

Distributed in Canada by Fraser Direct
100 Armstrong Avenue
Georgetown, Ontario L7G 5S4
Canada

Distributed in the U.K. and Europe by
F&W Media International, LTD
Brunel House, Forde Close
Newton Abbot
TQ12 4PU, UK
Tel: (+44) 1626 323200
Fax: (+44) 1626 323319
E-mail: enquiries@fwmedia.com

Distributed in Australia by Capricorn Link
P.O. Box 704
Windsor, NSW 2756
Australia

Visit our website at www.popularwoodworking.com or our consumer website at www.shopwoodworking.com for more woodworking information projects.

Other fine Popular Woodworking Books are available from your local bookstore or direct from the publisher.

16   15   14   13   12   5   4   3   2   1

ACQUISITIONS EDITOR: DAVID THIEL
DESIGNER: KELLY ODELL
PRODUCTION COORDINATOR: MARK GRIFFIN

READ THIS IMPORTANT SAFETY NOTICE

To prevent accidents, keep safety in mind while you work. Use the safety guards installed on power equipment; they are for your protection.

When working on power equipment, keep fingers away from saw blades, wear safety goggles to prevent injuries from flying wood chips and sawdust, wear hearing protection and consider installing a dust vacuum to reduce the amount of airborne sawdust in your woodshop.

Don't wear loose clothing, such as neckties or shirts with loose sleeves, or jewelry, such as rings, necklaces or bracelets, when working on power equipment. Tie back long hair to prevent it from getting caught in your equipment.

People who are sensitive to certain chemicals should check the chemical content of any product before using it.

Due to the variability of local conditions, construction materials, skill levels, etc., neither the author nor Popular Woodworking Books assumes any responsibility for any accidents, injuries, damages or other losses incurred resulting from the material presented in this book.

The authors and editors who compiled this book have tried to make the contents as accurate and correct as possible. Plans, illustrations, photographs and text have been carefully checked. All instructions, plans and projects should be carefully read, studied and understood before beginning construction.

Prices listed for supplies and equipment were current at the time of publication and are subject to change.

METRIC CONVERSION CHART

TO CONVERT	TO	MULTIPLY BY
Inches	Centimeters	2.54
Centimeters	Inches	0.4
Feet	Centimeters	30.5
Centimeters	Feet	0.03
Yards	Meters	0.9
Meters	Yards	1.1

1	¼" × 1" (6mm × 25mm) dowel
1	penny (any minting date will work!)

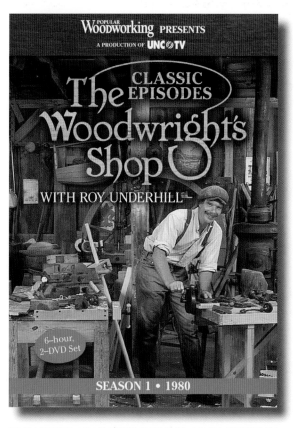

IDEAS. INSTRUCTION. INSPIRATION.

These and other great *Popular Woodworking* products are available at your local bookstore, woodworking store or online supplier.

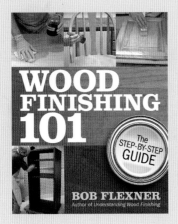 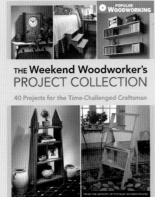 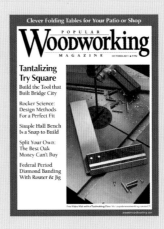 

WOOD FINISHING 101
By Bob Flexner

Wood finishing doesn't have to be complicated or confusing. Wood Finishing 101 boils it down to simple step-by-step instructions and pictures on how to finish common woods using widely-available finishing materials. Bob Flexner has been writing about and teaching wood finishing for over 20 years.

paperback • 128 pages

WEEKEND WOODWORKER'S PROJECT COLLECTION

This book has 40 projects from which to choose and, depending on the level of your woodworking skills, any of them can be completed in one or two weekends. Projects include: a game box, jewelry box, several styles of bookcases and shelves, mirrors, picture frames and more.

paperback • 256 pages

POPULAR WOODWORKING MAGAZINE

Whether learning a new hobby or perfecting your craft, *Popular Woodworking Magazine* has expert information to teach the skill, not just the project. Find the latest issue on newsstands, or you can order online at popularwoodworking.com.

SHOPCLASS VIDEOS

From drafting, to dovetails and even how to carve a ball-and-claw foot, our Shop Class Videos let you see the lesson as if you were standing right there.

Available at shopwoodworking.com
DVD & Instant download

POPULAR WOODWORKING'S VIP PROGRAM

Get the Most Out of Woodworking!

Join the Woodworker's Bookshop VIP program today for the tools you need to advance your woodworking abilities. Your one-year paid renewal membership includes:

Popular Woodworking Magazine (1 year/7 issue U.S. subscription — A $21.97 Value)

Popular Woodworking Magazine CD — Get all issues of **Popular Woodworking Magazine** from 2006 to today on one CD (A $64.95 Value!)

The Best of Shops & Workbenches CD — 62 articles on workbenches, shop furniture, shop organization and the essential jigs and fixtures published in **Popular Woodworking** and **Woodworking Magazine** ($15.00 Value!)

20% Members-Only Savings on 6-Month Subscription for Shop Class OnDemand

10% Members-Only Savings at Shopwoodworking.com

10% Members-Only Savings on FULL PRICE Registration for Woodworking In America Conference (Does Not Work with Early Bird Price)

and more....

Visit *popularwoodworking.com* to see more woodworking information by the experts, learn about our digital subscription and sign up to receive our weekly newsletter at *popularwoodworking.com/newsletters/*

FOLLOW POPULAR WOODWORKING